DEAR WHITE CHRISTIANS

PROPHETIC CHRISTIANITY

Series Editors

Bruce Ellis Benson
Malinda Elizabeth Berry
Peter Goodwin Heltzel

The PROPHETIC CHRISTIANITY series explores the complex relationship between Christian doctrine and contemporary life. Deeply rooted in the Christian tradition yet taking postmodern and postcolonial perspectives seriously, series authors navigate difference and dialogue constructively about divisive and urgent issues of the early twenty-first century. The books in the series are sensitive to historical contexts, marked by philosophical precision, and relevant to contemporary problems. Embracing shalom justice, series authors seek to bear witness to God's gracious activity of building beloved community.

PUBLISHED

Bruce Ellis Benson, Malinda Elizabeth Berry, and Peter Goodwin Heltzel, eds., *Prophetic Evangelicals: Envisioning a Just and Peaceable Kingdom* (2012)

Jennifer Harvey, *Dear White Christians: For Those Still Longing for Racial Reconciliation* (2014)

Peter Goodwin Heltzel, *Resurrection City: A Theology of Improvisation* (2012)

Johnny Bernard Hill, *Prophetic Rage: A Postcolonial Theology of Liberation* (2013)

Randy S. Woodley, *Shalom and the Community of Creation: An Indigenous Vision* (2012)

Dear White Christians

For Those Still Longing
for Racial Reconciliation

Jennifer Harvey

WILLIAM B. EERDMANS PUBLISHING COMPANY
GRAND RAPIDS, MICHIGAN / CAMBRIDGE, U.K.

Published 2014 by

Wm. B. Eerdmans Publishing Co.

2140 Oak Industrial Drive N.E., Grand Rapids, Michigan 49505 /

P.O. Box 163, Cambridge CB3 9PU U.K.

www.eerdmans.com

Printed in the United States of America

20 19 18 17 16   7 6 5 4

Library of Congress Cataloging-in-Publication Data

Harvey, Jennifer, 1971-

Dear white Christians: for those still longing for racial reconciliation / Jennifer Harvey.

pages   cm.   — (Prophetic Christianity series)

ISBN 978-0-8028-7207-4 (pbk.: alk. paper)

1. Racism — Religious aspects — Christianity.

2. Race relations — Religious aspects — Christianity.

3. Reconciliation — Religious aspects — Christianity.

I. Title.

BT734.2.H275   2014

277.3'083089 — dc23

2014026867

Substantial portions of chapters 4 and 5 were previously published as "White Protestants and Black Christians: The Absence and Presence of Whiteness in the Face of the Black Manifesto" in *Journal of Religious Ethics,* 39:1 (2011): 131-46.

Portions of chapter 6 were previously published and are excerpted from *Buffalo Shout, Salmon Cry,* copyright © Herald Press 2013, Waterloo, Ont. Used with permission.

Substantial portions of chapter 7 were previously published as "Which Way to Justice? Reconciliation, Reparations, and the Problem of Whiteness in U.S. Protestantism" in *Journal of the Society of Christian Ethics* 31:1 (2011): 57-78.

Contents

Acknowledgments

This work has been a long time coming, and my first thanks go to the many communities — most of them Christian — who have engaged with me on race and racial injustice over the past years in ways that have provoked and challenged my thinking. It was insights and passions shared in a variety of such engagements that led me to clarity about the need for this book and to the primary argument within it. The communities of which I speak are too numerous to name, but two deserve special mention. Thanks to the Urbandale United Church of Christ and First Unitarian Universalist Church of Des Moines for having provided me two of the most substantive contexts in which to think about these matters aloud and "try them out" with real live people in Iowa.

I also acknowledge with gratitude colleagues and administrators at Drake University, where I teach. The Drake University Center for the Humanities, ably led by Craig Owens during the period in which I was granted funding, provided critical resources for travel, recording equipment, and the final stages of the manuscript. I appreciate, too, the faculty research programs supported by the College of Arts and Sciences Dean, which allowed me to purchase books and hire an assistant for the initial research and to do interview transcription. Nora Sullivan and Alexandra Hilgart, both students at Drake, deserve recognition for having served in these latter capacities. Given its well-deserved reputation for delivering on its commitment to teaching excellence (a commitment in line with my own), Drake and those who are part of it certainly do a mighty fine job supporting faculty like myself in our research and writing.

Acknowledgments

Malinda Elizabeth Berry first saw value in this project and encouraged me to see it through with Eerdmans. She also spent the last weekend before it was complete sitting close to her computer and providing me with supportive and critical feedback. Peter Goodwin Heltzel and Bruce Ellis Benson, editors of this series along with Malinda, did the same. I am grateful to all three of them for seeing in this project a set of ideas worth sharing with others and for their willingness to include it in their important and timely Prophetic Christianity series.

Most heartfelt thanks go to the faithful Christians who allowed me to interview them for this book. I was utterly inspired and challenged by my time with Episcopalians in Baltimore and New York. Not only did I leave those conversations re-energized and hopeful about the future, I cannot say enough how much I appreciated the risk these groups took in speaking to me with candor, humility, and passion. In particular, I am grateful to the Reverend Canon Angela Shepherd, Canon for Mission for the Diocese of Maryland, who invited me to Baltimore, set up the interviews, hosted me graciously, and otherwise made it possible for me to engage reparations beyond the theoretical level.

In New York, I owe thanks to the Reverend Dr. Mary Foulke, who not only similarly arranged for my time with the Reparations Committee there, but who started me on this journey into anti-racism back when we were both students at Union Theological Seminary. Mary was the first white person I knew who was willing to insist that justice-seeking white people could not only learn to do our own work and do it well, but who created environments in which we did learn to do it. Thanks as well to Nell Braxton Gibson for her leadership in New York and her generous provision of key materials to me after my visit.

The Reverend Dr. Melanie Harris has long been a heart friend and soul sister. But she supported me, and this book, every single day in the last months. I only hope I faithfully show up for her in the ways she has shown up for me.

As I sit completing this manuscript, my children are sleeping soundly in their beds and my beloved partner is resting after having supported our family in a million extra ways while I worked toward this deadline in what has proven to be a grueling final month. Words always fail when I attempt to describe my gratitude for the family who supports so much of what I do and who I am in the world. The presence of Harper and Emery in my life deepens my resolve to keep working for a world more just than the one that was bequeathed to me. It also puts me in daily touch with an experience of profound joy, even while living in a world desperately needing *just* transformation. The presence of Chris Patterson in my life, quite simply, continues to be a gift and surprise. I never knew such an experience of *home* could exist, let alone that it could exist in Iowa. Now that I do, I cannot fathom what it was like to have lived without it. Thank you.

Introduction

I am a white Christian (and parent, partner, teacher, and feminist) who still longs for racial reconciliation. This book emerges from some of the deepest yearnings of my spirit and directly from anti-racism work to which those yearnings have led me for nearly two decades. It is written, therefore, from a place of empathy for and identification with other Christians who feel frustration, outrage, and sometimes despair over the extent to which racial brokenness and interracial alienation continue to characterize not just our civic communities and nation but, more painfully, our faith communities. And this book is written to those faith communities.

I begin by emphasizing my identification with other justice-minded Christians because this book is, in many ways, very critical. It directly questions the adequacy of what I see as the prominent way liberal, progressive, and prophetic Christian communities respond to race — both communities that are predominantly white, as well as many of those we might describe as multiracial. It tries to be specific and demonstrate carefully why our responses to race and racism are so inadequate; to explain why we should, in fact, not be surprised that so many decades now past the point at which some white Christians finally acknowledged racism as a problem that we remain so inefficacious in realizing justice and a racially transformed church.

This may be a hard word for some to hear. But the reasons for saying it nonetheless include my being convinced that framing and pursuing responses to race through a vision of reconciliation, as we do in justice-seeking Christian contexts, has proven to be a fundamentally flawed approach. As long as we persist in it, reconciliation itself will remain out of reach.

1

In this way, then, as critical as this book is, it is also — or tries to be — deeply constructive. I committed at the outset of this project to devoting a significant portion of it to helping readers imagine possibilities and to providing concrete examples that model the kinds of responses to race for which I argue in these pages. Rather than simply point out what it is we are doing inadequately, I have sought here to give clear direction about what it is we should be doing instead and how we might envision steps in that direction.

Quite simply, however, the most important way in which this book is constructive has to do with the spirit in which it is written. I write from a place of shared commitment with those who have spent so much energy earnestly thinking about, talking about, and working for racial reconciliation. At every moment of my critique, even at its most deconstructive, I come from a place of passionately longing for us — for me — to do better, radically better.

Reconciliation Has Failed

In the many years I have spent teaching, dialoguing, and otherwise engaging in anti-racist work within Christian faith communities, over and over again I have encountered the powerful hold that "reconciliation" has on the white Christian imagination. Rooted in our understanding of the beloved community vision that emerged during the civil rights movement, as well as in our efforts to better embrace and value the racial differences that seem to divide us, we speak about robust and just interracial togetherness as that toward which we need to journey in our efforts to realize a racially transformed church.

When I speak to justice-minded Christians I almost always ask them, "How many of you believe we are to be about the work of reconciliation? How many of you believe we should be creating an inclusive church?" Almost every hand goes up in response to these questions. "Reconciliation" fundamentally frames the ways that many justice-minded Christian communities, but especially those communities that are predominantly white, conceptualize our work on race.

The basic critique of this book, then, is that this "reconciliation paradigm" as I call it here (a notion I will explain carefully in chapter 1) has failed us. The fact that we have been working for interracial, multiracial, diverse, and just reconciled faith communities for some time and have yet to see almost any sustained movement toward realizing such communities is a powerful indictment of the adequacy of reconciliation. Moreover, our failure to have realized these communities should also command our attention and lead us to the insight that, perhaps, something different is required (this argument is explored in chapters 2 and 3).

More powerful still is the reality that in clinging to a reconciliation paradigm for understanding race, we have basically ignored what actually transpired in this nation, but also within the church, in the final years of the civil rights movement. While we rightly find historical and theological precedent for today's visions of reconciliation in the civil rights movement, by the end of the 1960s many, many Christians of color (and, given the specific focus of this work, I should say many Black Christians specifically) were insistent and clear that our integrationist visions of reconciled beloved communities were utterly inadequate. But when Black Power offered its analysis, firing the imagination and conviction of many Black Christians, white Christians' response was not to respond to what we heard. Instead we fled.

The final years of the civil rights movement were anything but peaceable between Blacks and whites who had been allies in the movement. In fact, racial alienation deepened in this period. It deepened precisely because Black Power's claim that the civil rights movement had missed critical pieces in the racial puzzle was regarded by many Black Christians as fundamentally correct. But white Christians would have none of it.

When we continue in our reconciliation visions today, then, we refuse to remember this history. We ignore the betrayal and devastation Black Christians felt when Martin Luther King Jr. was assassinated and the fact that even King had begun questioning whether he had misjudged and been overly optimistic about the state of the white soul. We miss that the Black anger and white denial that characterized the end of the civil rights movement remain powerful in our relationships today because white Christians have not collectively gone back, re-engaged, and apologized for our recalcitrance. White Christians have yet to ask in the wake of failed reconciliation, "Wait a minute, just what was that analysis and diagnosis Black Christians insisted on in the late 1960s? If, nearly fifty years later, we are still struggling to realize reconciliation, might it be possible that what Black Christians were saying *then* (and have continued to say ever since) is something white Christians still need to hear *today?*"

My answer to that question in this work is a resounding "yes." And thus enters the constructive argument.

We Need a New Paradigm

The Black Power movement offered a different paradigm for understanding race. Instead of emphasizing reconciliation, Black Power insisted clearly and without apology that redistribution (of resources and power) and repair were not only necessary, but were the only appropriate way to think about racial relations in the United States, given the *actual* state of things. In this book, I call this analysis the "reparations paradigm" (a notion I explore in chapters 4, 5, and 6).

Drawing on this history, my argument is relatively straightforward: a reparations paradigm continues to be the necessary and appropriate way for Christians, especially white Christians, to understand and respond to race in the United States generally and in our faith communities specifically. In making this argument I draw on what happened when James Forman, backed by many African American clergy, placed the Black Manifesto before the eyes of the white church in 1969. The Black Manifesto made a simple, evidence-based demand: white Christians were complicit in Black oppression and thus reparations were due.

From that point I go on to demonstrate both the ways in which reparations themselves — namely, reparations for slavery — but also a paradigm of reparations (which insists we must understand race in ways that center around history, the degree to which racial identities emerge from that history, and the structural dimensions of our relationships across lines of difference) offers a much more adequate understanding of race and a process for envisioning responses to it if justice is what we truly seek.

A reparations paradigm can be brought to bear on interracial relationships relative to any community — not only between whites and African Americans — and goes beyond reparations for slavery. In chapter 6 of this book, I attempt to identify the scaffolding intrinsic to a reparations paradigm that allows us to better understand and respond to race regardless of which particular racial groups are involved. I then give three examples of how a reparations paradigm might shape our work for racial justice in regard to the environmental crisis, immigration, and mass incarceration.

At the same time, I believe strongly that a powerful and formative moral, social, political debt continues to inhere in white and Black relations relative to the history of enslavement, and for that reason the final two chapters of this book look specifically at reparations for slavery. In these chapters I consider movements for reparations that have been pursued overtly in the past ten years in two Protestant denominations, honing in with the most attention on work in the Episcopal Church (chapters 7 and 8).

I exercise great care to make a persuasive case for a reparations paradigm, and explain precisely in the pages that follow what a reparations paradigm is and might mean. Thus, I do not presume the reader should yet understand what I mean by such a term. Still, let me say here just a general word about what a reparations paradigm would do if it came to frame our work on race in the church.

A reparations paradigm slows us down in our racial visions. It requires us to not move so quickly, given the actual situation in which race locates us right now — with its legacies of unaddressed violence, oppression, subjugation, and devastation for which those of us who have benefited have yet to apologize, let alone make meaningful repair — to presume that interracial relationships and beloved community are even possible. A reparations paradigm requires us to ask the question that seems unthinkable to many white Christians: that, without repentance and repair having come prior, why would we even assume interracial relations to be desirable or beneficial to Christians of color?

A reparations paradigm presumes that if we continue to live in an unacknowledged history of brutal injustice, harm done, white hostility to and violence against communities of color — histories with legacies that are alive and well in the present — then speaking of reconciliation may do more harm than good, may cover more than it discloses. Deployed in Christian contexts a reparations paradigm *insists* that repentance and repair must come first. And for them to come first, we must also know and name carefully what the harm has been and how it continues in the present. We must have a sense of what it is we propose to stop and to redress the damage done.

Living into a reparations paradigm is difficult. It requires dwelling in painful truths. But it is honest in ways that, I am convinced, are potentially liberating and transformative for all of us.

A Few Notes on Audience, Focus, and Language

Before turning to the work, a few explanations are warranted in regard to questions I anticipate might arise about the way I pursue the case herein.

1. Audience

First, the primary communities I engage as I describe the reconciliation paradigm are the same communities to whom I write. I plead here for the engagement of a reparations paradigm by those we might describe (or, better, who have self-described) as prophetic evangelicals,[1] as well as by those who practice their faith within self-consciously progressive pockets of mainline Protestantism (the Episcopal Church, Lutherans, the Presbyterians, Methodists, some Baptists, and the United Church of Christ, for example). In many ways these two cohorts of Christians are rather different. Their histories, especially in terms of race, diverge significantly.

When prophetic evangelicals take up matters of justice, they are more likely (though not exclusively) to think in terms more consistent with piety traditions. Here individual transformation and radical commitment is key. Meanwhile their mainline siblings tend to be more likely (though not exclusively) to think in terms of structures and resolutions to be implemented. Changing institutions is prioritized. Both of these approaches have deep merits and both have weaknesses.

My discussion of both of these groups throughout this book — mainline Protestants and prophetic evangelicals — is not intended to reify a fixed boundary distinguishing them. The distinctions I draw merely serve to lift up the resolutions and curriculum mainline Protestants have produced in their work on race and the radical commitments to justice that prophetic evangelicals pursue, specifically those living in intentional communities.[2] In terms of institutional differences, the National Council of Churches (NCC) would be the relevant umbrella organization for mainline Protestants, whereas for prophetic evangelicals it would be the National Association of Evangelicals (NAE). But while the NCC has a longer history of engaging race and racial justice overtly than does the NAE (which is why Protestant denominations get attention in the discussion of the Black Manifesto and prophetic evangelicals do not), I have no interest in making any claims here about either of these communities engaging race more adequately than the other. And again, I also presume there is overlap between these groups.

This work, then, is not an analysis of either of these groups of Christians, nor a detailed discussion of the differences and overlaps between them. I write of these groups because they both — albeit with nuances to which I do give some attention — have articulated a sustained commitment to racial reconciliation. Readers looking for a detailed analysis of how prophetic

1. See "Introduction" in *Prophetic Evangelicals: Envisioning a Just and Peaceable Kingdom*, ed. Bruce Ellis Benson, Malinda Elizabeth Berry, and Peter Goodwin Heltzel (Grand Rapids, Mich.: William B. Eerdmans Publishing Company, 2012).

2. Peter Goodwin Heltzel problematizes these distinctions in *Jesus and Justice: Evangelicals, Race, and American Politics* (New Haven, Conn.: Yale University Press, 2009).

evangelicals are in the midst of a transition in their work on racial justice (which is, I believe, happening right now) or for an in-depth discussion of all the programs mainline Protestants have constructed and pursued over the past several decades, will find this book a disappointment. Never fear, there is other outstanding scholarship available on precisely those matters.

This work makes a case for a paradigm shift in communities that use reconciliation as the primary way to talk about their racial vision. In my experience both prophetic evangelicals and mainline Protestants do this to a significant degree. And it is explaining and emphasizing the need for the shift to which this book is devoted, not to a detailed scholarly treatment of the groups.

My clarity that this work is neither an analysis of these groups nor a comprehensive account of all they have done on race is also a way of saying from the outset that it is possible this work may at points use language to describe these groups that is less precise than what a detailed scholarly analysis of them might demand — or that there may be dimensions of their work or groups active within their ranks that are not given attention. Saying so is not an excuse designed to preempt legitimate critiques readers might raise about either of these matters. Furthermore I have, of course, attempted to write in such a way that these communities will recognize themselves, and if they do not then this work is appropriately critiqued for its inadequacy. But the point remains that the argument and emphasis here is neither the groups themselves, the differences or similarities between them, nor strengths and weaknesses they respectively manifest rendering either group more or less likely to engage a reparations paradigm in a real and meaningful way. (That would, however, be an interesting book.)

The argument here is simply and urgently a case for the appropriateness, efficacy, and adequacy of a reparations paradigm for engaging race and responding to our longings for justice. White Christians need to take the counterintuitive risk of actually letting go of the reconciliation paradigm to which we are so deeply wedded (at least for now), even as the state of being reconciled continues to be the vision of what the just and transformed racial communities for which we long looks like.

Even while I do not primarily write *about* these communities, I do write directly *to* them because I believe their longing for justice and reconciliation is sincere. And I believe that if any white Christians are likely to take up the challenge laid out in this work, they are the ones.

I also write to these communities because in many ways I recognize them as "my people" — though in very different ways. I was nurtured in evangelical faith communities and attribute the liberationist, feminist Christian convictions I hold today to the fervor of and commitment to my own search for piety and radical transformation. I found Black liberation theology because of my evangelical worldview. The sincerity and all-encompassing nature of that faith, so characteristic of and nurtured by evangelicalism, shaped my walk in this world in ways that ultimately led me beyond the evangelical theological world — seeking theological responses to questions about my own identity and developing political commitments that I could not answer within it. But, even as I joined the ranks of mainline Protestantism officially when I was ordained as pastor in the American Baptist Churches (U.S.A.), I attributed my arrival to that place to what I had come to know first about God and world in the Conservative Baptist world of which I was an active part for the first twenty years of my life. It was through dwelling long in that world that I arrived at a place of believing fervently in justice and knowing a relentless call to embody that justice commitment in every way possible in my life. I am committed to justice because first I believed that truly God so loved this broken, aching world.

2. Focus

Second, I anticipate that some readers may ask why — with the brief exception of chapter 6 — I focus herein primarily on Black and white Christians. This is a legitimate question. To the degree it is asked as a critique, it is a critique that has traction. Many scholars have emphasized the artificiality and inadequacy of the Black/white binary in which so much thinking about and work on race in the United States continues to take place. Many scholars have accurately emphasized how often it is that scholarship (perhaps like that found in this book) focusing on relationships between white Americans and African Americans reifies that binary and perpetuates U.S. Americans' inabilities to think in terms more adequate for the pluralistic society that we not only have increasingly become, but in many ways have always been.

An important dimension of this critique is that overemphasizing Black and white relations can serve to render invisible, and thus further subjugate, racial and ethnic communities whose experiences fall outside the Black/white binary and yet who also have compelling justice claims and rich cultural and political heritages deserving attention. If pluralism is our racial reality in the United States, scholars have an obligation to theorize in ways that better enable us to think in pluralistic terms and seek forms of justice that honor pluralism.

I am convinced by each of these critiques and yet have still chosen in this book to focus on white and Black American relationships primarily. This conscious decision stems from my sense that there remain persuasive and important reasons to continue to work on *that* set of relationships. Doing so does not in and of itself mean I am ignoring the veracity of the concern about needing more theorizing for pluralism.

In addition, sometimes critiques of the Black/white binary seem to fall prey to the insinuation that somehow we have moved beyond the importance of such work, a case that cannot really be made unless one is prepared to assert we have actually and meaningfully transformed relationships between Blacks and whites. Another insinuation in this charge is that the Black experience takes up more space than it should relative to other racial groups; this insinuation has its own problems. In addition, the important call for better theoretical work on racial pluralism is too often taken up — from my perspective — by white U.S. Americans who find it easier to talk about difference and engage race regarding issues other than those relating to African Americans. (For example, my white colleagues are much more eager to talk about programming and practices that increase diversity in our teaching institution than they are about relating to the African American communities in our own city of Des Moines, Iowa.) I am suspicious of this for obvious reasons.

The degree to which both African and Native American history and experience represent the first and still-uncontended-with interracial encounter here (European/African/Native) and continue to form the fundamental basis of U.S. economic prosperity (for some) merits ongoing work on these relations. So saying is not a case against seeking and constructing theories and models that allow us to engage the complexities and intersections of pluralism. Nor is it a trope in one of those dead-end conversations about any oppression being "worse" and thus more "worthy" of attention than any other. It is simply a case for continuing direct work on these particular matters and histories as deeply and attentively as any others in our rapidly changing demographics.

There are other specific reasons I chose to focus on white and Black Christian relationships. I have long been and remain deeply interested in and passionate about the United States' "original sins" of genocide and slavery.[3]

---

3. A phrase invoked by ethicist Larry Rasmussen in the 2002 Dietrich Bonhoeffer Lectures in Public Ethics, "Costly Grace: Race and Reparations, Theological and Ethical Readings of Communities."

I wanted to engage movements for repair actually taking place, and it so happens that reparations for slavery are being given attention in a substantive way in some Christian communities. In addition, I believe that the era of Black Power deeply impacted Black/white Christian relationships within the church and remains underrepresented in the self-understanding of white Christians today. Finally, the reader will note that I attend to reparations for slavery without taking up reparative responses to Native nations — despite my deep interest in those matters as well. That is simply because though the United States' "original sins" are thoroughly interrelated, responses to the distinct histories and legacies of Native/white relations merit their own lengthy treatment (as would be true in relation to the experiences of any other racial communities). I have given some such treatment elsewhere, but here the focus is reparations for slavery.[4]

Having said all of that, with informed nuance and careful attention to the distinct and particular histories, I find a reparations paradigm applicable regarding the experiences of any racial community that has had meaningful encounters with white U.S.-American communities. In chapter 6 I provide three short explanations, then, of how a reparations paradigm might shape justice responses to race beyond the issue of reparations for slavery. It is my hope that doing so will inspire and invite Christians longing for reconciliation to deploy a reparations paradigm for whatever racial justice work seems most befitting and salient in their own contexts.

3. Language

Third and finally, please note that I use the language of "whiteness" extensively throughout this work. While the language of white privilege and, with it, the particular relationships of white people to histories and contemporary structures of white supremacy have been given increasing attention by justice-seeking white Christians in recent years, this term may still feel strange to some readers. It is my hope that the analysis I provide herein makes clear why this language is important, explaining carefully and making a solid case for how honing in on the particular problem of whiteness is

---

4. See Jennifer Harvey, "Dangerous Goods: Seven Reasons Creation Care Movements Must Advocate Reparations," in *Buffalo Shout, Salmon Cry: Conversations on Creation, Land Justice, and Life Together,* ed. Steve Heinrichs (Waterloo, Ont., and Harrisonburg, Va.: Herald Press, 2013).

critical in our justice work. In fact, what I have described elsewhere as the "moral crisis of being white" is a primary phenomenon around which the need for a reparations paradigm turns.[5]

Despite decades of calls from Black activists, scholars, and theologians, white Christians' attempts to address racism have largely failed to acknowledge the problem of whiteness. In fact, a reconciliation paradigm makes it almost impossible to do so — even as a reparations paradigm makes it almost impossible not to. The term "whiteness" in this book is intended to signal not only white people but, more broadly, the phenomenon of white perpetration and complicity; to point to the deep and formative relationship that exists between white people and white supremacy.

The concept of whiteness assumes that human body-selves that happen to be of lighter skin tones become socially recognizable and categorized as "white" even as those same body-selves encounter and interact with the structures and systems that maintain racial hierarchy. In other words, people who are "white" are not white in some essential way. Rather, we are racially formed and shaped by way of — and as we respond to — the same systems that enable white supremacy. As I argue beginning in chapter 2 of this book, racial identities are always formed (positively and negatively) in relation to systems of injustice.

It goes without saying that African Americans' historical experiences of and struggles against racial oppression are of first importance when considering matters of race and racial justice. But, by and large, the perpetrators of racial oppression have been people categorized as "white," as have the beneficiaries of the wealth generated through appropriation of lands belonging to indigenous peoples and enslavement of people of African descent. These historical realities are formative in U.S. history, and Christian churches have been deeply implicated in them. The problem of whiteness is thus critical when thinking about and responding to race. If whiteness is the central reality in the existence of racial injustice, then being able to name, analyze, and deconstruct it is necessary in working toward justice. Yet very little of our efforts or understanding in anti-racist work in Christian contexts has been devoted to such work, nor has the phenomenon of whiteness even been named a problem. Furthermore, as I will argue in this book, the reconciliation paradigm we use to think about race makes it very difficult to do so.

As a Christian ethicist working in the liberationist tradition, I sub-

---

5. See Jennifer Harvey, *Whiteness and Morality: Pursuing Racial Justice Through Reparations and Sovereignty* (New York: Palgrave Macmillan, 2007).

scribe to the conviction that a norm of "justice" is at the heart of Christian practice and identity. I understand "just" in the tradition of ethicist Beverly Harrison, who describes it as "rightly related community."[6] As such, justice is a state of relations that must be actively pursued, as well as being the relevant terrain in which the caliber of our racial relationships is to be assessed.[7] When whiteness is absented from our analysis of the problem of racial injustice, racism becomes conceived as a problem pertaining primarily to Black people or other people of color, even among those who would agree that theological or moral imperatives exist for ending oppression. Yet without a direct acknowledgment of white behavior and the active participation of white people in our racial relationships, without the choice to take full ownership of and responsibility for white agency, without work to understand what it is about whiteness that makes it difficult for white people to do so, it is impossible for us get to the root of racial brokenness. For all of these reasons then, the urgency of making whiteness visible and challenging it directly — something that a reparations paradigm not only makes possible, but actually demands — is a primary commitment of this work.

Having laid out the arguments, clarified the choices, and described the ethos and sensibility that informs the pages that follow, I invite the reader now to simply engage. Even while this book makes no pretense of having answers to all of the challenging questions that such a paradigm raises, I hope that the work contained herein at least successfully secures a real hearing for a reparations paradigm. Let us, therefore, begin.

6. See Beverly Wildung Harrison, "The Dream of a Common Language: Toward a Normative Theory of Justice in Christian Ethics," in *Justice in the Making: Feminist Social Ethics* (Louisville, Ky.: Westminster John Knox Press, 2004), 14-29.

7. This claim is fleshed out in greater detail in Harvey, *Whiteness and Morality*.

PART ONE

Reconciliation? Where We Are and Why

CHAPTER ONE

A Reconciliation Paradigm

Christians concerned about racial justice often repeat Martin Luther King Jr.'s proclamation that eleven o'clock on Sunday morning is the most segregated hour of the week.[1] If you have spent much time at all in mainline Protestant worship spaces, you have almost certainly heard someone make this claim.

This statement refers to the fact that most churches in the United States are overwhelmingly composed of only one racial group. In startlingly few congregations do people worship regularly together across racial lines. Setting aside for now the question of whether this situation is best understood as "segregation," the perception that racial separation characterizes churches today as much as it did in King's day is rooted in factual accuracy. Data from a recent study show that what was true by the end of the Civil War remains so today. Not only are mainline Protestant denominations overwhelmingly white (91 percent), with as little as 2 percent of the membership identifying as African American and 3 percent as Hispanic, but even within denominations congregations tend to be composed of one racial group or another. In other words, the 9 percent who identify racially/ethnically as other than white tend to worship in their own separate churches even within the same denomination. Meanwhile, white Christians constitute 2 percent of the membership of historically Black denominations.[2]

---

1. Martin Luther King Jr., interview by James Miller, transcript, December 18, 1962, www.wmich.edu/library/archives/mlk/q-a.html.

2. See the Pew Research Religion & Public Life Project "Religious Landscape Survey," http://religions.pewforum.org/portraits.

The authors of *United by Faith: The Multiracial Congregation as an Answer to the Problem of Race* define a racially mixed church as one in which no group comprises 80 percent or more of the congregation. If we include churches beyond mainline Protestantism, only 5.5 percent of congregations in the United States meet this standard. Of these, the authors write, only half are truly racially mixed because the other half are congregations in transition, which will, ultimately, end up composed of one racial group.[3]

There are many reasons such divisions exist. These include the cultural cohesions and connections needed and created by new immigrant communities, realities of linguistic differences, and a myriad of other dimensions of social life that might make multiracial/ethnic community more challenging for and the familiarity of uniracial/ethnic community more appealing to people of color.

In regard to the longest interracial relationship constituting the U.S. church, that of whites and African Americans, history provides the most obvious reasons for such stark division. In fact, the history out of which the Black church developed makes it unsurprising that congregations remain racially separated. At the end of the Civil War, when newly freed African Americans had the opportunity to attend a church of their choosing (rather than one chosen for them by their enslavers), a majority left for Black congregations and denominations. Harold T. Lewis describes the movement of Blacks out of the Episcopal Church at this time as a "wholesale Exodus."[4] The only way in which the Episcopal Church may have been unique in this regard is that this exodus happened later than it had in other denominations. Among Baptists, for example, organizational structure made it possible for Black Christians to leave and start their own churches earlier.

Meanwhile, this is to say nothing of the experience of free African Americans in the North, both before and after Emancipation, and the ways northern history informs today's racial demographics. The African Methodist Episcopal Church, for example, began because Blacks in the North refused to be treated as second-class citizens within their houses of worship. Even Christian movements that had multiracial origins (such as the Church of God) or resisted segregation after the Civil War (such as the Congrega-

---

3. Curtiss Paul DeYoung, Michael O. Emerson, George Yancey, and Karen Chai Kim, *United by Faith: The Multiracial Congregation as an Answer to the Problem of Race* (New York: Oxford University Press, 2003), 2.

4. Harold T. Lewis, *Yet with a Steady Beat: The African American Struggle for Recognition in the Episcopal Church* (Valley Forge: Trinity Press International, 1996), 40.

tionalists) eventually "caved in to [the] pressure" of white racism and with time became uniracial.[5]

Whether the pressures of racism were direct or indirect, the history of Christian churches in the United States on the whole is this: white churches became "more white" as Blacks created their own racially affirming worship spaces and opportunities for religious leadership.

Given decades upon decades of overt racism in the United States, even after legal enslavement came to an end, and given the centrality of white Christian participation in this racism, it would be more surprising today if our churches did *not* remain racially separate! The Black church was born long before most white Christians believed inclusion and diversity were important. Indeed, given what this legacy represents, namely African Americans' creative refusal to comply with racist religious practice, the existence still today of vibrant and robust African American spiritual communities and religious institutions would be better seen as a happy reality.

Moreover, given the concerns about racism and diversity that presumably precipitate the 11:00-hour statement, at least when it is articulated by white Christians, a more logical question would be to ask why more white Christians do not simply join African American churches or denominations. In short, it is clear that the segregated-hour statement is much more complicated than it might appear at first glance.

In addition to historical factors, there are other reasons for our racial separateness. As Jason E. Shelton and Michael O. Emerson document through extensive interviews in *Blacks and Whites in Christian America,* significant differences exist between white and Black Christianity. Aside from sharing the basic beliefs confessed in the Apostles' Creed "black and white believers often radically differ in their faith-based thoughts and practices."[6] The differences are fascinating. They range from the contrast between "academic" and "experiential" models of Christianity, to different understandings of morality and the relationship between faith and works, to widely divergent levels of ease with including beliefs that might be considered outside the bounds of "orthodox" Christian doctrine within one's religious matrix.[7]

All of Shelton and Emerson's interviewees agree that these differences exist. A few attribute them to innate qualities within white and Black cul-

5. DeYoung et al., *United by Faith,* 53, 54.

6. Jason E. Shelton and Michael O. Emerson, *Blacks and Whites in Christian America: How Racial Discrimination Shapes Religious Convictions* (New York and London: New York University Press, 2012), 56.

7. See Shelton and Emerson, chapters 4, 6, and 7.

ture. But most of the African American pastors and scholars the authors engage describe the differences as a direct outgrowth of whites' and Blacks' different racial histories and experiences.[8] For Black Christians, for example, a powerful and direct connection with God has emerged in relation to the need to survive the intense and relentless racial violence of U.S. history and the racial oppression that persists today. This resulting experiential center of Black Christianity can be correlated with much higher rates of prayer and a tendency toward more affective worship practices. In contrast, for whites, who less often face questions of basic survival and typically can assume their needs will be met in the social and political milieu, the option of philosophizing about God (instead of experiencing God directly in times of dire need) has always been more available. White racial experience helps account for what Shelton and Emerson's interviewees describe as a more academic and abstract approach within white Christianity. This approach tends to emphasize belief and doctrine over the action and experience that is more central within Black Christianity.[9]

For many reasons, then, the statement about eleven o'clock as the most segregated hour contains real complexity that should give us pause: It makes certain assumptions about what the problem of race in the church is. It references a reality that is born of powerful past and present social dynamics that deserve to be carefully understood. And it is accompanied by specific (but often unspoken) longings about what the church or churches should be, look like, or do. Each of these matters requires further inquiry. Having said that, it is worth beginning such an inquiry by looking more closely at why Christians invoke this statement. There is something theologically important going on here, and a first, critical step in engaging more successful practices and postures in relation to racial justice is to understand what that is.

The Perceived Problem, the Perceived Solution

While the issues flagged above complicate how we should understand the reality of racial division in our churches, the popularity of the "segregated hour" adage tells us something important about predominant Protestant understandings of race and racism. It is significant, for example, that despite

---

8. See Shelton and Emerson, chapter 4, which includes data from interviews with African American pastors.

9. Shelton and Emerson, 71-78.

the histories that help explain why our religious communities reflect race the way they do, we invoke the adage not merely as a descriptive fact but as a lament.

For many justice-oriented white Christians, our lack of racial mixing on Sunday mornings is a problem. For some it is even "the problem" when it comes to the continuing presence of racism in the church. Separation, segregation, or some other lack of Christian unity across racial lines seems to evidence barriers, dislike, mistrust, and non-acceptance.

Most mainline Protestant denominations have explicitly named diversity and inclusion as Christian values for at least two decades. In the context of our eleven o'clock lament, racial separateness seems therefore to demonstrate our failure to embody those values. If the premise of diversity is that difference is to be celebrated and embraced, separate worship must mean we are still resistant to difference somehow and hold negative views of those whose racial identities are distinct from our own. If the premise of inclusion is that everyone feels welcome and that our congregations attentively create environments in which this is the case, separation must mean some have been made to feel they do not belong — otherwise they would be "here."

Moreover, if separateness is the problem, then the logical solution becomes togetherness. We use the common theological term "reconciliation" to describe this vision. We speak of the Christian community as "being one in Christ," employing metaphors about family, about brotherhood and sisterhood, to talk about who we should be to one another and what our fellowship should be like. Versions of this interpretation of the problem of racial division and the reconciliation for which Christians long in its wake can be seen in most Protestant publications produced in the past twenty years.

This reconciliation paradigm shows up in both mainline Protestantism and prophetic evangelicalism. Depending on the context, the reconciliation paradigm brings with it slightly different nuances. These are important and will be given attention in chapters 2 and 3. However, these nuances do not fundamentally alter the paradigm itself, nor the ways in which it ultimately frames, discusses, and subsequently responds to the challenge of racial division.

My use of the word "paradigm" is intentional here. Paradigms are powerful. A paradigm might be considered a framework that shapes how we understand a situation at its most fundamental level. A paradigm contains within it operative assumptions about how we see and comprehend the basic nature of a problem. As a result it necessarily informs the kind of solutions or responses we identify, as well as which responses we perceive to have the most urgency or even recognize as viable. In other words, a paradigm becomes itself an interpretation explaining what is going on and establishing the range of possibilities we might therefore engage.

We might compare the power of a paradigm to the power contained in the construction of a question. Imagine, for example, that you are wearing a T-shirt and I ask you, "Is your sweater green or blue?" Any answer you give to my question ("green" or "blue") already contains within it the same error innate to the question itself. The only way to respond adequately to my query is to refuse the question altogether: "It's not a sweater. It's a T-shirt." James Cone provides a theological description of this same phenomenon.

Since its advent during the rise of the Black Power movement, Black liberation theology has shared some of Black Power's critiques of both the goals of integration and the method of nonviolence. Whites would thus regularly ask Cone, "So, do you believe in violence?" Seeking to expose the deep-seated assumptions and hypocrisies contained within that question — namely that it was legitimate to place those who were oppressed and literally being killed for their resistance under heightened moral scrutiny for *their* adherence to "nonviolence," without talking seriously about the violence of their oppressors — Cone always refuses the question. Rather than answering "yes" or "no," he always responds, "Whose violence are we talking about?"

These comparisons are meant to make clear both what I mean by paradigm and why it is so important in regard to race. An interpretive paradigm matters. If we begin with the wrong paradigm, it becomes difficult to arrive at the right set of concerns, emphases, and responses.

In the context of mainline Protestant curriculum and prophetic evangelical communities, we have put the highest premium on the need to build relationships of authenticity and mutual regard across lines of racial difference in order to seek "togetherness." The originating question is posed as "Why are we still so divided?" The lament is "Eleven o'clock is still the most segregated hour of the week." Thus the overwhelming emphasis becomes the need to heal division, to come together in just and mutual ways across that divide. This basic framing of the question or problem of race — with its emphasis on division or failed inclusion and its vision of unity and interracial togetherness — is what I describe here with my use of "reconciliation paradigm."

According to the reconciliation paradigm in mainline Protestantism, God desires the human family to be in authentic community. Divisions along racial lines are, therefore, nothing less than a violation of God's will. Consider the 1999 policy statement issued by the Presbyterian Church (USA), *Facing Racism: A Vision of the Beloved Community:* "We violate God's intention for the human family by creating false categories of value and identity, based on identifiable characteristics such as culture, place of origin, and skin color."[10] Seeing such identifiable differences as a source for celebration, rather than as a cause for differently valuing one another, is essential for putting us on the path away from division and toward racial reconciliation. While warning against creating "false categories of value and identity," this same Presbyterian statement calls its members "to embrace racial and cultural diversity as God-given assets of the human family."[11]

Like many other denominations, the PC(USA) has exerted considerable effort advocating and educating their congregations to adopt multicultural frameworks for worship and community life. In 2004 the Presbyterian Peacemaking Program published a curriculum titled *Living the Gospel of Peace: Tools for Building More Inclusive Community.* In this six-part study, Eric H. F. Law encourages participants to recognize the ways in which racial and cultural differences can lead to communication challenges and, as a result, exclusion of one group by another.[12]

This phenomenon is more complex than the possibility that any given group might on any given day exclude any other. Law also insists that congregational members take seriously the ways in which access to social power varies depending on one's racial or cultural identity, exacerbating the already existing challenges differences can create. In other words, it's not simply the challenge of differences themselves. The substantive challenge is the way that social power and difference combine so some groups (in the United States, usually white Christians) regularly end up in dominant positions. Law uses his account of power to encourage Christians to measure our proximity to the cross as a way of assessing whether we are among the group who needs to relinquish (and, thus, better share) power — something, he claims, Jesus consistently asked the powerful to do.[13]

Throughout the curriculum Law claims that diversity is a core value in the biblical record: the Tower of Babel is a story in which God challenges us to abandon our ethnocentrism, and Pentecost is an account of the church's

10. Initiative Team on Racism and Racial Violence, *Facing Racism: A Vision of the Beloved Community* (Louisville, Ky.: Office of the General Assembly, 1999), 1.

11. *Facing Racism*, 1.

12. Eric H. F. Law, *Living the Gospel of Peace: Tools for Building More Inclusive Community* (Presbyterian Peacemaking Program, 2004). See sessions 1, 2, and 4.

13. Law, session 5.

call to create inclusive, diverse community.[14] This curriculum is a perfect example of what the reconciliation paradigm looks like and the extent to which it shapes the way Protestants think about racism, division, diversity, and inclusion.

Presbyterian Mark Lomax writes, "The Christian church in the United States repeatedly has claimed interest in racial reconciliation. Many, if not most, Christian communions have gone so far as to establish denominational offices of racial and ethnic concerns, create and approve policies of representation and inclusion, and host forums, seminars and workshops addressing racial distrust, disharmony and division."[15] The accuracy of Lomax's words can be seen with even a cursory look at the website of any major denomination. The lists of publications and pronouncements are long. For example, in the United Church of Christ there exists a 1993 declaration calling the UCC to be a "Multiracial and Multicultural Church," a 2003 call to become "An Anti-Racist Church," and a 2008 curriculum urging all UCC congregations to implement a "Sacred Conversation on Race."[16] Prior to its publication of *Facing Racism* and Law's curriculum, the PC(USA) named racial healing and reconciliation its major emphasis in 1996. It emphasized racial tension in 1997.[17] These lists only scratch the surface. We can see strikingly similar work, publications, and processes in the Methodist Church, the Christian Church (Disciples of Christ), the Episcopal Church, and many other denominational bodies.

White evangelicals have a different history and have been slower in the post–civil rights era to come to active interest in, let alone dismay about, the 11:00 hour than have their mainline siblings. In fact, far from promoting a vision for racial reconciliation, Lisa Sharon Harper — herself an evangelical — claims that both the beliefs and conduct of white evangelicals bear significant responsibility for the ongoing racial divide in the nation as a whole.[18] More tellingly, Harper engages evidence that the deepest racial divide in the United States today actually exists within evangelicalism itself

14. Law, sessions 3 and 6.

15. Mark A. Lomax, "Reparations: Getting to the Ground Level," *Horizons* 17, no. 7 (November/December 2004): 19.

16. See the following: http://www.ucc.org/justice/multiracial-multicultural/pronounce ment.html; http://ucc.org/justice/racism/anti-racist-church.html; http://www.ucc.org/ sacred-conversation/.

17. *Facing Racism*, 6.

18. Lisa Sharon Harper, *Evangelical Does Not Equal Republican or Democrat* (New York and London: New Press, 2008), 13.

— found in the distance between the worlds and worldviews of Black and white evangelicals.[19]

But in recent years, some progressive white evangelicals have begun to articulate a passionate concern about matters of race with increasing vigor and visibility. Harper claims these developments represent a return to the political and social commitments that historically characterized evangelicalism and that they are the fruits of faithful, lonely labor begun in the late 1960s by African American evangelicals such as John M. Perkins and Tom Skinner, and white evangelicals like Jim Wallis, Ron Sider, and Tony Campolo. These leaders insist that the good news of the gospel means a commitment to work not only for personal transformation — the emphasis for which twentieth-century evangelicalism has been most associated — but also for social reform.[20] Harper traces key moments in this movement's history in which this focus manifested in regard to matters of race and racial justice, then claims that a tipping point was reached in 2000, when Brenda Salter McNeil preached to 20,000 young people and future evangelical leaders at the triennial Urbana student missions conference that they were to be the "Reconciliation Generation."

The call, claims Harper, was to a new kind of evangelicalism, and younger evangelicals are demonstrating a passionate willingness to respond to it.[21] This evangelicalism understands, in the paraphrased words of Tom Skinner in 1970, that God actively desires to see justice realized in the world, and that the good news means the redemption not only of the relationship between an individual and the divine, but of all relationships.[22] This means racial relationships and racial justice matter in spiritual terms.[23]

---

19. Here Harper relies on data accumulated and interpreted by Michael O. Emerson and Christian Smith in *Divided by Faith: Evangelical Religion and the Problem of Race in America* (Oxford and New York: Oxford University Press, 2000). See Harper, 13.

20. Harper, 44. Harper goes on to describe this dual focus as getting lost when white evangelicals allowed themselves to be galvanized by the Religious Right, starting in the early 1970s, in order to "perpetuate discrimination against African Americans." This is an ironic and painful betrayal of their nineteenth-century ancestors who had worked actively against slavery in order "to free African Americans from bondage." Harper, 79. Peter Goodwin Heltzel argues in *Jesus and Justice* (New Haven, Conn.: Yale University Press, 2009) that prophetic Black evangelicals, from Martin Luther King Jr. to John M. Perkins, hearken to a prophetic intercultural future, offering a counter-narrative to the conservative white evangelicalism of the Religious Right.

21. Harper, 160.

22. Harper, 153.

23. See Soong-Chan Rah, *The Next Evangelicalism: Freeing the Church from Western Cultural Captivity* (Downers Grove, Ill.: InterVarsity Press, 2009), for an excellent example of recent scholarship on race emerging out of prophetic evangelicalism.

The emergence of a reconciliation paradigm among evangelicals is a story worth telling (and Harper tells it well). Though manifesting some important differences from how mainline Protestants understand the reconciliation paradigm, as with mainliners the paradigm here tends to be articulated with some degree of focus on the particular responsibility of white people to renounce racism. But the overarching framework is about racial division as one manifestation — albeit a critically important one — of the hostility toward each other and the relational brokenness that is innate to the human condition, and about the pursuit of healing and togetherness as interracial reconciliation work for which we are all responsible.

It is among an increasingly visible cohort — a loosely affiliated network who identify as New Monastics as well as others who have been referred to as part of an intentional Christian community movement — that racial reconciliation has become particularly central. These Christians attempt to live out their understanding of the gospel in ways that go beyond merely ascribing to particular theological views. They seek to cultivate day-to-day living that runs radically counter to U.S. culture and, in many ways, to institutional church culture.

Perhaps the best way to convey the character of this movement is through the origin story of The Simple Way community in Philadelphia. Rob Moll of *Christianity Today* gives this account:

> "How can you worship a homeless Man on Sunday and ignore one on Monday?" said the sign outside St. Edward's Cathedral in Philadelphia. Inside, a group of 40 homeless families were joined by students from Eastern University to protest the eviction of women and their children from the abandoned Kensington neighborhood church. In 1996, the story was all over the news as a community activist group and a crowd of Eastern students fought the eviction by living in the church, sleeping on pews, and worshiping each Sunday. Shane Claiborne and other students left Eastern's campus in St. Davids, drove the 20 miles into Philly, and unpacked their things in the nave.[24]

Eventually these young people formed a permanent community in this same neighborhood. Since 1996, communities like The Simple Way have been established in numerous places among the poor, in both rural and urban parts

---

24. Rob Moll, "The New Monasticism," *Christianity Today* (September 9, 2005), at http://www.christianitytoday.com/ct/2005/september/16.38.html.

of the United States. Shane Claiborne explains that many of those involved have learned to read the gospel anew — through the eyes of the poor.[25]

Follow Me to Freedom: Leading and Following as an Ordinary Radical, co-authored by Claiborne and longtime pastor and deeply respected community activist John M. Perkins, provides a glimpse of the centrality and understanding of the reconciliation paradigm among these evangelicals.[26] In the course of discussing what Christ-like leadership and meaningful discipleship look like in a broken world, Perkins and Claiborne discuss the challenge of race numerous times. Perkins writes:

> Reconciliation assumes equality; that all people are equal. For people who look different and live different lives to become friends, we first have to be reconciled. For me to be reconciled to you, I have to feel and see dignity in you, not just accept you because the Bible tells me to or because it is comfortable.[27]

Seeing dignity does not come by overlooking difference through emphasizing a shared human identity that ignores race. Rather, Perkins lifts up the stories of Moses and Esther. Each of these biblical examples needed to affirm his or her unique ethnic identity in a system attempting to obliterate it. Their stories teach us that failure to embrace and affirm our God-given identities is nothing less than deadly. Perkins thus concludes,

> God wants whites to be white, not un-white. The same is true for all ethnicities. I didn't just happen to be black. My mother was black, my grandmother was black, my great-grandfather was black. I'm intentionally black. . . . *God intended you to be who you are* [emphasis in the original].[28]

This understanding is not unlike mainline Protestant's insistence that differences are part of God's design and intention and are thus to be celebrated.

Claiborne similarly reflects on the meaning of difference. He claims "Caesar's world" demands that we all be the same or conform to certain "boxes." In contrast, he claims: ". . . our God is a God of diversity. Our God is an artist. The kingdom of God is a place where every person is unique,

25. Moll, "The New Monasticism."
26. Shane Claiborne and John M. Perkins, *Follow Me to Freedom: Leading and Following as an Ordinary Radical* (Ventura, Calif.: Regal, 2009).
27. Claiborne and Perkins, 56.
28. Claiborne and Perkins, 32.

just like our fingerprints."[29] This reflection on the divine intentionality of difference comes after Claiborne describes The Simple Way's dilemma as it began to recognize how white its membership and long-term leadership was, a seeming contradiction of the community's yearning "to be about the work of reconciliation" and its desire to "reflect the diversity of God's family."[30]

Here again the logic of the reconciliation paradigm is in clear view: if being constituted as "white" impedes the work of reconciliation, then a lack of interracial or mulitracial diversity is key evidence of a nonreconciled or broken state. This state is presumably caused by buying in to Caesar's world and failing to embrace racial differences.

For Perkins and Claiborne there is nothing easy about reconciliation work. As one of the earliest and most visionary evangelical leaders on this front, Perkins has always made clear that the journey into a state in which diversity is welcomed, embraced, and recognized as part of God's plan, where we actually acknowledge dignity and live into the equality of all, will bring with it real tensions and challenges.[31] Nonetheless, that authentic mutual interracial togetherness is the vision toward which the reconciliation paradigm leads.

Another prominent figure, Jonathan Wilson-Hartgrove, is a white southerner who writes in *Free to Be Bound* of his journey to come to terms with racism and to understand racial reconciliation as central to the meaning of Christian discipleship.[32] He and his wife, Leah, who is also white, started Rutba House, a community in the African American section of a deeply segregated Durham, North Carolina. Jonathan Wilson-Hartgrove describes numerous humbling lessons he and Leah experienced as they became deeply invested in this neighborhood and as he journeyed from participant to associate minister at the historically Black St. John's Missionary Baptist Church. As he reflects on these experiences, Wilson-Hartgrove engages the theology of James Cone, at one point arguing in support of Cone's understanding of Jesus as Black.[33]

Like Perkins in particular, there is nothing abstract or easy about Wilson-Hartgrove's understanding of racism, neither in terms of his theological understanding nor his practical living. He never downplays the evil

29. Claiborne and Perkins, 91.

30. Claiborne and Perkins, 91.

31. Harper, 53.

32. Jonathan Wilson-Hartgrove, *Free to Be Bound: Church Beyond the Color Line* (Carol Stream, Ill.: NavPress, 2008).

33. Wilson-Hartgrove, 86, 91.

in which white Christians are implicated and thus assumes reconciliation cannot happen without a significant commitment by whites against racism. However, *Free to Be Bound*'s ultimate conclusion is that race is, at its essence, a divider beyond which a relationship with the Christ calls us all. Reconciliation, in this view, is the goal, and this goal calls us out of and enables us to transcend our racial differences in the context of our primary identity as one in Christ.

Recent scholarship by evangelicals thinking about race in the church has also contributed to efforts to argue for reconciliation. Here, too, we see the problem of race understood primarily as a problem of division and racial togetherness as the necessary solution. The authors of *United by Faith* insist that our 11:00 hour of racially separate congregations has powerfully negative consequences for the broader society. In contrast, they argue, multiracial congregations "can play an important role in reducing racial division and inequality and this should be the goal of Christian people." Indeed, these authors go so far as to argue that multiracial congregations might be an important part of a larger strategy to help realize racial reconciliation in the nation as a whole.[34]

In the context of taking a strong stance for multiracial congregations as a core value in Christian visions of the church, *United by Faith* carefully acknowledges the deep and long history of white racism that has led to uniracial congregations. It also attends to the theological reasons separation exists — namely that people of color have needed uniracial churches to be able to honor the God-ordained dignity of all against what was being encountered when worship took place with white racists.[35] The authors make clear that uniracial churches have played some of the most important roles in terms of political activism for communities of color, engaging on behalf of those who experience racism. They are clear that multiracial congregations must not lose this role.[36]

In fact, *United by Faith* is more explicit than is most of the literature coming out of mainline Protestantism that the call for multiracial churches does not mean people of color should all become part of white churches.[37] Rather, they warn against the dangers multiracial worship poses if dominant voices (in other words, white ones) hold most of the power and set the

---

34. DeYoung et al., *United by Faith*, 3.
35. DeYoung et al., 133.
36. DeYoung et al., 135.
37. DeYoung et al., 128.

cultural norms for the entire congregation. White cultural styles, they write, can impede the "faith development" of people of color, and careful attention must be given to creating structures that work against white cultural domination and enable truly diverse styles of worship to manifest.[38]

After providing this history and these warnings about the dangers of embracing racial togetherness as the ecclesial goal without giving adequate attention to power imbalances, the authors of *United by Faith* engage biblical teachings, emphasizing Jesus' life and ministry, to ground their reading of the importance of diversity. They cite Jesus' multicultural set of followers, his call to be a house of prayer for all nations, and the diversity of the early church, then conclude,

> Therefore, we even go so far as to say that a Christian, by biblical definition, is a follower of Jesus Christ *whose way of life is racial reconciliation* [emphasis mine].[39]

In the analysis of these authors, coming together across racial differences in ways that are just and eschew the domination of any one racial group is the very definition or would represent the realization of racial reconciliation. Moreover, reconciliation lies so deeply at the heart of Christian identity and the meaning of discipleship that the imperative of working for it far outweighs any risks that multiracialism might pose.[40]

In both mainline Protestant denominations and in social justice–committed evangelicalism there exist some contradictions in the arguments made regarding the importance of unity and diversity. On the one hand, the reconciliation paradigm seems to claim that racial identities do not innately pertain to who we are as human beings created in God's image. This version of reconciliation assumes that our separateness betrays a failure to understand our shared humanity as something that transcends our differences. The implications of this assumption seem to be that reconciliation would come if we honored the truth that at our core we are one and *the same.*

On the other hand, these Christians argue that we must do better at learning about, understanding, and appreciating real differences among racial groups. This claim assumes that separateness comes from failing to value diversity enough. Reconciliation in this version becomes a matter of

38. DeYoung et al., 137.
39. DeYoung et al., 128.
40. DeYoung et al., 129.

genuinely embracing *particularities,* or the ways in which *we are not the same.* This is quite a different take on what is at stake in calls for interracial reconciliation than one emphasizing our shared humanity.

Whether understood primarily as a problem of not recognizing our essential sameness or undervaluing our innate differences, these contradictions are worth noting. Like the suggestion at the beginning of this chapter, that history complicates the eleven o'clock hour lament, they hint at problems with the reconciliation paradigm on which the lament rests. These contradictions might shed light on why so much attention and so many attempts to teach and advocate for racial reconciliation — and the diversity, inclusion, and proliferation of meaningful interracial relationships by which we apparently would know it had been realized — have failed to result in the kind of Christian fellowship for which many of us claim to long. At this point, however, it is sufficient merely to emphasize that despite the contradictions just named, there is general consensus among white Christians interested in racial justice that reconciliation, sought through committed attempts to cultivate just interracial relations of mutual regard, remains a primary appropriate response to the problem of racism.

Historical and Theological Precedents for Reconciliation

Despite the potential problems in the paradigm of reconciliation, there are good reasons white Christians are so concerned about racial separation and emphasize reconciliation as a key theological vision for the life of the church.

First, given that the Black church or other racially separated congregations were born because of rampant racism in white churches, it makes sense for white Christians to worry that a lack of racial mixing indicates the same kind of racism remains prevalent. It is also reasonable to conclude that moral judgment of our recent racial history should also mean we reject phenomena that were outgrowths of this history (i.e., the prevalence of uniracial congregations). More important, exclusion based on difference has been one of the more overt ways racism has manifested in much of U.S. racial history, including in the life of the church. During the civil rights movement much attention and rapprochement by movement activists was directed at white congregations that literally barred interracial traffic in their churches.

Contemporary Protestant views of race were deeply shaped by the civil rights movement, which targeted the central problem of segregation — racial separation imposed and enforced for the purpose of racial domination.

The civil rights movement deeply informed what Black and white Christian activists saw as evidence of the hold racism had on the church (namely the uniracial parish) and thus shaped the goals of their ecclesial social-change work. This work included not only desegregation efforts directed toward the more intransigent white congregations, but also a vision of a multiracial, fully integrated church. A brief overview of just one denomination's civil rights journey makes clear how much impact the civil rights movement had on the mainline Protestant understanding of racism. In the wake of *Brown v. Board of Education,* the Episcopal Church's official response was not only to assert that the courts had made the correct decision, but also to state that the church needed to cultivate "interracial fellowship" throughout the denomination.[41] This perspective was by no means representative of the views of much of the EC's membership or many of its leaders, however, especially in the South. And what transpired in the denomination departed radically from this official position.

Church historian Gardiner H. Shattuck Jr. recounts years of subsequent struggle by Black and white Episcopalians to put the denomination's stated principles into action. In the period immediately following *Brown,* Shattuck writes, in locations where Blacks were putting themselves on the front lines at great peril, the denomination did nothing to support them other than issue statements and engage in theological debates over whether civil disobedience was legitimate.[42] When Black and white Episcopalians organized in 1958 to demand that the church unequivocally join the struggle and actively condemn racial prejudice — rather than catering to the ambivalence or hostility many dioceses held toward integration — the church responded by endorsing an official statement that insisted any moves toward integration should be slow.[43]

This denominational response compelled the same group of activists to found the Episcopal Society for Cultural and Racial Unity (ESCRU) in December 1959. During its active years ESCRU challenged the Episcopal Church to take on pro-segregation priests and bishops, provide support for Episcopalians working in the civil rights movement, and end racial admission criteria for any school, hospital, or other institution with which the EC was affiliated.[44] In fact, Martin Luther King Jr. himself had applied for his son's admission to

41. Gardiner H. Shattuck Jr., *Episcopalians and Race: Civil War to Civil Rights* (Lexington: University of Kentucky Press, 2000), 67.
42. Shattuck, 79.
43. Shattuck, *Episcopalians and Race,* 95-98. Lewis, *Yet with a Steady Beat,* 149, 150.
44. Shattuck, 99-100.

an all-white Episcopal private school in 1961. But, despite the denomination's official stance on *Brown*, his son was denied on the basis of race.[45]

Pictures of ESCRU members picketing Episcopal churches they saw as racially intransigent, the revocation of the license of the priest who had helped prompt King's application (and who had co-founded ESCRU), and the murder of an ESCRU activist reveal how deeply the civil rights movement embroiled this denomination in internal strife and struggle.[46] (In response to the murder of the ESCRU activist, many white Episcopalians complained not about the murder, but about the fact that the church had not stuck to its 1958 resolution condemning civil disobedience, which they saw as causing the discord.)

Having been so internally challenged by movement activists, then, the church became deeply marked by specific goals of the civil rights movement. For example, one of ESCRU's main goals became to end all single-race parishes. In other words, like the broader social movement that birthed it, ESCRU framed its analysis through the lens of segregation and integration.[47] Segregation was the injustice; integration (reconciliation), the solution.

Meanwhile, the fact that ESCRU is officially remembered as one of the more prophetic and impactful institutional voices in Episcopalian civil rights history indicates the extent to which the segregation/integration lens that framed its work remains prominent today.

The Episcopal Church's dramatic history of internal racial turmoil is not particularly emblematic of, nor radically divergent from, the civil rights experience of any other denomination.[48] My point is simply to make clear the encompassing historical precedent for Protestants' contemporary focus on the problem of racial separateness. If the conflict within the EC resulted directly from the refusal of white Christians — both clergy and laity — to embrace the call for interracial fellowship and reconciliation within their congregations and civic communities, it is no wonder that a concern about separation and its constructive alternative (interracial togetherness) continues to dwell so centrally in Protestant visions and assessments of race today.

45. Shattuck, 136.
46. Shattuck, 157, 136, 139.
47. Shattuck, 101.
48. Notably and perhaps relatedly, the Episcopal Church was the only Protestant denomination that did not eventually split over slavery a century prior. It may have, therefore, had more tensions within its ranks than did other denominations in which persons who may have had different allegiances to the North or South were already denominationally separated.

Moreover, legalized segregation became the major target of the broader civic context of activism in which Christians were engaged during the civil rights movement, adding another layer of historical precedent for contemporary understandings of race and racism among Protestants.

By the end of the civil rights movement, thanks to the contributions of groups like the Student Nonviolence Coordinating Committee (SNCC), Malcolm X, the Black Power movement, and even King's own experience of racial hostility and violence when he tried to organize in the North (where oppression of Blacks was devastating though integration had been the norm for a long time), the adequacy of the perception that segregation was "the" most important problem for Blacks in the United States was increasingly called into question. But despite alternative diagnoses of the problem of race, the story of the civil rights movement is overwhelmingly told and re-told in the United States as a story of the pursuit and successful achievement of integration.

Many northern white Protestants' formative experiences of actively resisting racism come directly through this history. For many more, who did not take part directly or who were children during this period, the civil rights movement's attention to the evils of segregation was the first time and definitive way they came to understand racial justice. Even if developed from afar, a self-consciously sympathetic stance for racial justice that developed as a result would understandably be particularly attuned to the segregation/integration divide. Many white Protestants who were of age during the movement continue to exercise significant lay participation and clerical leadership in the church today. All of these realities further explain why the perception of racial separation as the major problem of racism is so prevalent among mainline Protestants.

There is also important theological precedent for Protestants' concept of racial reconciliation as the antidote to racism. For King and other Christian civil rights leaders, while the struggle for justice was a struggle to secure legal rights, theirs was not merely a secular, legal vision of equality. James Cone has thoroughly explored the theological dimensions of this dream. King's dream was rooted in the liberal democratic tradition of the United States and thus was avowedly political. But it was political by way of having been nurtured in the Black Baptist tradition. Cone writes of

> . . . the central assumption of King's dream: that America was a Christian nation which had failed to live out the true meaning of its destiny. That destiny was defined by the nation's moral vision of freedom and justice

and its religious identity as the Kingdom of God, the "beloved community" that King referred to so often.[49]

As an encompassing vision of authentic human community and right relations, this dream had long been part of the Black religious imagination and had a broader moral and spiritual mandate and character than simply the achievement of legal equity. Historian Charles Marsh echoes Cone when he writes that King envisioned a place at which "the kingdom of God met the American dream."[50] This meeting place was the "beloved community."

The struggle for civil rights, exemplified by the attempt to successfully realize integration, was rooted in this vision of beloved community, the motivating theological concept behind which was "love."[51] White Protestant Christians shaped by the civil rights movement bought into this vision wholeheartedly.

For King and other movement leaders, alongside the devastating consequences it had for those it marked "second class," one of the primary sins of segregation was the way it violated human unity and destroyed the possibility of real human community. In contrast, the beloved community heralds images of reconciliation. It is a state of being in which division and enmity do not characterize church or society. It is a place in which authentic relationships exist across various kinds of difference.

In order to convey the theological significance of this vision, Cone describes its evolution in King's thought. Cone explains that King's earliest impulse was informed by his commitment to justice. In the case of the Montgomery, Alabama, bus boycott, for example, justice meant "the right to ride the bus . . . free of the paralysis of crippling fear."[52] But the justice vision did not require the political goal of integration. Cone emphasizes that even while King believed in integration early in his career, he knew one could not publicly pursue it in the South and live to tell about it.[53]

The first demands of the Montgomery Improvement Association (MIA), then, were not that anyone be allowed to sit wherever he or she wanted. Rather, instead of requiring Black citizens to stand if the "colored section" was full

49. James H. Cone, *Martin & Malcolm & America: A Dream or Nightmare* (Maryknoll, N.Y.: Orbis, 1992), 121.

50. Charles Marsh, *The Beloved Community: How Faith Shapes Social Justice, from the Civil Rights Movement to Today* (New York: Basic Books, 2005), 49.

51. Cone, *Martin & Malcolm & America*, 214.

52. Cone, 62.

53. Cone, 63.

and the "white section" was not (the practice to that point), seating would become "first-come, first-served seating, with blacks starting from the rear and whites from the front."[54] The MIA also initially demanded that bus drivers be required to treat all passengers with courtesy and that the bus company allow Blacks "access to jobs as drivers for bus service in their neighborhoods."[55] This was not initially, therefore, a movement demanding integration.

It was only as the boycott gained national and international visibility, writes Cone, that the goal become integration — a shift that reflected a concordant shift in King's theology. Cone writes, "The oneness of humanity, informed by creative divine love, began to move to the center of [King's] thinking."[56] Justice, in its political expression and understood on its own terms, meant the struggle for simple desegregation — equal treatment before the law. But love "bestowed a deeper significance on justice." Justice understood in the context of love could not tolerate segregation, and thus full-blown integration had to become the goal.[57]

This transformation came about because of King's *theological* vision of the oneness of humanity.[58] Integration was the full instantiation of beloved community called into being by God's love for all humanity.

Civil disobedience was deployed in order to realize justice, which was a precondition for achieving love. And King's commitment to nonviolent civil disobedience intentionally honored the humanity of all the actors in the civil rights struggle — including those who defended segregation. Nonviolence was not just the most practical strategy; it was the only way to express love in activism.[59] In this way, every dimension of the wrenching, deadly struggle for rights with which we so closely identify this prophetic Black pastor — with whom justice-committed white Christians wish to be identified — was of a piece with the pursuit of beloved community.

Cone's reading of the entirety of King's life and thought suggests that it is arguable whether Protestants today who invoke the reconciliation paradigm understand King's notion of beloved community in its fullness. Not only do white Protestants tend to skip over King's latter days, in which he became much more pessimistic about the state of the white soul and the realization of beloved community, but they also tend to understand deseg-

54. Cone, *Martin & Malcolm & America*, 63.
55. Cone, 63.
56. Cone, 64.
57. Cone, 64.
58. Cone, 64.
59. Cone, 61.

regation and integration in ways that miss the deeper theological realities required to conclude integration has truly been made manifest.

More provocatively, Cone argues that given the depth of its rootedness in the faith of the Black church, which relentlessly insisted on Black dignity and integrity despite white treatment, King's Christian faith actually placed him closer to Malcolm X than to white Christians.[60] Such a suggestion gives King's life and vision a more radical edge than one encounters when Protestants today talk about "beloved community." To put it bluntly, few white Christians embrace Malcolm X. In other words, it is questionable whether we appropriate this vision with depth and fullness.

There are also real questions about the extent to which — then and now — the vision of racial reconciliation adequately addresses other realities in the challenge of race. For example, it is possible to see ways in which a reconciliation paradigm misses important nuances that exist in the differences between segregation, separation, and integration. A brief return to the eleven o'clock lament indicates the degree to which we are predisposed to flatten the significant differences between segregation and separation. Even the brief history provided earlier in this chapter makes clear that it might be as true to describe eleven o'clock on Sunday morning as our most separated hour, rather than our most segregated one. We have already seen why it is important to respect the possibility that racial separation — even if it means falling short, for now, of beloved community — plays an important role in the lives of Christians of color.

Even though the authors of *United by Faith* believe separation does not ultimately serve the interest of racial equality and flies in the face of what Christians are called to in the gospel, they carefully note the distinction between segregation and separation in a manner that exhibits respect for the phenomenon of separation. They emphasize that the emergence of separate congregations is rooted in the rejection by communities of color of racist Christianity and white Christians' general unwillingness, even when they reject overt racism, to give up leadership and control.[61]

They are right to emphasize such dimensions of multiracial communities. Even the most well-intentioned whites succumb to such dynamics. Our history of racial justice work is replete with examples of multiracial ventures and coalitions fallen short because of white participation that, though presumably well intentioned, failed to relinquish control and continued to en-

---

60. Cone, 122, 123.
61. DeYoung et al., *United by Faith,* 111-113.

gage in patronizing and/or dominating ways. Becky Thompson documents account after account of interracial coalitions that fell apart because whites would not or could not share decision-making power.[62]

In addition, significant data exist that indicate a high percentage of even those whites who actively reject and attempt to "unlearn" racism continue to exhibit deep-seated but discernible anti-Black biases.[63] These real risks force these authors to conclude,

> . . . when we bring people together with different identities, collective memories, and histories we put them at risk for losing their identities and their faith, and possibly allow the world to lose their unique perspective of God.[64]

In the context of the racial landscape of U.S. Christianity, *United by Faith* makes clear that it is Christians of color who are at risk for such loss in calls for interracial unity, not white Christians. In this regard these authors are cautious when they call Christians of color away from racial separation and to multiracial community, making the point repeatedly that numerous important values have been realized in the separation of Black Christians.

The implications of confusing separation with segregation are significant and can result in racial justice pursuits leading to profound injustices. This happened in the civil rights era. For example, one of ESCRU's goals was to end all single-race parishes in the Episcopal Church.[65] On its surface such a goal was thoroughly consistent with the extent to which single-race parishes bespoke the sin of segregation, and with the integrationist outcomes of the "beloved community" vision.

But in failing to distinguish between separation and segregation, this goal failed to acknowledge the fundamentally different nature of a Black parish led by a Black priest than a white parish led by a white priest. Even when their existence was a result of imposed segregation, Black-led African American parishes became worship spaces in which Christians were living out critical racial autonomy and empowerment away from the more

62. Becky Thompson's book *A Promise and a Way of Life: White Antiracist Activism* (Minneapolis: University of Minnesota Press, 2001) gives a challenging and inspiring analysis of some of these ventures.

63. Michelle Alexander, *The New Jim Crow: Mass Incarceration in the Age of Colorblindness* (New York: The New Press, 2010), 103-105.

64. DeYoung et al., *United by Faith*, 114.

65. Shattuck, *Episcopalians and Race*, 101.

overt constraints and impositions of white racism. Such parishes lived a Christianity that they could not have lived within the context of a larger, white-dominated parish.

In contrast a white parish resulted from and was maintained through the active choice to embrace a white racist Christianity. These two environments could not be more distinct. Of course, no Black parish ever forbade white civil rights activists from entering and worshiping with them during the struggle. But, obviously, the same cannot be said of white parishes.

During the height of its activism, ESCRU's well-intentioned but ill-advised focus led to their complicity in the Episcopal Church's decision to close numerous Black parishes. Instead of increasing financial support to struggling Black congregations, northern bishops — who were wary of being accused of supporting "segregated" parishes — simply shut them down.[66] Northern Black parishes were integrated into white ones.[67] The reverse, of course, never happened.

Historian Shattuck writes, "The white liberal approach to 'integration' (i.e., absorbing black parishes into white ones) proved to be an essentially one-way proposition that further undermined the black presence in the Episcopal Church."[68]

Shattuck explains that even Black priests who had been ardent supporters of integration began to realize by the mid-1960s that Black Power within the denomination — minimal as it may have been to begin with — was being even further eroded by integration.[69] Rather than working to strengthen Black parishes, ESCRU actively encouraged African Americans to leave these parishes, thus weakening their own churches.[70]

By 1965 six Black clergy in the denomination were sufficiently troubled by the institutional outcomes of ESCRU's agenda that they issued a "Declaration of Concern." Three years later they founded the Union of Black Clergy and Laity.[71] Lewis writes,

> While ESCRU may have been somewhat successful in its attempt "to arouse the conscience of the Episcopal Church and lead it into effective action with its own life," black Episcopalians found that such effective

66. Shattuck, *Episcopalians and Race,* 167.
67. Lewis, *Yet with a Steady Beat,* 152.
68. Shattuck, 167.
69. Shattuck, 167.
70. Shattuck, 169.
71. Lewis, *Yet with a Steady Beat,* 154.

action as was implemented did not result in an appreciable improvement of their lot, which in the 1960s had been of necessity subsumed in the white liberal agenda.[72]

In other words, among other ways ESCRU may have operated out of a white perception of the problem of racism, its ("white liberal") failure to understand the difference between segregation and separation and its related focus on interracial "unity" led to more, rather than less, marginalization of Black Episcopalians.

Precisely these kinds of dangers continue to exist in the reconciliation paradigm. Yet to discuss them at length here would be to get a bit ahead of ourselves. While the reconciliation paradigm already showed signs of real trouble by the mid-1960s, what matters at this point is to understand how powerfully white Protestants were shaped by the civil rights movement — by the teachings of its powerful leaders and the reconciliation vision of the beloved community — as well as the extent to which the reconciliation paradigm manifests in progressive evangelical movements today.

The vision of beloved community and the reconciliation paradigm it portends continue to motivate and influence mainline Protestant denominations' anti-racism curriculum and programming. *Facing Racism,* the subtitle of which is *A Vision of the Beloved Community,* is an excellent example. Here the authors of the PC(USA)'s 1999 policy statement describe "beloved community" as a contemporary example of a "vision rooted in the biblical vision of God's will for human relationships. . . ." They continue:

> All persons are mutually linked and meant to live and grow in relationship with each other as we share a common destiny. . . . "The Beloved Community" symbolizes that network of human relationships where diversity is embraced.[73]

The UCC's 1991 *Pastoral Letter on Racism and the Role of the Church* named racism a "sin and idolatry" and called Christians to "renew their commitment to be a people grounded in the love and justice embodied in Jesus Christ and the beloved community that King envisioned."[74] The UCC's 2008

72. Lewis, 155.

73. *Facing Racism*, 3.

74. As quoted in the United Church of Christ, "Sacred Conversation on Race: Immerse Yourself (Resource Guide)," 2008, 16.

"Sacred Conversation on Race" refers to this 1991 lament and call to renewal, and goes on to identify numerous systemic issues that continue, seventeen years after the letter, to get in the way of our ability to realize beloved community.[75] And, in its comprehensive anti-oppression curriculum, *Seeing the Face of God in Each Other,* the Episcopal Church offers the following explanation as to its ultimate goal:

> The goal of this program is the transformation of the racist structures of North American society through the creation of multicultural, antiracist institutions — *inclusive, beloved communities* [emphasis added].[76]

In short, King's vision made its theological mark. Whatever problems we might begin to see with the reconciliation paradigm today, here we have important, substantive, and meaningful theological precedent for Protestant visions of racial division and the time, energy, and effort we put into articulating the pursuit of racial reconciliation.

Acknowledging these historical and theological precedents for reconciliation is important. Much of this book argues that the reconciliation paradigm is inadequate for the way Christians — white Christians in particular — should think about and understand race in today's historical moment. It would be easy to read this argument as a mere critique of, or perhaps even disrespect for, the profound activism and theological brilliance of the civil rights movement. But that would be a mistake. I have no desire to argue against the powerful courage and transformations wrought by the movement. Cone's words deserve attention here. He writes,

> Who can doubt that those who suffered in the black freedom movement made America a better place than before? *Their suffering redeemed America from the sin of legalized segregation.* And those blacks among us who lived under Jim Crow know that was no small achievement [emphasis in the original].[77]

Despite my critique of the ways the reconciliation paradigm fails us today, it will, I hope, be clear in what follows that my claim is not that recon-

75. "Sacred Conversation on Race," 16.

76. *Seeing the Face of God in Each Other: A Manual for Antiracism Training and Action, A Positive Vision of the Unity That Can Be Achieved Through Christ,* Social Justice Ministries, Episcopal Church Center, Antiracism Committee of the Executive Council, 2003, 1.

77. James H. Cone, *The Cross and the Lynching Tree* (Maryknoll, N.Y.: Orbis, 2013), 89.

ciliation is undesirable, nor that robust, truly inclusive diversity in Christian fellowship is not an important and desirable outcome of good racial justice work. Quite the opposite is the case. One reason I am eager to demonstrate the problems with the reconciliation paradigm, and argue instead for a reparations paradigm, is precisely because reconciliation (like the robust, multiracial community by which we might conclude we have actually achieved it) *is so desirable.* And it is my deeply held conviction that the way we currently focus on and understand race in white Protestant contexts is undermining our ability to actually realize reconciliation, the beloved community. I believe we have missed a crucial prior step — one that, as long as we fail to take it, will keep reconciliation forever out of reach.

There were many important reasons King and other activists focused their efforts and energy in the ways and through the frameworks that they did. There were also many challenges to their frameworks. These became increasingly prominent in the latter years of the civil rights movement with the rise of Black Power. It is imperative for white Christians today to take seriously Black Power's critique of the civil rights movement, a critique white Protestants rejected at the time and remain largely unaware of or open to today.

But my interest in Black Power and the reparations paradigm upon which it insisted is not in its critique of King and other civil rights leaders who focused on integration. My interest is in Black Power's critique of whiteness, its theological challenge to white Christians, and in what it had and still has to say to the church.

White Christians ran away from Black Power with much greater fervor than that with which they embraced King and his vision of integration. I am convinced that within the paradigm of reparations offered by Black Power exists our greatest hope for eventual reconciliation.

Conclusion

A reconciliation paradigm dominates the way justice-committed Christians understand race and think about the problem of racism. This paradigm laments the reality of racial division (or separation) in our churches and faith communities and sees this division as a primary indication of racism. This paradigm thus advocates a pursuit of just racial togetherness across lines of racial difference as a central ethic in Christian life through which racism will be eradicated.

While these visions of reconciliation do pay some attention to the ways that structural justice and injustice influence our ability to achieve diverse, multiracial communities — and certainly assume that mutuality and justice must characterize the interracial relationships we seek — the presence of racial diversity remains the primary way justice-committed Christians measure the achievement of racial reconciliation.

Some versions of this reconciliation paradigm warn against the danger of confusing separation and segregation. But most give inadequate attention to the important difference between the two, as well as to the historically compelling reasons our racial lives are separate.

Furthermore, within the reconciliation vision there often exist unaddressed contradictions over whether we are to transcend race in order to honor our God-created sameness or to embrace it in order to celebrate our God-created differences. In many of its expressions reconciliation gives heightened scrutiny to single-race churches (typically white ones) without adequately honoring the legacy of Black empowerment and cultivation of separate meaningful and vibrant worship communities. Rarely is the radically different work required of white and Black Christians made the center of attention.

Reconciliation matters and matters deeply. Diversity is a good. And the theological arguments some Christians (like those introduced in these and subsequent pages) make for it are, in many ways, very sound.

But while the work of this chapter was to develop understanding of the nature and prevalence of the reconciliation paradigm among mainline Protestants and prophetic evangelicals, and to give it a generous and historically and theologically contextualized reading, many of the problems with the reconciliation paradigm have already emerged. The next step in envisioning a more adequate approach to racial justice is, therefore, to more directly take on and explain the problems inherent to the reconciliation paradigm. These problems may then become the starting point for exploring a more adequate paradigm for approaching race and racial justice.

CHAPTER TWO

There Is No Racial Parallel

The prolific attention Protestant denominations have given to reconciliation makes the problem of racial division with which chapter 1 began stand out starkly. Surely the civil rights activists who conceived "beloved community" as the realization of integration would see our current ecclesial racial composition as evidence of failure.

If Protestants have done anything but ignore the problem of separateness, instead working hard to put their commitment to racial reconciliation at the center of their denominational identities, why is it that the eleven o'clock Sunday morning adage remains so powerful? Related questions emerge in relation to prophetic evangelicalism. Among this group, a visible commitment to emphasizing race and reconciliation is more recent, but its youth alone does not explain why similar levels of racial separation exist in these contexts as well.

Since prophetic evangelicals' commitment to reconciliation emerged in the mid-1990s, material produced both by and about what David Janzen calls the "intentional Christian community movement" (a more recent phenomenon) regularly notes how "white" it is, usually framing its demographics as a problem or, at least, a perplexing state that needs to be addressed. When Janzen studies these communities on the issue of racial reconciliation (to which he devotes a full chapter), he can find only three that are truly multiracial. Notably, he describes these three as "exploratory exceptions" in the movement as a whole.[1] He explains further,

---

1. David Janzen, *The Intentional Christian Community Handbook: For Idealists, Hypocrites, and Wannabe Disciples of Jesus* (Brewster, Mass.: Paraclete Press, 2013), 135.

The New Monastic communities I know have a few persons of color, but usually not people in leadership who might attract others. The racial diversity among them is the result of mixed marriages, adoptions, recent immigrations, or individuals attracted by the support network available as they go through a hard time of life. *But there is a hurdle that most communities can't get over to arrive at substantial diversity* [emphasis mine].[2]

If we are truly committed to reconciliation, it is incumbent on us to dig deeply and ask of both mainline and evangelical Christianity, "What is going on here?" Why is it that so much focused energy and attention on reconciliation has not yielded something new and different?

Despite its important historical and theological precedents, the reconciliation paradigm is, at best, incomplete. At worst it is woefully inadequate for our current efforts to understand and, more important, respond effectively to the challenges of race in our lives as Christians. Our emphasis on reconciliation misses critical aspects of what race is, and as a result it causes those of us who rely on it to fundamentally misunderstand important truths about the nature of racism and racial division. These misunderstandings directly undermine our hopes for actually realizing racial reconciliation.

As we will see in this chapter, the largely unaddressed problem of whiteness throws the very notions of reconciliation and diversity into utter conceptual chaos.

By "whiteness" here, I mean a direct and unflinching recognition of the relationship all white people have to white supremacy, along with the many ways this relationship affects those of us who are racialized as white. Honest, careful scrutiny of this chaos not only forces us to conclude that reconciliation is the wrong paradigm for how the church thinks about race today; it also begins to provide important clues about why and about what kind of understandings might be needed instead.

Two exercises help illustrate this "conceptual chaos," generating insights that allow us to unpack specific problems with the reconciliation paradigm. First, imagine asking a Protestant congregation to identify five unique and positive characteristics they associate with their racial identity. In other words, they are requested to list racial characteristics they can wholeheartedly celebrate. By definition, any characteristic affiliated with unjust privilege or dominance must be excluded from the list.

2. Janzen, *The Intentional Christian Community*, 137.

After they have had time to ponder, participants are invited to share their results. What would you expect these to be?[3]

More than likely, white people in the room will experience profound discomfort with this exercise. Most will claim they could not identify anything unique and positive about their racial identity. If anyone does identify an attribute, he or she will probably list it tentatively. (And if that happens, others in the room may even question whether the attribute named is actually unique to whiteness and/or whether it exists because whites have had unfair societal advantages.)

Some white folks will try to identify positive traits by way of their racial/ethnic roots (German, Italian, Irish, etc.). But in most cases these roots will be admitted as so distant as to not be particularly meaningful. Overwhelmingly, the sentiment expressed will be confusion.

In sharp contrast, more than likely, people of color in the room will have little difficulty with this exercise. Most will identify a host of unique and positive characteristics they associate with their racial identity — that is, characteristics to embrace and of which they are proud. Most will be able to describe dimensions of what their racial identity means in their life and how it shapes their self-understanding and relationships with others who identify as part of the same racial group.

Each time I use this exercise, the white people in the room ultimately agree that the exercise throws them into distress and disarray. Each time I use it, the contrast between how white folks and folks of color experience this exercise is stark and dramatic. It is usually sufficiently stark that I do not even have to point it out in order for everyone present to take note of it.

Now imagine a second exercise. This is one I often use with my college students. I ask them what they would think if they saw a group of African American students walking across our campus, carrying signs that stated "Black is Beautiful." They respond that they would interpret such a scene as a statement of community pride, a celebration of Black History month, or a protest of some sort of racial incident. Most indicate they would have a positive and supportive response were they to encounter this scene.

Then I ask my students if they would have a similarly supportive response if they encountered a group of white students carrying signs that stated "White is Beautiful." They usually get quiet at this point. They squirm

3. This exercise was inspired by Joseph Barndt and adapted from his book *Dismantling Racism: The Continuing Challenge to White America* (Minneapolis: Augsburg Fortress, 1991).

in their seats. They shake their heads vigorously: "no." They would not support nor wish to be perceived as supporting this group.

"Why not?" I ask them. "We talk about valuing diversity here. Shouldn't that include all kinds of diversity? If we can't include 'white,' what kind of diversity are we talking about?" They stumble to explain that calling white "beautiful" seems like an endorsement of white supremacy or a rallying cry for the Ku Klux Klan. They are not sure why our commitment to diversity does not make it possible for these "white" signs to communicate the same message as do the "Black" signs. But they are very clear the signs are not the same.

From here, we explore the possibility that there must, therefore, be some incoherence in how we understand and prioritize diversity.

These exercises expose a fundamental problem with the reconciliation paradigm. Whether it flows out of the integrationist vision of beloved community that emphasizes our shared humanity, or insists on our ability to learn to thoroughly embrace one another's divinely created differences, reconciliation implies a need to bring the *whole self* to the table if we are to be in authentic relationship with other selves. But such holistic authenticity is nothing short of impossible if one or more of the parties involved have no clear sense of self.

How can a vision of reconciliation that entails celebrating "God-given" racial differences be made manifest if a significant proportion of those being reconciled embodies a difference that creates such ambivalence and discomfort, or if those parties have no way to speak clearly about their racial selves, let alone invoke a positive racial identity? White people cannot continue to talk seriously about reconciliation without first digging into the conundrum these exercises expose.

Race as a Social Construction

These exercises reveal important truths about the reality of race. What is going on here, in large part, is that "race" is not a clear, pre-existing, and self-evident category based on our innate biology. Instead, categories of race, or racial identities, are the ongoing, living embodiments of history and of material and structural relations. Categories of race and racial identities are also embodiments of the political, social, and moral agency (capacity for choice) that people live in, through, and in response to those histories and material and structural relations. This is the phenomenon scholars refer to when they claim "race is a social construction." To claim that race is a social construction may sound abstract, but it is by no means irrelevant to everyday life for those of us longing for reconciliation. This theoretical way of understanding race is pregnant with moral meaning and ethical significance that justice-committed Christians would do well to take seriously. To say that race is a social construction is to suggest that even though we hold "common sense" notions about what race is — for example, we just know it or think we know it when we see it — race is not something pre-wired into the human body. It is not something already there that we can then point to or take note of in a second act. It is not an essential reality that exists before or outside of human social activity. Instead, in a sense, race actually comes to exist in the act of pointing and taking note. Race is very real. But it becomes so only in the interactions between different bodies and laws, economics, education, the criminal justice system, and a nearly infinite number of other institutions and processes.

An example may make this claim more concrete. Imagine someone walking down the street late at night. If that person has physical features typically recognized by society as "white" — light skin, a certain kind of hair, etc. — a passing police officer might slow down and make sure that person is not lost. In contrast, if that person has features recognized as "Black" or "Latino/a" — darker skin, a certain kind of hair, etc. — that same officer might instead slow down and ask him for identification or suggest she is involved in some sort of illicit activity.

Race in this example is not the skin tone or the hair type. These phenotypes are not meaningful in and of themselves. In this example race exists at the meeting point between certain bodily features and the activity of profiling that takes place in response to those features.

Race becomes real — it is built, or constructed — as physical attributes *are given* meaning. It is constructed at the intersection of human physiology and individual, collective, and institutional activity. And, significantly, the legal, political, religious, and economic processes that *make reference* to bodies (in the activity of constructing race) do so in order to organize power relations or distribute social resources differentially.

Other concrete examples of this can be found in Ian Haney López's work emphasizing the role of law in constructing race. López recounts an 1806 case in which three generations of women who had been enslaved (deemed "Black") sued for freedom on the grounds that their line of descent came through a "free maternal ancestry." The only "evidence" of this they could bring to the court was "their faces and bodies." "The fate of the women rode upon the complexion of their face, the texture of their hair, and the width of their nose," writes López. After several witnesses testified that "the hair of Hannah . . . [was] the long, straight, black hair of the native aborigines of this country," the court freed the women. Obviously the physical attributes of hair are not in and of themselves meaningful. But here we see how they became so as reference was made to them in order to allocate and distribute power (in this case, literal legal freedom or enslavement).[4] The combination of these references, the legal determination, and the subsequent social status ascribed to the women (by determining they were "Indian" and thus "presumably free," rather than "Black" and "presumably slaves") created "race."

Similar cases with different resources at stake arose in the middle of the twentieth century, the period during which naturalization was restricted to white immigrants. Courts were frequently asked to rule not whether "whites only" naturalization was legitimate policy, but whether certain peoples (from Mexico and South Asia in particular) should be considered "white." The courts considered a variety of assumptions about what race is, references to physical attributes, and even anthropological theories (since discredited) to determine who was "really" white and thus distribute or deny the social resource of citizenship.[5]

Race is real. Race is powerful. But race is also a social construct. This understanding of race begins to shed light on the conundrums of whiteness. In the United States constructions of race have never been morally neutral. Racial construction processes have always meant and continue to mean today that persons with phenotypes marking them as "white" receive better treatment, greater social access, and more institutional benefits than those with phenotypes that mark them "of color."

In other words, the construction of race is deeply and directly linked to white supremacist social structures. In this way it becomes clear that "white" and "Black," for example, are not parallel differences. Each has real and distinct material meanings and different relationships to social structures. The realities of injustice embodied in these distinctions have moral implications that mean "white" and "Black" cannot be seen, let alone celebrated and embraced, in the same way.

4. Ian Haney López, "The Social Construction of Race," in *Critical Race Theory: The Cutting Edge*, 2nd ed., ed. Richard Delgado and Jean Stefancic (Philadelphia: Temple University Press, 2000), 163-164.

5. See Ian Haney López, *White By Law 10th Anniversary Edition: The Legal Construction of Race* (New York: New York University Press, 2006).

A brief look at the U.S. history in which "race" first emerged can help us wrestle with this recognition and its implications. On this land base the origins of race lie in the enslavement of people of African descent and the genocide and displacement of indigenous peoples by people of European descent. Despite the way U.S. Americans usually retell the tale, the earliest European imperialists/colonists/settlers who arrived in the Virginia region — the area from which most of the "founding fathers" hail — were not seeking religious freedom. These were English elites pursuing wealth, and they quickly learned that tobacco would be their source for amassing it.[6] Lucrative tobacco production requires large swaths of land and vast amounts of labor. The stage was thus set for English relations with Native peoples and African peoples.

A powerful religious, economic, and ultimately, racial trajectory cuts through the 1600s with direct implications for the meaning of race today. In the earliest years of the Virginia colony, plantation workers were shipped from England to serve as the primary labor source (1610-1618); they arrived as tenant farmers who had some prospect of becoming self-sufficient landholders (on indigenous lands, of course). Within a decade, however, this system of production had transformed into an indentured servant system as colonial elites attempted to decrease their labor costs in order to increase profits.[7] By the time the ship the *Tristram and Jane* arrived in Virginia in 1637, all but two of its seventy-six passengers were indentured servants from Europe who were to serve a period of at least seven years before their release.[8]

Over the course of the 1600s, the range of experiences of European servitude varied: indenture time increased with the ongoing drive for profit, voluntary emigration gave way to people brought against their will and sold upon arrival, terms of service were unilaterally changed or ignored.[9] In short, indenture was a system of outright exploitation. But it never approached anything like the exploitations of chattel slavery.

In this same period there exists the first documented presence of African peoples on this land base (1619).[10] Their arrival was aboard a Dutch ship, and while little is known about their precise status, it was certainly in

---

6. Theodore W. Allen, *The Invention of the White Race: The Origin of Racial Oppression in Anglo-America*, vol. 2 (New York: Verso Books, 1997), 53.

7. Allen, *The Invention of the White Race*, 54, 74, 97.

8. Allen, 108.

9. Allen, 125, 126.

10. Charles Johnson and Patricia Smith, *Africans in America: America's Journey Through Slavery* (San Diego: Harcourt Brace, 1998), 36, 37.

the form of servitude and the result of forced relocation.[11] Scant historical records exist to tell us much about the experience of African peoples in the colony for the next twenty years. Some scholars claim the historical records indicate that Africans' experiences were similar to that of European indentures. Others argue that even though chattel slavery was not yet fully established, Africans' geographical, religious, and physical differences from Europeans make it likely their experiences were more severe. (I would emphasize that the larger context of the rapacious, violent imperial processes taking place on the continent of Africa means we should be wary of overstating the similarity of the African bondage experience to that of European indentures.) But it is inarguably clear that in the year 1640 something dramatically important for the construction of race took place.[12]

Three indentured servants stood accused of the same crime. They had run away together from their owner. After they were caught, they were put on trial and punishments were meted out. First, they were all sentenced to being whipped. Then the two servants of European descent were sentenced to four extra years of servitude. From the ruling:

> The said three servants shall receive the punishment of whipping and to have thirty stripes apiece. . . . One called Victor, a Dutchman, the other a Scotchman called James Gregory, shall first serve out their times according to their indentures, and one whole year apiece after . . . and after that . . . to serve the colony for three whole years apiece.

But then the third servant, a person of African descent, was sentenced. And unlike his European counterparts, John Punch was made a servant for life. Again, from the ruling:

> The third being a negro named John Punch shall serve his said master of his assigns for the time of his natural Life.[13]

There exist no historical records of a European servant ever receiving such a sentence.[14]

The use of the word "negro" in this ruling is critical. This was not the

---

11. Winthrop D. Jordan, *The White Man's Burden: Historical Origins of Racism in the United States* (London: Oxford University Press, 1974), 26, 27.

12. Jordan, *The White Man's Burden*, 40.

13. Johnson and Smith, *Africans in America*, 41.

14. Jordan, 42.

first time physical differences were noticed and named on this land base — the English were already quite practiced at describing Native and African peoples in ways that differentiated them from themselves and did so in order to mark superiority and inferiority and justify certain kinds of treatment. But this 1640 case marks the first time on this land base, as far as existing records indicate, that physical difference was invoked specifically and clearly as a means to assign a radically different servitude status to an African person *vis-à-vis* his European counterparts. "Negro" is a word drawn from the Spanish to refer to physical appearance. "Negro" is the pivot on which this devastating ruling and the history it ushered in turned.

From this point, lifelong enslavement increasingly became the norm for people of African descent, while freedom (or, at least, non-enslavability) became the norm for people of European descent.[15] This is the history of the horrifying and relentless march toward the institutionalization of slavery in what would become the United States — a history too few of us here know well. It is the history of one of the most comprehensive, brutal, inescapable system of enslavement the world has known. It is the history of one of the most massive and intergenerational transfers of wealth from one group of people — secured through physical dislocation, bodily brutalization, and labor exploitation — to an emerging nation and others granted normalized access to that nation's resources.

This history is that of race being constructed right before our eyes. Race was literally built here as moves to institutionalize chattel slavery relentlessly tangoed with discourses that referenced the look of various bodies. The moment John Punch was called "negro" and made a slave for life is emblematic: specific references to physical differences in bodies became the primary mechanism for marking enslaved and free. "Negro" was a physical reference made to contain African-descended peoples as legally enslavable. It was also through reference to physical differences that Native peoples were declared "savage" in nature — in a context wherein a presumed savage status "justified" dispossession and genocide at the hands of the "nonsavage." Native American history is deeply interrelated with that of chattel slavery. It, too, features a racial formation process, though it manifested in distinct

15. This transition took only a generation but, as Johnson and Smith describe, its steadfastness and quick expansion beyond the Virginia region is terrifying. See their work, *Africans in America*, 42, 43. A detailed and more technical account of this process, including attention to primary sources and documents in which we see this scaffolding being built, can be found in my book *Whiteness and Morality: Pursuing Racial Justice Through Reparations and Sovereignty* (New York: Palgrave Macmillan, 2007).

ways for a number of reasons, the study of which goes beyond the scope of this book.[16]

A critical and revelatory historical fact completes this European-Native-African triangle. According to historian Winthrop Jordan, from the initial contact until the mid-1600s, the terminology the English most often used to describe themselves was "Christian."

"Christian" became the identity category distinguishing the English from the "heathen" and "savage" (African and Native peoples). Heathens and savages were considered inferior "others" who might therefore be legitimately treated as such from the perspective of the colonial-imperialists making such determinations.

From the mid-1600s to 1680, however, Jordan claims that the English began to refer to themselves primarily as "English" and "free." This is notable because during the same period a shift was taking place in the social milieu. At first, though oppression ran rampant, it was so unwieldy and complex that who was master/servant and in what kind of labor and economic situation was not entirely predictable based on physical differences (remember Victor, James Gregory, and John Punch were *all* indentured servants). But the lifelong chattel enslavement of people of African descent soon became justified and institutionalized through a variety of legal codes, prolific rhetoric, and powerful ideology ("negro" rendered Punch enslavable for life). At this point the dispossession and genocide of Native people remains a central component in the story, in ways that overlap with though differ from the experience of people of African descent. Finally, and most significantly, the unequivocally *racial* apex of this story came at the end of the century. Jordan writes: "after about 1680, taking the colonies as a whole, a new term of self-identification appeared — *white* [emphasis in the original]."[17]

"White" literally came into existence as a racial identity through the construction of the same systems built to enact and sustain systemic violence against and complete subjugation of the darker skinned.

What I describe here is a profoundly different matter than simply saying "white people committed violence against African Americans and Native Americans." In that understanding someone who happens to be white was involved in violence and atrocity. Even if guilty of participation, a gap of sorts exists between the person and the violence. In the framework I propose

16. See *Whiteness and Morality* for a more complete analysis of this process including attention to the Native American experience.

17. Jordan, 52.

there is no gap. The light-skinned were actually racialized as white through violence. "Whiteness" literally and directly emerged from violence as a socially real, meaningful, and recognizable category. It was constituted by and forged through systems and structures of violence and oppression. White racial identity itself meant complicity and violence.

The implications of this emergence and its meaning should shake us to our core; this is a difficult and potentially reality-changing truth with which those of us who are white need to tarry and attempt to absorb deeply. This account of the genesis of "race" in the United States — the origins of "white" in particular — should render that which seems so familiar and normal (namely the easy self-understanding "I'm white") suddenly unfamiliar, aberrational even. The implications of the particular emergence and meaning of whiteness should literally jar us. For this legacy bequeaths a crisis that resides in our very bodies and demands responses from us that are radically different from those we have collectively made to this point.[18]

Moreover, the depth of this crisis not only sheds light on the consternation and discomfort whites experience in the exercises with which this chapter began; it is not easily taken up in a racial paradigm that blankets every challenge of race with a harmonious vision of reconciliation.

Race "Connects Our Faces to Our Souls"[19]

In the history of racial origins on this land base, we observe the processes through which "race" was constructed. While the shapes of such processes differ in different eras (obviously, the specific mechanisms and discourses are not the same today that they were in 1640), the basic process remains the same: physical attributes become referents that legal codes and/or social practices use to relegate different bodies to different statuses, creating racial categories.

Ideologies contribute too. They provide justifications and explanations to which people turn, and a worldview-shaping lens through which

18. See George Yancy, *Look, A White!: Philosophical Essays on Whiteness* (Philadelphia: Temple University Press, 2012). In this work Yancy frames the white subject as the one gazed upon and gestured toward with a gasp ("Look!") — an expression of shock typically directed toward the Black racial subject (the "Negro") by the white gaze. The notion of "tarrying" with the strange, deep problem of whiteness, thus resisting the temptation to move too quickly to attempt resolving it, is also Yancy's.

19. López, "The Social Construction of Race," 165.

racial horrors are seen by some — though never by those on the receiving end — as "normal." Ideologies thus massage and enable these processes to function more smoothly. For example, while legal codes clarified categories for disparate treatment through recognizing skin, blood, and hair, Christian rhetoric in this era of slavery claimed that God ordained some people to the status of slave and others to that of master. Not only was slavery, thus, part of God's orderly design for human society, but disrupting the natural order was actually wrong.

During Jim and Jane Crow, white Christian rhetoric insisted that God intended races to remain separate, and any kind of mixing was an abomination (a radically different interpretation of the Tower of Babel than what Eric H. F. Law proposes).[20] Scientific claims joined the ideological scene as well. As the legitimacy of slavery came up for increasing debate among people of European descent in the 1700s, science "proved" that people from Africa were more naturally equipped to labor in the hot sun and that African women were physically constituted in ways that made them uniquely strong and different than women of European descent.[21] Thomas Jefferson, who manages somehow to be remembered still by white U.S. Americans as an architect of "freedom," was a particularly prolific consumer and producer of these purportedly rational, scientific reasons that Blacks were destined for enslavement.[22]

White supremacy has thus constructed (and continues to construct) the categories of "black" and "white." But an additional and equally powerful component of this equation explains the confusion generated by the exercises at the beginning of this chapter: human agency.

White supremacy has never been the sole determiner of racial identities. The construction of race is never a one-way process in which white supremacy has the final word. Remember the claim made earlier in this chapter: "categories of race and racial identities are *also* embodiments of the political,

20. See my discussion of Law's work in chapter 1. Eric H. F. Law, *Living the Gospel of Peace: Tools for Building More Inclusive Community* (Presbyterian Peacemaking Program, 2004), Sections 3 and 6.

21. There is a thick canon of work analyzing endless ways in which differences between white and Black women were argued and claimed. For one particularly compelling account of the experience of Black women read through the lens of ethics, see Emilie M. Townes, *Womanist Ethics and the Cultural Production of Evil* (New York: Palgrave Macmillan, 2006).

22. For an in-depth discussion of Thomas Jefferson, see Jordan, *The White Man's Burden,* chapter 12. Also see Peter Goodwin Heltzel, "Freedom Dreams: Thomas Jefferson, Sojourner Truth, and the Promise of Freedom" (chapter 4), in *Resurrection City: A Theology of Improvisation* (Grand Rapids, Mich.: Eerdmans, 2012).

social, and moral agency that *people live in, through, and in response* to those histories and material and structural relations." Human agency (our capacity for choice) also and always participates in giving racial identities meaning.

People of African descent always rejected both the legal status white supremacy ascribed to "blackness" and the ideological claims that to be "black" meant one was legitimately destined for servitude. People of African descent reinterpreted Christian Scriptures, risked life and limb by running North, came back again for family members, revolted, petitioned the U.S. government to recognize their rights, and on and on. People of African descent created spirituals, the blues, literary canons, religious traditions that critiqued, refused, defied, and completely repudiated in creative and poignant ways the ideologies of white supremacy that attempted to constrain and define them.

In the process of this collective and sustained subversive action, African Americans forged identities that were unique and easily distinguishable from white supremacy's agenda. One might usefully say that the "blackness" that white supremacy constructed, disparaged, and subjugated has been repeatedly transformed, re-created, embraced, and celebrated as "Blackness" over the course of U.S. history.

Like people of color, those with light skin have exercised profound moral agency in response to white supremacy. An ethical tragedy, however, "whiteness" emerged as people of European descent flourished by largely complying with supremacist social processes and reaping the wealth that came from that compliance. The agency of the light-skinned has had disastrous moral consequences for the construction of "white" and for white racial identity.

Although a majority of whites on this land base were not slaveholders themselves, all occupied Native land, and most refused to disrupt the institution of slavery. Even those whose economic interests were harmed by the existence of slavery benefited from it in various ways. Moreover, slavery could not have functioned were not most whites — rich or poor, third generation or new immigrant — willing to allow it to continue. As long as the system could rely on light-skinned people to choose not to be a safe haven when African peoples ran away, and to choose to serve as overseers, to mill the cotton that moved from South to North, to rely on wages earned in that production to feed their families, and on a myriad of other similar behaviors that ensured slavery functioned, it did not matter that most whites did not themselves own slaves.

In the process of these collective and sustained actions of compliance, people of European descent forged identities that were defined by and indistinguishable from white supremacy's agenda. One might usefully say the "whiteness" that white supremacy lauded and rewarded has been repeatedly endorsed, embraced, and accepted as "whiteness" over the course of U.S. history.

The point here is not that individual white people or communities are innately sinful or uniquely immoral. The point is not that we continue to endorse these heritages. Most of us assuredly do not. The point is not that there have never been individual whites who struggled against white supremacy as allies with and for communities of color. Such people have always existed. In fact, that few of us know white resistance histories any better than we know the history of slavery is unfortunate, because we would likely be more successful in our efforts to live out transformative justice if we did, drawing on the wisdom and experiences of such forebearers.[23]

The point most certainly is, however, that (unlike communities of color) those of us who have come to be white by way of U.S. racial projects have failed to collectively or in a sustained manner resist and refuse white supremacy over and over again. In the course of this failure we have allowed the meanings white supremacy gives to whiteness to define our own white racial identities.

People of color tend to engage successfully in the first exercise with which this chapter began precisely because they have written a story for themselves utterly different from that which white supremacy has attempted to write for them. In the second exercise, "Black" can be claimed as "beautiful" because the agency of people of African descent has made it so. But white racial identity has emerged as those deemed white have lived in active or passive complicity with racially unjust practices and have continually accrued, even until today, the material benefits of those histories and their contemporary manifestations. And while the particular benefits of white supremacy for different groups vary dramatically, this is true even for the less economically well-off among us, the female, and the gay or lesbian.[24]

23. Tim Wise says something similar when he states, ". . . how helpful might it be (in terms of lessening our [white] anxiety and allowing us to embrace the multiracial and multicultural future) if we knew about the history of white antiracism, multiracial solidarity and allyship?" He goes on to urge us to learn the stories of the following: Jeremiah Evarts, William Shreve Bailey, John Fee, Helen Hunt Jackson, Sarah and Angelina Grimké, Robert Flournoy, George Henry Evans, Matilda Gage, Catherine Weldon, Lydia Child, Anne Braden, Will Campbell, Virginia Foster Durr, J. Waties Waring, Constance Curry, Bob and Dottie Zellner, and Mab Segrest. *Dear White America: Letter to a New Minority* (San Francisco: City Light Books, 2012), 151.

24. See, for example, Aida Hurtado, *The Color of Privilege: Three Blasphemies on Race*

White people struggle with the first exercise because we have not engaged in a collective and sustained disruption and refusal of white supremacy. As a result, identifying unique and positive characteristics is nearly impossible and claiming white as beautiful is unthinkable: to do so reiterates a supremacist stance. Whereas "Black is beautiful" endorses an identity of creative resistance, "white is beautiful" endorses an identity that has overwhelmingly been constituted by white supremacy and racial dominance. We and my students are right to be troubled by that invocation. Simply put, "white" as a racial category today cannot and does not endorse or refer to a collective identity of resistance.

In the context of this land base and nation-state, which remains racially hierarchical and dominating, to understand that race is a social construction means to recognize that "white" as a racial identity contains within it a moral crisis. To put it a different way: to be white is to exist in a state of profound moral crisis.

This is not a crisis of our choosing. And, perhaps more frustrating, it is not a crisis to which there are any obvious or immediate solutions. But many of us have gained sufficient awareness of this crisis that we become deeply uncomfortable when challenged to talk about our whiteness — especially if asked to do so in positive terms or in the context of "valuing diversity." I believe that recognizing and acknowledging this crisis provides a powerful and clarifying starting point — if a difficult one — in addressing so much of our moral confusion about race.

Recognizing and acknowledging my "whiteness" as a state of profound moral crisis requires me to take a very different view of racial identity than does John Perkins when he says, "God wants whites to be white."[25] If the history described above has given "white" its moral and material meanings and if today's structural realities continue those trajectories, it makes no sense to say "God wants whites to be white!" In fact, this history suggests that those of us who are white must be called to some sort of intervention and interruption in regard to our whiteness.

Virtually nothing in the actual formation of "white" *as a racial identity* (which is not the same as saying "nothing in our identity as people who

and Feminism (Ann Arbor: University of Michigan Press, 1997). Hurtado analyzes the ways white women's access to the economic resources of white men through familiar relations undermines even the most ardent white feminist's ability to challenge whiteness and white racial privilege and thus our abilities to live out solidarity with women of color.

25. Shane Claiborne and John M. Perkins, *Follow Me to Freedom: Leading and Following as an Ordinary Radical* (Ventura, Calif.: Regal, 2009), 32.

happen to be white"), to this point in U.S. history, is anything we dare say "God wants." We will all be so much better served if we put this truth — an honest acknowledgment of the moral crisis of white identity — on the table in full view; rather than attempt to flatten the distinct problem of whiteness and white racial identity to fit a paradigm of our shared struggle to embrace those who are different (as though this were something with which whites and people of color wrestle similarly). Such a move might allow us to contend collectively with the moral crisis in ways that reveal more effective responses to racial division and injustice than we have lived out to this point.

Indeed, understanding what race actually is and the histories and structures from which it emerges suggests that the challenge of embracing difference — however real — may be among the least of our justice problems. The concrete structures and histories that are the source of our alienation from each other are the far more serious problem. And the deeper problem still? The reality that these structures and unredressed histories continue to racialize us. In failing to respond to them, white people actively allow white supremacy to continue to constitute our identities.

Race, writes Ian Haney López, "connect[s] our faces to our souls."[26] López means here something deeply akin to what I am trying to describe. Race has been and continues to be constructed. It is a process through which people — human communities — live out behaviors and make choices in response to unjust legal, economic, and political structures. These choices shape our very humanity, as we are all thoroughly and differently racialized in this ongoing, dynamic exchange.

In the context of our contemporary U.S. racial landscape, then, what is there for white people to embrace as unique and positive? That whites are stymied by the opening exercises makes complete sense. And the causes and nature of this crisis begin to gesture toward the work that is required — work we will be capable of only if we allow ourselves to see our very racialization in this unfamiliar but deeply historical and reality-based way.

A Universal Ethic versus a Particular One

The reconciliation paradigm justice-seeking Christians overwhelmingly advocate claims that difference is a good that should be embraced and celebrated. But historical realities complicate and even implode that claim. To

26. López, "The Social Construction of Race," 165.

put it bluntly, racial differences are not different in the same way. The moral crisis of whiteness throws the reconciliation paradigm into complete chaos because "whiteness" is a difference we simply cannot and should not embrace and celebrate — at least not yet.

Moreover, the alienation and brokenness we experience is not a problem for which those of us who are white and those of us who are people of color or African American share equal or even similar responsibility.

As we deepen our understanding of how and why the reconciliation paradigm fails in light of a historical overview that reconfigures our understanding of what race is, an important concept needs to be introduced. At its most basic level, the reconciliation paradigm rests on a *"universalist ethic"* for conceptualizing matters of race.

To speak of a universalist ethic is to describe a standard presumed to be so truthful and essential (so universal) that it can be legitimately brought to bear in regard to all of us, no matter our particular racial identity. A universalist ethic presumes that the fundamental common denominator on which we should focus is our sameness — on what it is we supposedly all share.

True to its name, such an ethic speaks in universal terms about uniracial parishes, racial differences, and interracial divisions. For example, it views white uniracial congregations the same as Black uniracial congregations — namely it sees them as similarly problematic in their uniracialness. Difference is something "we" should "all" want to learn about. Our differences are similarly unique and valuable and, thus, equally embraceable. "The problem" of race or racial division is a problem against which all Christians are called to work in similar ways.

The universalist ethic that leads to these interpretations of the challenge of race names the humanness underneath our differences as the most relevant category of analysis. It urges us to learn to embrace our differences because difference is something we all, as humans, share. Indeed, our first exercise offers a perfect example. The presumption that it would even make sense to ask people of color and white people the same question about unique and positive characteristics inherent to their racial identities (a question we have now seen makes little sense) can only come out of a universalist ethic.

A universalist ethic tends to use a good deal of "we" language to speak about all of us in relationship to racial brokenness and division. The internal logic of its universality means it cannot effectively employ the language of distinction, such as "we whites" and "we African Americans." Rather, it has to assume at an underlying level that Black and white racial identities are somehow parallel.

Digging more deeply into what race actually is begins to shed light on why a universalist ethic (and the reconciliation paradigm that depends on it) is bound to fail us. First, even if it is true on some abstract level that underneath our differences we are the same, none of us actually knows what that means. Have you ever engaged a human who had no sex, no gender, no race, no embodiment? We only ever know people as humans through particularities.

In other words, the "truth" of our human sameness has virtually no meaningful impact on day-to-day lives. It is a relatively useless abstraction. But whether universalism assumes our racial difference is just a veneer of some fundamental sameness or asserts that our differences are equally beautiful and thus to be equally valued, it fails to describe the actual reality of race belying both of those assumptions.

In political and moral terms "white" is clearly not an identity that is an easy or obvious parallel to Black, Latino, Native American, or any other racial/ethnic identity. What we share in our diversity is not some innate identity category that God created and we therefore need to always affirm. What we share are histories and social structures — and those that mark the white/Black/Native American divide are particularly deep. This sharing makes our identities themselves, our relationships to racial division, and our responsibilities when it comes to injustice anything but the same.

Meanwhile, the confusion of whites in our first two exercises, the notion of race as a social construction, and the historical overview that lifts up a mere fraction of the devastating realities innate to that construction evidence the nonparallel natures of whiteness and blackness. This not only proves inadequate the universal ethic that presumes all differences are different in the same way. It reveals how whiteness is a moral crisis that those of us who are white must challenge head-on — to its depths and in concrete ways over a long enough period of time — that its meanings might be radically and utterly transformed. We need an ethic that both insists and focuses on the distinct relationship and responsibility of whites for the particular problem of whiteness.

Problems with the reconciliation paradigm and the assumptions about difference on which it rests become most clear when we move away from a *"universalist"* way of talking about race and difference and, instead, bring a *"particularist ethic"* to bear on the discussion. A particularist ethic recognizes that there is no one shared standard against which we might measure or interpret our experiences of race, nor one to which we may all be held similarly accountable. Rather, we can begin to speak of the *"particular"* problem white racial identity brings to bear on reconciliation, the particular relationship of white people to matters of race and racial injustice. (As well, we can speak of the particular relationship of people of color to matters of race and racial injustice.)

When we do so, incoherence is not the result. Rather, allowing particularity or distinction to be our starting point allows us to analyze and meaningfully discuss the differences between blackness and whiteness, as well as to ascertain the different work required of differently racialized groups in the context of white supremacy.

Another important outcome is that the structures, histories, and injustices that result in such particularity — that, in fact, give our identities (and our agency in response to those realities) distinct meanings — become central in our attempts to envision and work for racial justice. This focus leads us to a very different and more adequate paradigm for responding to race than the reconciliation paradigm can offer. In short, given the construction of race and U.S. racial history, only a particularist ethic is able to support the kind of understanding imperative for meaningful and effective responses to our *actual* racial situation.

Racial division is a real problem. For one thing, we have significant evidence that whites move into more active anti-racist postures only after being exposed to robust and significant diversity such that they make meaningful and sustained relationships across racial lines. Our separateness makes it more difficult for white people to be deeply aware of and take on the crisis of whiteness in ways that contribute to the flourishing of all.

Moreover, a lack of robust, authentic diversity in our day-to-day lives — including in our churches — deeply impoverishes white lives. I underscore here my unwillingness to say that the same is necessarily true for communities of color. In fact, having to contend on a regular basis with certain kinds of white racial embodiments is often quite taxing and costly to people of color.[27]

But the racial problem, or the problem of racism — the *actual* racial situation in our faith communities — is not separateness itself. And togetherness is certainly no solution. Separateness is merely a symptom. The real problem is what our differences represent, how they came to be historically, and what they mean materially and structurally still. Racial separateness is evidence of the extent to which our differences embody legacies of unjust

---

27. "Research suggests that whites who attend church with people of color are more likely to have progressive attitudes than other whites." Curtiss Paul DeYoung, Michael O. Emerson, George Yancey, and Karen Chai Kim, *United by Faith: The Multiracial Congregation as an Answer to the Problem of Race* (New York: Oxford University Press, 2003), 137.

material structures. Racial separateness is a to-be-expected outcome of the reality that our differences literally contain still painful and violent histories that remain unredressed and unrepaired. Racial separateness reveals that our differences are the very manifestation of ongoing forms of racial injustice and white supremacy. A paradigm that cannot meaningfully incorporate this understanding within its very framing of the problem cannot begin to realize its own hoped-for ends.

On a related note, racism is not primarily a pattern of thought, though it includes such, any more than our racial differences are morally neutral.[28] Even if and when we reject the "thinking" on which these histories were based — namely that some races are better than others — or reject the way claims of racial superiority and inferiority express themselves today, we have not done much to directly engage the reality of race that comes into view in this chapter. This is yet another reason the reconciliation paradigm as white Protestants articulate it is so rarely, if ever, realized despite how much energy and effort we put into advocating and working toward it.

Racism and racial injustice are actual material conditions that shape all of our lives and mediate all of our relationships with one another. These material conditions, which began in the era of enslavement and continue powerfully still today, are the source of our alienation from each other. Loving difference without addressing these conditions as a way of demonstrating that love is a recipe for failure.

Race does indeed connect our faces to our souls. If race is produced in significant part by the social structures in which we live, the histories we inherit, and our agency-filled responses to all of this, then it is fair to say that the white soul is in great peril. Recognizing that race is a social construction helps us to be clear that setting our souls right is not and cannot be merely a matter of coming to the right ideas and attitudes on difference. As important as genuinely appreciating difference may be for an array of other reasons, setting our souls right can be done only through justice-filled engagement with and responses to those very same structures that racialized our human bodies in the first place and continue to racialize us on a daily basis.

---

28. Mary McClintock Fulkerson writes of this phenomenon. She notes ". . . the lack of correlation between beliefs about equality of the races and persons with disabilities and successfully diverse churches," and her qualitative study that identifies ". . . the practices that brought people *physically* together in settings of equality that provided the crucial minimal conditions for altering bodily proprieties toward comfort with the other." Mary McClintock Fulkerson, *Places of Redemption: Theology for a Worldly Church* (New York: Oxford University Press, 2007), 200.

In order for us to meaningfully and coherently develop a vision of justice-filled responses to the realities of race that exist in the distinct meanings, structures, and histories our identities represent, it would seem we need at least two things. First, we need to embrace an ethic that can meaningfully take up the particular problem of whiteness. Second, we need to embrace the shift in focus this particularist ethic demands.

Rather than setting our sights on the other who is racially distinct from us and from whom we are alienated — seeing transformation of that relationship as primary in our justice work — we need to set our sights on the sources of the alienation: seeing transformation of unjust structures and disruption of our complicity in those structures as primary in our justice work.

Conclusion

Pushing on notions of diversity and difference — the values out of which our eleven o'clock Sunday morning lament emerges and for which the reconciliation paradigm is the primary response — by focusing on the meaning of "white" as white people engage issues of diversity, we quickly discover the extent to which "whiteness" or the attempt to value "white" racial identity throws the reconciliation paradigm into chaos. Given what "white" is at present, white Christians cannot show up with our whole racial selves to engage in authentic interracial relationships — a showing up that the very notion of *"racial"* reconciliation requires.

In contrast, when we take seriously the history of race in the United States and the processes through which race comes to be real, socially meaningful, and constitutive of our collective lives, we begin to understand why this is the case, become unable to ignore the particular problem of whiteness, and gain insights as to why our attempts to realize racial healing and beloved community continue to fail. Namely attempts to interpret and respond to race by emphasizing separation as the problem instead of understanding it as a mere symptom will not succeed as long as the moral crisis remains unaddressed.

It is deeply ironic, perhaps, but it would seem that our only hope of realizing the very thing we say we most want — meaningful, robust, authentic multiracial communities of reconciliation — may in fact require us to give up and let go of that very thing, of reconciliation as our vision and goal. As long as the particular problem of whiteness remains unaddressed, the reconciliation paradigm and the universal ethic on which it rests will prove utterly inadequate and ill-suited to the challenges we face.

Meanwhile, as long as we continue to respond to the challenges of race and racism primarily through a reconciliation paradigm, we will be unable to emphasize and respond to the particular problem of whiteness. For the framework and logic of the universal ethic on which reconciliation rests foreclose the possibility of engaging in such a particular reading. The nature of race and U.S. racial history makes clear that the structural and material conditions of alienation out of which our differences actually emerge, rather than the differences themselves, must become the primary emphasis and inform the organizing logic of our response to the challenges of race.

It may also be ironic that hopeful possibilities actually emerge out of the despair racial division seems to provoke today among white Christians if and when we begin to let go of the reconciliation paradigm. This is because the same analysis that reveals why reconciliation fails also allows more adequate ways of engaging race that take seriously the structures, histories, violence, and other concrete realities that create our moral crisis and cause interracial alienation. Here it has become clear that a particularist ethic enables us to take seriously the difference that whiteness represents relative to blackness. And, like the universalist ethic, a particularist ethic also supports a specific racial paradigm. In chapter 4 we will begin to engage the reparations paradigm — a way of understanding and responding to race that both takes whiteness seriously and locates structures and histories in the center of its vision, even when considering the problem of interracial relationships.

Before turning to the reparations paradigm, however, two other explorations are needed. First, to fully embrace the possibilities that emerge if we let go — at least for now — of the reconciliation paradigm, we must make sure we have fully come to grips with as many dimensions of its inadequacies for our contemporary racial situation as possible. Thus, chapter 3 will identify another dimension of the problem with the reconciliation paradigm — namely the extent to which it privileges a white perspective.

Second, and somewhat contradictory, even as the reconciliation paradigm remains dominant in the thinking and actions of both mainline Protestants and prophetic evangelicals, there are, nonetheless, breakthroughs in these communities of some of the constraints reconciliation imposes. For example, at points attention to the structures that unjustly benefit and harm differently racialized groups is understood as part of the work of reconciliation, as is some discussion of the greater responsibility of white people for racism (given the nature of those structures). In my view, these breakthroughs ultimately succumb to the problems that reconciliation and a universalist ethic impose. But it is important to acknowledge them to ensure that these communities and their thinking are represented as fairly and adequately as possible.

More important, emphasizing points at which justice-seeking white Christians are already engaging race in ways demanded by a reparations paradigm may, in fact, make the move to embrace that paradigm — and the kind of racial justice work for which it calls — less of a stretch. In what follows, then, we will attend to both of these matters as a final step toward clearing the necessary analytical ground for presenting a convincing case for a reparations paradigm.

CHAPTER THREE

Reconciliation Is Not the Answer

By this point real inadequacies of the reconciliation paradigm are clear. It cannot attend to the specific problem posed by white racial identity, which complicates our vision of beloved community as diverse and reconciled community. This vision necessitates we all bring our whole, authentic racial selves to the table. But without having responded to the acute moral crisis that resides in white racial identity, white Christians are simply not prepared to do this.

Related, the reconciliation paradigm asks us to focus primarily on difference itself instead of on what our differences represent: our failure to understand the significance of the constructed nature of race. Even when reconciliation visions do acknowledge that our different racial identities position us differently in relation to social power, centering on difference *per se* as the problem leads to interpretations of and responses to race that are far different from those that would emerge from centering on the histories, structures, and material relations that constructed race. Centering on difference *per se* hinders our ability to hone in on whiteness (for the moral crisis is made visible only when we focus on the same histories and structures that constitute whiteness in the first place) and subordinates structural justice pursuits to relational ones.

With such clarity comes understanding of why it is that robust, multiracial communities and authentic, sustained relationships across lines of racial difference largely continue to evade us. A misdiagnosis — as we mistake symptoms for the underlying cause — of the reasons beloved community is so difficult to bring to fruition generates responses to race and racism that perpetuate that very misdiagnosis. Put differently, our responses to racial division reproduce the problems that begin with inaccurate assessments of the significance and meaning of that division. (Question: "Is your T-shirt green or blue?" Response: "Huh? It's a sweater.")

We have come quite a distance by this point, then, in exploring the case that a new approach to understanding and responding to race in justice-seeking Christian contexts is needed.

But our engagement of the reconciliation paradigm is not complete. There are other dimensions of the reconciliation paradigm that further render it inadequate. There are risks in taking this "inadequacy analysis" further. Too much deconstruction (of anything we hold dear!) can create conditions in which cynicism and despair set in. As well, by pressing harder still on the inadequacies of the reconciliation paradigm, I risk creating the perception that there is nothing at all good, helpful, or rightly focused in regard to racial justice taking place today among Christians (of any color) longing for reconciliation. That perception would be inaccurate.

But this risk is worth taking. Deep, clear understanding of the pitfalls and conundrums innate to the reconciliation paradigm and into which it inevitability leads leave us more open to considering a different paradigm — a paradigm that those of us who are white might quickly dismiss if we are not clear about the depth and extent of reconciliation's flaws.

We need to see *utterly* why reconciliation fails so we may risk ceasing our endless efforts to make it realize ends for which we long but for which it is woefully unequipped. The reconciliation paradigm has such a deep grip and garners such powerful loyalty in justice-seeking Christian contexts (for reasons laudable in themselves) that nothing less than a clear-eyed assessment of its shortcomings can begin to gain a hearing for a reparations paradigm, let alone to empower those of us longing for reconciliation to take the radically counterintuitive step of letting the reconciliation paradigm go.

The risks of further deconstruction, however, bring into focus a second responsibility of this chapter. After attending to additional dimensions of reconciliation's inadequacy, this chapter will focus on thinking and work among mainline Protestants and prophetic evangelical Christians that do manifest more adequate approaches to racism. These glimmers of anti-racist approaches seem to indicate that some in these groups ascertain the need for a particularist ethic (my language, not theirs), one that is capable of contending with the problem of whiteness and that is thus, at least in moments, unfolding despite the grip and logic of reconciliation.

It is important to emphasize these glimmers — as partial as they may be — in order to give as fair and complete a description as possible of the actual understanding of race and racism in mainline and evangelical thought today. But it is also important as insulation against cynicism and despair. These glimmers suggest that a move to a reparations paradigm is not a full and unprecedented break with everything white Christians longing for reconciliation have been doing and thinking to this point. (It is certainly not a break from what African American Christians have done and thought, and are doing and thinking.)

These glimmers of the logic at the heart of a reparations paradigm may, in fact, be one reason reparations itself has found a forum in several contexts among mainline Protestants (the focus of the final third of this book). And while we are a far cry from widespread recognition of the need for such a paradigm, such glimmers may mean we are more prepared than we might think to let go of the reconciliation paradigm and recognize what we stand to gain from heartily embracing new, more adequate ways of conceptualizing and responding to race.

Reconciliation Today as a "White" Vision

In addition to throwing the notion of reconciliation and the assumptions of diversity on which it rests into conceptual chaos, there is another way the problem of whiteness complicates our eleven o'clock Sunday morning lament. When pressed, some of the complexities of the lament — for example, that it ignores the legacy of Black church history — lead to the recognition that it privileges a white perspective on the meaning and goals of diversity, inclusion, and reconciliation.

I make this claim with some trepidation. I am aware that there are Christians of color — including African American Christians — actively at work promoting a reconciliation paradigm as a way forward (the multiracial authorship of *United by Faith* comes to mind). To be frank, as a white scholar it is somewhat uncomfortable to risk being seen as suggesting that any Christian of color may be advocating a framework overly inflected by "white" concerns.

Indeed, important nuances often attend people of color's reconciliation talk that are missing in predominantly white articulations of reconciliation (recall the care *United by Faith* exerts to articulate the reason separation has yielded many goods for Christians of color and the dangers multiracial congregations can pose to these same Christians). Some of these nuances will be given attention later this chapter.

In short, I venture into this fraught terrain lightly. But I venture nonetheless. I remain convinced that even when reconciliation is nuanced and addresses social power so as to work against privileging white concerns — and even in the rare cases when reconciliation is being worked on together by activists, thinkers, and communities in ways that can be described as truly multiracial — the reconciliation paradigm often succumbs and becomes overly attentive to white concerns at the expense of the concerns and needs of communities of color. That reconciliation today is largely a "white" vision is evident in at least three different ways.

First, white Christian concerns about our segregated hour overwhelmingly rest on the unspoken assumption that inclusion or diversification should happen primarily in one direction. Namely, "our" churches are too white and the fact that they do not include more people of color probably means racism is present.

While it is certainly the case that racism remains present in our churches and that their uniracial whiteness could be evidence of this, this concern is framed from a white perspective: "Why aren't there more people of color here, and what can we do to fix that?"

Consider the radically different question that results if we flip this assumption on its head, if we frame the concern from a perspective other than white. Instead of ambiguously bemoaning racial division at eleven o'clock on Sunday or implying that people of color should be made to feel more welcome within churches that are too white, imagine asking this: "Why don't more white Christians join historically Black churches?" Especially since we say we long for diversity and reconciliation, why don't we join churches in which people of color are in the overwhelming majority, including in leadership positions?

Most likely this question sounds unusual. Remarkably fewer of us have heard it in our churches. But it makes clear the degree to which the eleven o'clock lament as presently expressed tends to assume integration should happen one way: how can we diversify predominantly white churches?

Meanwhile, there is a long tradition of African Americans raising pointed warnings about such white longings. As James Cone puts it in his most recent publication:

> What most whites call "integration" (or in the language of today, diversity) is often merely "tokenism." There is very little justice in any educa-

tion institution [and, we could add here, "ecclesial institutions"] where black presence is less than 20 percent. . . . There is no justice without power; and there is no power with one, two or three tokens.[1]

As we will see, precisely this danger lay at the heart of the critique Black Power advocates lodged at the integrationist vision of civil rights activists.

Even if we envision a world in which racism ceased to exist in all congregations, I cannot imagine justice-committed Christians advocating that we achieve or maintain diversity by dissolving historically Black church communities. Few to none of us would be willing to say there is something innately wrong with the existence of the Black church. And well we should not! Surely many of us were distressed to read about the Episcopal Society for Cultural and Racial Unity's advocacy in this regard.

So it's simply not the case that uniracial parishes are innately the problem; nor do we see all uniracial parishes as similarly problematic. Our lament is really about *white* churches. The fact that we rarely state this dimension of our lament openly is a result of our universal approach to talking about race — as well as of our discomfort discussing the problem of whiteness itself.

The reality is that nothing prevents us from achieving diverse churches by simply integrating in the "other" direction. White Christians who claim to long for diversity could simply join Black churches, denominations, or other worship communities constituted and led primarily by Christians of color.

This suggestion, of course, brings with it other complexities, and I am not suggesting it in a serious way as an easy solution to the problem of racism. But the very suggestion exposes the extent to which the operative assumption in our concerns about racial separation, our work for diversity, and perhaps even our reconciliation talk is that of better and more robust inclusion of people of color in white churches.

In short, the eleven o'clock adage is at least deeply inflected by white concerns, if not utterly framed by a white perspective. We should not be surprised, therefore, that our attempts at reconciliation come up so short.

Having said that, this is one way Jonathan Wilson-Hartgrove's understanding of reconciliation stands out for its integrity. This white southerner writes of reconciliation only after having immersed himself deeply and for the long haul in a Black church, rather than in a predominantly white church longing to be more diverse. Despite a universalist ethic that ultimately asserts we are all called to reconciliation across our differences, Wilson-Hartgrove's

---

1. James H. Cone, *The Cross and the Lynching Tree* (Maryknoll, N.Y.: Orbis, 2013), 61.

consideration of race and racial relationships in *Free to Be Bound* is deeply particular.

Moreover, alongside his immersion in a Black church, Wilson-Hartgrove is also unapologetically clear that our failure to be reconciled is primarily the fault of white Christians.[2] A similar sentiment is articulated by one of the "exploratory exceptions" about which David Janzen writes. Chris Lahr, who is white and a member of The Simple Way community, is also an active member of a predominantly Hispanic congregation. When engaged as part of Janzen's study of racial reconciliation he says this:

> "Lots of white folks," [Chris] began, "want their church to become more diverse, which usually means, keep the same structures and wish that people of color will come and join them. But most people of color," he continued, "don't want to go where whites are in charge. If you want to be part of a diverse congregation, go to an African American congregation or a Hispanic congregation, lay down your power, and learn from them. . . ."[3]

I am not suggesting that either of these examples redeems the reconciliation paradigm by overcoming the problem of a white perspective. But in naming whiteness and addressing it in these ways, both Wilson-Hartgrove and Lahr convey a sensibility in which a particularist ethic — one more befitting the *actual* challenges we face as Christians — has partially emerged. This despite the powerful (and flattening) presence of a universalist ethic and reconciliation paradigm.

Yet the rareness of such sensibilities and the clarity with which they are articulated cannot be overstated. They are indeed, to borrow Janzen's term, "exceptional" among both mainline Protestants and prophetic evangelicals. Underscoring their exceptionality makes clear how deep-seated this unidirectional conception of inclusion and integration is among justice-seeking white Christians.

It seems worth noting — though theorizing this issue is beyond the scope of this book — that both Wilson-Hartgrove and Lahr articulate particularist understandings while remaining part of communities Janzen de-

---

2. Jonathan Wilson-Hartgrove, *Free to Be Bound: Church Beyond the Color Line* (Carol Stream, Ill.: NavPress, 2008).

3. David Janzen, *The Intentional Christian Community Handbook: For Idealists, Hypocrites, and Wannabe Disciples of Jesus* (Brewster, Mass.: Paraclete Press, 2013), 143.

scribes as still contending with the challenge of achieving "substantial diversity." In other words, their success in living robust interracial relationship has come by joining communities of color as part of their ecclesial life (a distinct institutional space from their home communities). I note this not as a critique of either Wilson-Hartgrove or Lahr, or their communities.

On the contrary, I find such bi-membership provocative and, perhaps, anecdotal evidence of what I am claiming here: that the goal of realizing truly multiracial community as the primary way of framing our work for racial justice is simply ill-suited; which is not the same thing as saying that reconciliation is not itself ultimately desirable. Perhaps these individuals — knowingly or not — have ascertained the failure of our current reconciliation paradigm and are living into their deep commitments to multiracialism (and reconciliation itself) by "integrating" in the other direction.

For now, the exceptionality of these perspectives further evidences the extent to which the reconciliation paradigm privileges a white interest in bringing more people of color "to us."

Second, we see a largely "white" vision evident in Protestant publications on racial division. Sometimes they name the truth that white folks and people of color have different work to do in pursuing reconciliation. But most are ambiguous at best about who does and who does not need to learn to appreciate difference in order to realize reconciliation.

These publications never state that people of color have as much learning to do as whites — a suggestion easily recognized as offensive. We all know that racism has not been a two-way street. But because they employ a universalist ethic, these publications are all but prevented from stating boldly and clearly the truth that it is white people in particular who need to embrace racial difference — or who otherwise have the bulk of responsibility for responding to racism.[4] Such ambiguity is present in Eric H. F. Law's *Living the Gospel of Peace* curriculum, for example, when an early chapter suggests that all of us should be equally interested in difference and fails to make clear that people of color already know a great deal — perhaps all they need to — about white people.[5] People of color have long had to know the ins and outs of whiteness in order to survive.

At the same time, Law's curriculum and many similar discussions in

4. This is not to say there are not challenges among different communities of color, but for any number of reasons there is a persistent challenge between whites and people of color that has a difference cadence.

5. Eric H. F. Law, *Living the Gospel of Peace: Tools for Building More Inclusive Community* (Presbyterian Peacemaking Program, 2004). See Sessions 2 and 3.

Protestant work on race do make clear that racism and structures of power exacerbate racial tensions and negatively impact our ability to reconcile. Most emphasize the reality that whites in the United States benefit from structural racism while people of color are harmed by it. Language and teaching about white privilege — the way white relationships to structures of oppression unjustly enable all kinds of social goods at the expense of those who are not white — are particularly prevalent.

But despite these glimpses of a particularist approach, it cannot be overstated that particularism does not permeate this material as a whole, lead to adequate exploration of the very different work required of different racial groups, or avoid the conundrums into which a failure to get at the root of the moral crisis of whiteness leads us.

The United Church of Christ's "Sacred Conversation on Race" is illustrative here because it goes further than most other denominationally produced material to specifically move participants beyond relationship building to actions. It emphasizes the need to cultivate skills for interrupting racism and becoming an "anti-racist ally," as well as the need to connect participating congregations with organizations doing work on structural justice.[6] In doing so the "Sacred Conversation on Race" attempts to enable white people in particular to take up our responsibilities in this work.

However, it is precisely the high quality of "Sacred Conversation on Race" that makes its introductory words (framing for congregations the nature of the work they are being asked to undertake) so telling. The multiracial group of authors quotes a UCC pastoral letter on racism to close the introduction with this:

> For those of us who are White, neither the sins of our ancestors nor our own past failures to confront racism, need mire us in guilt. For those of us who have suffered the ravages of racism, neither our rightful indignation nor our temptation to despair need keep us from trusting once again.[7]

Note here the attempt to speak differently to differently racialized participants in preparing them for this conversation. The challenges faced by and the responses needed from each group are identified as distinct. In these two

---

6. "Sacred Conversation on Race: Immerse Yourself (Resource Guide)" (United Church of Christ, 2008), 9.

7. "Sacred Conversation on Race," 6.

sentences the authors adopt a particularist ethic, undoubtedly out of their recognition that racism impacts our different racial identities differently. Such framing is welcome and appropriate.

But then note the assumptions this statement contains and the misunderstandings it thus perpetuates. The most troubling of these is the notion that it is people of color's responsibility to learn to trust again. I would not presume that, *at some point* in a journey of racial repair, trust might be important moral work for those who have been oppressed and victimized. In some ways it is simply not my place to weigh in on that question. But I cannot fathom, nor do I believe that any of us should accept, the suggestion that learning to trust is spiritual or moral work to be pursued simultaneously with the work required of whites.

I would similarly reject the insinuation that such work has the same moral weight as the work required of the dominant group, even if that work were identified as the work of repentance — which, perhaps more troubling, here it is not.

In few to no situations of harm and violence do we expect a victimized party to move to trust until there is evidence that the victimizer will unequivocally cease to victimize and thoroughly repent. In few to no situations is repentance accepted as anything other than an unequivocally rigorous and costly process of taking responsibility for changing one's ways and finding concrete, effective methods to demonstrate the sincerity of that repentance, by repairing the actual harm done to the greatest extent possible.

Further, I would argue that it is disrespectful, perhaps even dangerous, to expect people of color to start to trust unless and until this happens.

Moreover, as important as cross-racial talk might be for some purposes at some point in our respective racial-justice journeys, we should not accept the insinuation that trust can be cultivated merely by *talking* to those who continue to be complicit with domination. If trust is the goal, its cultivation depends on radically different criteria.

Finally there is the troubling insinuation that trust should be built "once again." Given the origin of white and Black relations in the slave trade and subsequent histories of race relations, one is hard-pressed to find a moment African Americans trusted whites to begin with. The only exception might be the modicum of trust that developed during the civil rights movement as some whites became actively supportive of the struggle.

But even then deep racial distrust re-emerged as the support of most whites — including those in mainline Protestant denominations — waned dramatically once the movement began to go beyond support for legal equality (to take up issues of job distribution, economic disparity, and more). Such distrust re-emerged with a vengeance as white Christians openly disparaged even Christian articulations of Black Power.

I suspect the authors of "Sacred Conversation on Race" would agree with the problems I just identified. It is not their intention, expertise, or even, ultimately, their analysis that is flawed here (the resource itself is quite good). Rather, it is more likely we can attribute these problems to the use of a universalist ethic, as well as to the organizing logic of the reconciliation paradigm — both of which channel our assessments in particular ways.

Given the overall Protestant understandings of race, the reconciliation paradigm is bound to show up in any work framed as a "conversation" — reproducing our already prevalent idea that coming together across racial lines to better relate to each other is what we most need to do better.

By placing their curriculum in the container of the reconciliation paradigm, the authors of "Sacred Conversation on Race" could not avoid the presumption that we "all" have something for which we are responsible relative to racial division. And if "our call is to trust that reconciliation is possible, but can only be achieved *by beginning the process together* [emphasis added]," it would stand to reason there is something we must each need to do for the other in our attempts to better relate.[8] Each racial group must owe something to each other racial group, and even if the precise work varies, it must be owed in somewhat equal measure.

On the one hand, this framing of the call reaffirms the (wrong) path whites are already inclined to take, in which our goals are to get to know people of color better and to value them more relationally. While both goals are good in some contexts, neither are good if not rooted fundamentally in the recognition of how deeply our relations are mediated by violent and subjugating structures through which whites benefit at the expense of people of color.

On the other hand, such framing completely flattens the unique responsibility of white people for taking massive collective action to disrupt our relationship to racism. And it leaves the vexing problem of "whiteness" demonstrated through the exercises in chapter 2 undisturbed.

But an even more significant problem here has to do with what this framing asks of and/or assumes about people of color.

This statement ("our call is to trust that reconciliation is possible, but can only be achieved *by beginning the process together*") asserts the very

8. "Sacred Conversation on Race," 6.

false notion that there is an equally pressing debt on every side of our racial challenge. To put it in the boldest terms possible, we should flatly reject any insinuation that people of color owe anything to whites collectively at this moment in our shared history. That insinuation is the most troubling of the "Sacred Conversation on Race['s]" introductory words.

A subsequent issue is also present: how or what communities of color stand to gain from engaging with whites in a reconciliatory posture goes unstated. The lack of recognition that a case might actually need to be made for the existence of such a benefit is noteworthy. It feeds into the already existing tendency of whites to hold a less-than-serious understanding of the severity and ongoing damage of historic racism. To the extent we do not or cannot address any of these matters directly, reconciliation privileges a white perspective.

Let me be clear: I am not unduly chastising the UCC. Myriad examples just like this exist in the body of Protestant work on race. And, frankly, the UCC has engaged in some of the finest work on racial justice among mainline denominations. Prophetic leaders of color have been part of this work and were part of the creation of this call for a "Sacred Conversation on Race."

This UCC resource is illustrative, however, precisely because it is of such high quality (a point to which I return in the second half of this chapter). The degree to which reconciliation cannot avoid privileging a white perspective is particularly evident in the introduction of a curriculum that on the whole *so carefully avoids such privileging and speaks with such specificity on whiteness.*

Given the pervasive misperceptions already present among justice-seeking white Christians in mainline Protestantism, any curriculum that similarly frames the call undoes its own best work before it can even get underway.

Reconciliation cannot seem to avoid reasserting conceptions of white and Black (or white and "of color") as parallel differences in our racial brokenness. It cannot seem to avoid putting harm done and unrepentant complicity with *perpetration* on the same moral plane as forgiveness and trust by the *perpetrated against.* It views our distinct racial responsibilities as appropriately pursued simultaneously, rather than as responsibilities that *might* become incumbent on people of color only well after white folks have faithfully and effectively addressed the moral crisis of whiteness.

Until we create and embrace frameworks that challenge the flaws we have allowed to become so embedded in the culture and ethos of our "diversity" work — and learn to see the specific challenge and work to which whites are (and have long been) called — a white perspective will continue to dominate in insidious ways.

Among evangelicals recognitions akin to those evident among mainline Protestants also exist. Discussions of race and diversity taking place among this group seem to acknowledge an impasse in the commitment to reconciliation that has something to do with whiteness. The Simple Way's monthly magazine, *Conspire,* recently devoted an entire issue to race ("Building the Beloved Community"), attending to this impasse.[9]

In addition, Shane Claiborne speaks of this directly in *Follow Me to Freedom,* co-authored with John Perkins. They, too, seem to recognize that white people bear the greater responsibility for the impasse.

Such awareness is evident in Janzen's consternation about the degree to which the intentional Christian community movement falls short of the ideal of being truly multiracial. At several points in his own assessment and in the responses he receives from the "exceptions" he interviews, it is implied that white people have a significantly greater share of work to do on the diversity problem than do the smaller number of African American and Latino Christians active in the movement.

Claiborne's account manifests awareness along these lines when he reports his community's struggle to "be about the work of reconciliation" yet having a primary demography of "young white folks." He describes calling up some of his "African-American and Latino brothers and sisters" who had critiqued The Simple Way for its whiteness "and asking, with tears in my eyes, for them to help us figure this out." He goes on to say that The Simple Way made "significant shifts" as a result of those conversations.[10]

This account steps into particularity by affirming that there are racially distinct things to be known about the problem of division (things of which, Claiborne seems to think, African Americans and Latinos may have a distinct, even authoritative, knowledge and perception). Clearly there is something about all of it that white people do not seem to get and need to get serious about learning.

Yet, despite this proto-emergence of a particularist ethic, in virtually every evangelical account of the challenge of race a universalist ethic ultimately judges "our" alienation from each other across racial lines and calls all Christians to work on this collective alienation in terms that perpetuate

---

9. See *Conspire* 5, no. 4 (Fall 2013).

10. Shane Claiborne and John M. Perkins, *Follow Me to Freedom: Leading and Following as an Ordinary Radical* (Ventura, Calif.: Regal, 2009), 90.

assumptions similar to those in the UCC example. In other words, while evangelicals seem to ascertain that whites bear greater responsibility for addressing the problem of racial alienation, they too presume we all have a "task" because alienation is assumed to be the fundamental problem (as the unrealized ideal of reconciliation). Thus particularity and distinct white responsibility is flattened.[11]

Ironically, we can observe this flattening most clearly in the very moments in which Janzen tries to get at the same whiteness problem he has boldly indicted. To get at it, he asks members of rare multiracial communities, "How can intentional communities become more racially diverse?" Thus, Janzen tries to see beyond the impasse by deploying a question that itself privileges a white perception of the problem.

It's no surprise that the leaders he asks — mostly of color — respond to him with answers about how to better achieve interracial togetherness. Given the framing of the question, how could they do otherwise ("Is your T-shirt green or blue?")?

While most of the respondents do direct attention to how a community structures itself and attends to internal interracial power dynamics, their responses are contained ahead of time by Janzen's question. The question pressures them to agree with Janzen's diagnosis of the problem (diversity) when this diagnosis is precisely what should be scrutinized — and with it his reiteration of the one-directional flow (how can "we" — the overly white intentional Christian community movement — diversify?).

What a different set of responses might have resulted if Janzen had asked a question more deeply rooted in the actual problem of race. For example, what if he had asked, "How can intentional communities become more active in disrupting racism and challenging the ways white supremacist structures continue to shape white Christian identity in the United States?"

Whatever answers he might have received, we should be clear that choosing to let go of the push toward diversity and *not* framing interracial togetherness as a solution would *not* mean Janzen was risking results that create greater racial separation than we experience now. Put differently, to invite a view that mostly white communities need to start by focusing on injustice and their distinct relationships to such injustice structurally —

11. This overarching universalism shows up in Claiborne and Perkins's book, Wilson-Hartgrove's use of reconciliation, Janzen's dialogue with multiracial communities, and almost anyplace in these works that "reconciliation" is used without intentional and careful theorizing attached to it.

rather than by focusing on relating to/with people of color — is unlikely to exacerbate the problem of uniracial demographics.

Like mainline Protestants, these evangelical communities could hardly become more uniracial! In fact, the actions my proposed framing of the question might lead to would require a careful posture of active listening to and knowledge of the needs and challenges faced by those who are racially different from ourselves in order to even know where to focus our work. Rather than asking people of color to focus yet more on white people (once we realize we have a problem) and assuming our concerns about diversity are the most salient, this proposed question asks how white people can show up for and with people of color, without placing on them the added burden of our expectation of relationship.

Reconciliation presumes personal and collective work that is spiritually and morally laudable. But the reconciliation paradigm is simply inadequate for the racial moment in which we find ourselves. It often fails to spell out clearly and carefully the radically different work required of whites and persons of color. It does not concretely lodge its understanding of our alienation and division in the structures and histories through which we are in relation to each other. And, finally, it tends to assume that forgiveness and trust are of equal urgency to the work of repentance and repair. Thus it privileges a white perspective at almost every turn. Even when we work to emphasize white privilege or white responsibility, the universalism on which the reconciliation paradigm rests will almost without exception lead us to the same result.

A third way we see reconciliation's largely "white" vision is in its prioritizing the work of relationship building (because of its emphasis on interracial relations). There are many reasons I am troubled by the tendency to prioritize relationships over action, even when action remains in the mix. But one that needs emphasis here is that the process of building relationships is often accomplished by urging people to share their diverse racial experiences and stories with each other.

There is an important logic to this strategy. Interracial relationships are critical to the work of justice, and sharing our experiences is critical to the work of human relations. In fact, we have substantial evidence that whites tend to become deeply invested in racial justice and anti-racism work only after they become invested in the lives of people of color through experiencing long-term, meaningful relationships. The power and impact of structural and personal racism, and passive white tolerance of these, become more visceral for whites when we see how real these are in the life of someone for whom we care. In any sphere of human life relationships are important, and story-telling is a key way in which we humanize ourselves to one another.

But, like prioritizing trust right alongside letting go of guilt, and like the presumption that people of color should be better included in white contexts (the one-directional integration flow), the expectation that people of color tell their stories and listen to white people tell theirs — an all but inevitable expectation when the paradigm is reconciliation — places an undue burden on people of color. White stories almost always include accounts in which we describe having lived out devastating complicity with racism.

There are no easy answers to this conundrum given the importance of story-telling. Nonetheless, expecting people of color to sit (again) and listen (again) to accounts of racism with which they are already all too familiar is ethically complicated and perhaps even immoral.[12]

This is not to mention that people of color have been telling their stories of encounters with racism and oppression endlessly for decades now. And overwhelmingly white people have failed to listen to them with sincerity and gravity.

People of color are typically the first "in the room" to call incidents of racism to our attention. Rarely do white people respond by jumping in to support them in these moments. Instead people of color often encounter white defensiveness, protestations of innocent intent, or challenges to do a better job proving racism is "really" present.

In other cases, when we do genuinely listen with open hearts and minds, there exists a widespread expectation among well-intentioned white folks that people of color need to educate us about race and racism. (This, unfortunately, is precisely the dynamic present in Claiborne's teary call to Christians of color to ask what The Simple Way is doing wrong.) This is a long-standing problem manifested by whites who claim interest in meeting the challenge of racism, and it is past time for anti-racist-oriented Christians to take it seriously in our writing and teaching on race.

By this point, vast bodies of scholarship engaging issues of racial justice, cross-racial dialogue, and the experiences of people of color with whites have well-documented how prevalent these dynamics are — and, more important, the toll they take on people of color. My concern here is not that stories are not valuable or should never be shared. Nor do I presume to speak for people of color, some of whom may want interracial forums in which

---

12. To return to the "Sacred Conversation on Race" this expectation is prevalent — though the resource is careful to create guidelines for making the space as safe as possible.

to tell their stories and be heard. Finally, I do not suggest there are never appropriate contexts within which to share stories.

But a story told and heard with the prior expectation or direct goal of reconciliation and relationship is very different from one shared and engaged through a reparations lens (as we will see in chapter 8). My concern is that here again the reconciliation paradigm privileges a white perspective by expecting and exacting things from people of color that are much more costly to them then they are to white people.

The reconciliation paradigm comes perilously close to reproducing each of the dynamics just described by assuming we all share an equal burden in teaching one another about difference or racism. As a result it meets white needs for racial education and learning much more than it meets needs that Black Christians or other Christians of color might actually have.

At the very least, we should be expected to make the case explicitly as to what Black Christians stand to gain from hearing more about white experiences — a case that is, in fact, rather difficult to make — rather than uncritically presuming the value of such hearings to Christians of color.

Each of these three examples of the ways reconciliation privileges a white perspective results because reconciliation misunderstands race and rests on a universalist ethic. Because universalism's bottom line is that we are all, at our core, one human family, reconciliation reinforces language and patterns of thought already pervasive among whites that presume we approach the problem of racial injustice from a position of relative sameness. We are all responsible to heal the divide. We are all responsible to tell our stories. We all must come to appreciate difference. We are all responsible for creating diverse, inclusive communities. We all stand to benefit in the same way from the creation of more diverse ecclesial communities. Yet, if we are honest, without significant nuance none of these statements is true.

There are likely many reasons we continue to present these statements as if they were true. They have become a kind of mantra among those of us longing for reconciliation. If not these "truths," what are the truths and what are we to do with them? How else can we understand the problem and the work? I think we continue to assert these claims and perceptions because we are not sure how to conceive the issues in a different way.

In addition, I suspect that we present them as true because we do not know what to do about the "white" part of things. But the inability of whites to speak about ourselves, as seen in our chapter 2 exercises, is not only indicative of our actual problem; it also makes the problem itself more difficult to respond to. But respond we must.

Whether or not we ascertain the chaos and conundrum it creates for us, we have yet to develop a sound and thoroughgoing set of practices that name and respond to the challenges posed by the moral crisis of being white. We have yet to admit and attend to the ways that whiteness leaves us so very far from the possibility of reconciliation. It is all but impossible to envision reconciliation without ignoring or silencing many dimensions of our actual racial situation as it stands right now.

It may be difficult to admit the ways reconciliation is not equipped to deal with the root of our alienation. Perhaps admitting the depth of our alienation and how very far we have yet to go — without having a roadmap for what to do in the wake of those confessions — is just too terrifying. So we keep repeating the same mantras over and over again.

Yet by taking a universalist approach to a situation in which the problem, our differences, and our relationships to race are *anything but the same,* we reproduce, rather than subvert, the most stubborn characteristics of racism and end up in the same places we've been since the close of the civil rights movement: with white diagnoses, needs, concerns, and hopes sitting at the center of our work on race.

Just like an approach to race that demands us to be color-blind in a situation in which people of color are already running on an unequal playing field, the universalism implicit in the reconciliation paradigm plays out in unequal ways and has radically different impacts on white communities than it does on Black communities. As long as we insist on continuing along that trajectory reconciliation will remain a white vision.

Inadequate But Not Irrelevant

To suggest that the reconciliation paradigm is inadequate is not to reject the desirability of authentic community across various kinds of difference as an appropriate, normative longing for Christians. I repeat this point because I am aware of the deep challenge my analysis poses — or hopes to pose — for justice-seeking Christians so committed to beloved community.

More important, it is urgent that this point not be missed because the entire basis of my critique comes out of a desire to articulate the conditions that must exist prior if we are to ever realize the diverse, authentic multiracial communities for which we claim to long.

To a similar end then, despite my ongoing clarity that justice-seeking Christians must identify and embrace a different paradigm, it is important to emphasize impulses that do exist in mainline and evangelical contexts that evidence more adequate understandings of the meaning of race, despite the grip of the reconciliation paradigm.

These impulses do not weaken my case for a new paradigm. Rather, such impulses stand to be strengthened and augmented by an explicit embrace of the reparations paradigm. Thus, at this point I want to highlight three broad examples of work or analysis that signal resonance with the kind of the thinking and action on race for which I have started to make a case — and about which a reparations paradigm, emphasized in the remainder of this book, is explicit.

First, in *The Schools(s) for Conversion: 12 Marks of a New Monasticism*, published by the Rutba community, those communities who are part of this movement attempt to discern and describe the commitments and postures they share in common. In regard to race, the fourth mark is notable. Here new monasticism is described as being marked by a "lament for racial divisions within the church and our communities combined with the active pursuit of a *just* reconciliation [emphasis added]."[13]

Martin Luther King Jr.'s beloved community was not a sentimental vision of unity and love. He knew that beloved community and authentic love could not come into existence without the prior actualization of freedom and justice.[14] Indeed, the notion of "beloved community" itself as the kingdom of God encountering the American dream, as historian Charles Marsh put it,[15] necessarily assumes that power relations and unjust structures have been transformed in ways consistent with biblical notions of what the kingdom of God looks like. Precisely such nuanced qualification of "beloved community" and "reconciliation" with "just" is evident in this mark.

The historical genealogy of new monasticism pairing "just" with "reconciliation" in this first example traces back to John Perkins. As suggested in chapter 1, Perkins has long been and continues to be an iconic leader among these communities. As Peter Heltzel points out in *Jesus and Justice,* when Shane Claiborne was asked to join the boards of the Christian Community Development Association (CCDA) and Sojourners, he chose CCDA so John

13. Rutba House, ed., *The School(s) for Conversion: 12 Marks of a New Monasticism* (Eugene, Ore.: Wipf and Stock, 2005), as quoted in Janzen, 137.

14. James H. Cone, *Martin & Malcolm & America: A Dream or a Nightmare* (Maryknoll, N.Y.: Orbis, 2012), 121 and 214.

15. Charles Marsh, *The Beloved Community: How Faith Shapes Social Justice, from the Civil Rights Movement to Today* (New York: Basic Books, 2005), 49.

Perkins could be his mentor, instead of Jim Wallis. Claiborne wanted to be mentored by an African American faith leader to deepen his understanding of white supremacy, communities of color, and faith-rooted community development.[16] Perkins's leadership is credited as bearing significant responsibility for race and racism having emerged as an urgent focus and concern among today's generation of young evangelicals.

Thus Perkins's early explicit work on reconciliation bears attention. Perkins has long advocated nuanced and complex notions of reconciliation and refused to conceive of it in the abstract. He has also refused to separate his notion of reconciliation from two other critical postures. For Perkins, "reconciliation" is only one of "three R's." The two *that come prior* are "relocation" and "redistribution."

When Lisa Sharon Harper explores Perkins' vision, she finds a use of "reconciliation" that is best understood as a call to be neighbors to each other and break down walls by coming together in interracial community (she uses the word "interethnic").[17] On its face, this use may not seem so different from the notion of reconciliation I have been critiquing throughout this book, but Harper's analysis goes on to indicate otherwise.

Nothing about Perkins's notion of reconciliation, Harper notes, should be misunderstood as easy or "feel-good." Real tensions are always present in genuinely interracial community, because the kind of community for which Perkins calls is the kind that only emerges when those with different worldviews and distinct experiences encounter each other in a sustained way. This comes to be only after those with power and privilege have literally relocated — the first "R" — to live with and among those without.[18]

Relocation — physically moving and rooting oneself elsewhere — precedes any possibility of reconciliation and assumes that white and/or economically privileged evangelicals relocate themselves among the poor and racially marginalized.

The second "R" — redistribution — is also non-negotiable and even more interesting here. Redistribution does not mean those with privilege enacting great charity or generosity toward those with less. Instead, writes Harper,

16. See Peter Heltzel, "The Christian Community Development Association: A Quiet Revolution," chapter 7, in *Jesus and Justice: Evangelicals, Race, and American Politics* (New Haven, Conn.: Yale University Press, 2009), 160-177.

17. Lisa Sharon Harper, *Evangelical Does Not Equal Republican or Democrat* (New York: New Press, 2008), 53.

18. Harper, 52-55.

Perkins' understanding of redistribution is much more radical, much more costly, and much more Christian than sharing resources. Christians must redistribute both their personal resources and their systemic privilege. *Christians must press for public policies that redistribute public resources as well* [emphasis added].[19]

How serious, systemic, and material is such an expectation becomes clear when we learn that historically one of Perkins's attempts to advocate for such redistribution took the form of an argument for reparations.

In the 1970s, Perkins contended that a savings account should be established for all African American children in the United States to serve as funding for college, saying that this was an appropriate response to the legacy of slavery.[20] This was only one of many public policies in support of which Perkins has spoken, although it no longer seems to be an active point of advocacy for him. Yet such clear, material attention to the very conditions and structures through which white and Black relationships are primarily mediated — the history of slavery and its long-term consequences — directly counters the universalist, difference *per se* notions of unity that dominate so much of evangelical (and mainline Protestant) understanding and discourse on race.

Perkins certainly speaks of cultivating relationships across racial lines in ways consistent with the prevalent notions of the reconciliation paradigm I have laid out here. But in his analysis and advocacy, the personal transformations that make reconciliation across lines of difference conceivable to begin with are a direct and inseparable outgrowth of active participation in radical, systemic, and structural changes in our relationships to the material and historical realities of race.

In the process, it's fair to say, the meaning of "reconciliation" itself is transformed. It ceases to function in quite the same way. It becomes less of a paradigm in which an abstract ideal and final goal is laid out ahead of time, with all pursuits of that goal then dictated by it (constraining and channeling them: namely the goal is authentic interracial diversity; pursuits are relentlessly calibrated toward realizing diversity). Instead, reconciliation functions more as a possibility that may emerge only if and as the first two "R's" are being vigorously pursued. (The diversity and cross-racial engagement spoken of in mainline Protestant contexts comes nowhere near the kind of sustained

19. Harper, *Evangelical Does Not Equal Republican or Democrat*, 57.
20. Harper, 57.

interracial encounter implied by the literal relocation Perkins presumes is necessary prior to reconciliation talk.)

Perkins's work represents theological and historical precedent for the modification of "reconciliation" by "just" in the fourth mark of new monasticism. To some degree then, racial reconciliation should be heard as inflected by these precedents any time it is articulated by these communities. This is especially true because most of these communities have come into existence only after the kind of relocation that Perkins advocates has taken place.

Another example of understanding that our different relationships to structures impedes our interracial relations emerges when Janzen engages two of the "exceptions." I have already critiqued his question "How can intentional communities become more racially diverse?" But it's notable that when he asks it of Leroy Barber, who is African American, the first answer he receives is structural: "If the organizations aren't willing to make some real structural changes I don't see it happening."[21] Implied in Barber's response is that, on its own, valuing the ideal of diversity and inclusion — having the right intentions — is insufficient.

Janzen receives an even more interesting response from Anton Flores-Maisonet, who is Puerto Rican. When Janzen asks Flores-Maisonet how intentional communities can become more diverse, Flores-Maisonet responds that authentic relations of diversity *must already exist* among those planning such a community: there must be "a diversity of relationships already in the dreaming stage." Says Flores-Maisonet, ". . . [W]e need to first come to authentic relationships [with the poor] before we import our idea of community."[22] Diversity simply cannot be realized as a later stage.

So much of the focus on reconciliation in evangelical worlds assumes that creating mutual, authentic, interracial diversity is itself the work of reconciliation — the goal. (Otherwise, for example, the white demography of The Simple Way would not be flagged by Claiborne as a concern relative to the communities' desire to be doing reconciliation.) Yet Flores-Maisonet's analysis implodes this notion.

If multiracial relationality is required *prior* to any formation as a community (if it is to be a defining characteristic of that community), then not only can you not simply form as a white community that then goes about the work of reconciliation, but the entire framework of reconciliation itself is ill-conceived. Reconciliation is either already there (diverse multiracial

21. Janzen, *The Intentional Christian Community Handbook*, 137-138.
22. Janzen, 140.

community) and thus need not be articulated as the primary goal; or it is not there and is not going to be realizable later.

Flores-Maisonet's analysis is not only sound and utterly consistent with the evidence we already have that our best attempts have failed to realize the diverse, reconciled ends that we seek. Taken seriously his analysis reveals an impossible conundrum: to reach the goal we envision as the ideal outcome (multiracialism), we have to have already lived into that manifestation (multiracialism).

He may not have intended it, but the impossibility and inevitable failure Flores-Maisonet points to reveals the failed logic of reconciliation and its lack of viability as a paradigm. This implosion, however, is productive! Like Perkins's second "R" (redistribution), it is evidence of analysis and awareness already present among evangelicals, even if not widespread, that suggests a readiness for a completely different paradigm, one that is more deeply consistent with the logic that emerges in a reparations paradigm.

Unfortunately, the evidentiary record in reading evangelicals' understanding of reconciliation suggests how easily and often it is decoupled from the other two "R's." Harper provides a crisp analysis of what such decoupling looks like when she contrasts the Promise Keepers' emphasis on racial reconciliation — which ignored relocation and redistribution — and reconciliation's failure among this group.[23]

Even in Perkins's recent co-authored work with Claiborne little is said about the first two "R's" in explicitly racial terms. And Barber, after offering Janzen insight into how the structures of intentional communities might inhibit true inclusion and diversity, goes on to describe his own communities' approach with young people who come to spend a mission year with Community Fellowship this way: "We talk about structural racism," he says, "but *the solution is embodied in relations of different ethnicities together in community.* This strong intentional year of service is like a rite of passage, a year of formation into a new way of life, learning to reconcile relationships as we go [emphasis mine]."[24]

A board member of Perkins's organization, Barber makes clear this is a departure from Perkins's view. And it may be the case that such an approach works more adequately for realizing transformative justice in a context where the leadership is a majority of people of color inviting white Christians in, rather than were the invitation other way around. Regardless, it is clear that

23. See Harper, chapter 4, in *Evangelical Does Not Equal Republican or Democrat*.
24. Leroy Barber, quoted in Janzen's *Intentional Christian Community Handbook,* 136.

even with the historical genealogy of reconciliation as one of three "R's" and analysis like that of Flores-Maisonet, this emphasis on personal relationships across lines of difference as the primary way to engage race remains the most common and widespread understanding of reconciliation among evangelicals.

A second broad example signaling resonance with a reparations paradigm is that the emphasis on reconciliation as it comes out of mainline Protestantism is almost always accompanied by attention to the ways structures of racism make reconciliation more difficult to realize (as noted in the first half of this chapter). The problem of "white privilege" as a social phenomenon has been given increasing attention in curricula and teaching in recent years and is described as a problem about which white people in particular need to become aware.

This dimension of analysis suggests that the problems we face in realizing reconciliation go beyond merely interpersonal hostility to difference, and it attempts to link anti-racist challenges to the structures that make alienation more severe.

So, for example, while the introduction to the Episcopal Church's *Seeing the Face of God in Each Other* (quoted in chapter 1) makes beloved community the goal and emphasizes the need to embrace difference as a central, universalist ethic in its educational program ("the creation of multicultural, antiracist institutions — inclusive, beloved communities" is described as the way broader racist structures will be transformed),[25] it also devotes sustained attention to the problem of white privilege. It understands structures that advantage and disadvantage us differently, depending on our racial identities, as complicating our attempts to embrace difference; and it names the dominance of whiteness as a problem of greater severity than other kinds of hostility toward difference. This is a strong move toward particularism.

> We must not forget that a principal reason for oppressive systems is the combination of ignorance and fear of the "other." This is compounded, in turn by *the primary obstacle to overcoming racism:* unearned white skin privilege [emphasis added].[26]

25. *Seeing the Face of God in Each Other: A Manual for Antiracism Training and Action, A Positive Vision of the Unity That Can Be Achieved Through Christ,* Social Justice Ministries, Episcopal Church Center, Antiracism Committee of the Executive Council, 2003, 1.

26. *Seeing the Face of God,* v.

The curricula moves from chapters on appreciating diversity and reducing prejudice to a chapter titled "Social Analysis," which helps participants study issues of power in our social lives. A later section explores the problem of institutional racism, and part 3 of the curriculum is titled "Coping with Dominant White Culture." Here, *Seeing the Face of God* teaches multicultural competency in both individuals and organizations. And it presumes savvy understanding of the structural dimensions of white dominance and its impact on white people and people of color is part of acquiring such competency. This nuancing mirrors the fourth mark: reconciliation must be qualified by "justice" to be realizable and true.

Seeing the Face of God takes it a step further. Not only must reconciliation be just, but actively pursuing justice enables the realization of reconciliation.

In its clarity and the depth of attention it gives to the problem of whiteness, white dominance, and white people, *Seeing the Face of God* looks very much like the "Sacred Conversation on Race." The "Sacred Conversation on Race" is a resource guide, not a detailed curriculum, so does not provide a detailed method for working through white privilege, for example. But it does give congregations specific pointers about issues that must be given attention for the Conversation to have integrity. These include attention to white privilege and that groups determine to end each session with a "tangible and specific commitment to action."[27]

In the course of responding to frequently asked questions, the authors address the following question: "How can we have a sacred conversation on race when all the members of our congregation are White?"[28] Their answer is nuanced and insightful. They make clear that perceiving racism as a problem primarily about people of color is itself a problem. Whites are enmeshed in and impacted by racism and need to do our own work. This is work we can do, the authors say, even if no people of color are in the room. The authors go further and disrupt the line of thinking that presumes whites should be taught by people of color:

> It can be very important for White people to learn how to talk about, analyze, and confront racism without depending on People of Color to be their teachers. It should not be the responsibility of People of Color

27. "Sacred Conversation on Race," 22.
28. "Sacred Conversation on Race," 25.

to educate White people about the realities of racism any more than it is their responsibility to always, in every situation, name and challenge racism.[29]

Not only does this analysis move away from a paradigm that frames the problem as primarily a diversity problem — thus interrupting at points the universalizing logic of reconciliation — it also moves this resource strongly in the direction of a high level of particularity and attention to the many dimensions of the problem of whiteness.

Such discussions of white privilege and institutional power structures appear as subsets of other denominations' statements and curricula as well, though in few materials are they as thoroughly developed as in these two. Still, the presence of such analysis indicates readiness for a different paradigm that would more fully support the logic and clarity revealed in such good analysis — analysis that cannot be given attention or brought to fruition over the long term when framed by a reconciliation paradigm.

A different kind of example among mainline Protestants also merits mention. Even with its strong reconciliation orientation, there is an important moment in the Presbyterian Church (USA)'s *Facing Racism* in which a self-critique is made about the denomination's involvement in the civil rights movement.

The critique begins with the statement that the fundamental principle informing the denomination's civil rights advocacy — "the belief that racism was a consequence of personal prejudice and ethnic pride" — was flawed.[30] It goes on to say that white Presbyterians have overemphasized integration and failed to understand what the Black Power movement did: namely ". . . that integration and racism are quite compatible."[31]

This self-critique emerges from the document's attempt to wrestle with the recognition that alienation remains deep and beloved community largely unrealized within Protestant Christianity. In so doing, the document locates contemporary alienation in historical realities, rather than in mere personal hostility toward difference. It also recognizes that separation itself is not the problem, nor integration necessarily the solution. This latter recognition is particularly unusual among Christians longing for reconciliation. Lastly, in

29. "Sacred Conversation on Race," 26.

30. Initiative Team on Racism and Racial Violence, *Facing Racism: A Vision of the Beloved Community* (Louisville, Ky.: Office of the General Assembly, 1999), 5.

31. *Facing Racism*, 6.

its positive invocation of what the Black Power movement knew (which white Christians overwhelmingly rejected), the document significantly gestures toward the need for a particular ethic for understanding race.

Facing Racism does not follow through on its own interruption of the reconciliation paradigm, which looms large and regularly returns to universalist conceptions of our racial situation. Nonetheless, the relationship between how adequately we understand the problem and the kinds of solutions we end up advocating is emphasized in terms very similar to the direction a reparations paradigm would take us. Particularly notable here is that the critique offered by Black Power went far beyond reconciliation, debunking the premise of integration. (It's worth noting that the negative outcomes Black Power predicted would come from integration have in many ways come true.)

A third and final important area in which a commitment to reconciliation exists, yet avoids many of the problems we have been analyzing deserves attention at this juncture. While not directly associated with the two groups primarily under consideration here, a growing body of activism and scholarship — being theorized and lived by Christian activists, scholars, laity, and pastors — has taken up reconciliation as the way to frame work for justice and peace in response to systemic social violence, oppression, and alienation.

This work is particularly interesting in that it seems to bring together the emphasis on personal transformation especially salient among evangelicals and the social analysis emphasized among mainline Protestants. This approach perceives relationships and relational healing as intrinsically related to and manifestations of unjust social power and oppression, and it sees attending to and restoring justice in concrete and structural ways as relational work.

Reconciliation studies are rooted in two related but distinct areas. The first is restorative justice approaches for responding to crime and punishment.[32]

In the context of the criminal justice system, restorative justice shifts the lens for interpreting and responding to crime away from retributive, punishment-based treatment of perpetrators (whose actions are seen, primarily, as a violation against the "state" and who thus must serve time in

---

32. In U.S.-American contexts, Howard Zehr is considered the most influential thinker and activist on this front. Restorative justice advocates exist in local contexts all over the nation to deploy restorative justice approaches in their criminal justice systems — especially in relation to youth offenders.

prison as a payment of their "debt to society"). The shift is toward perceiving crime as a phenomenon that breaks and damages the web of relationships in which we all live, with a view toward identifying the actual harms experienced by a victim as a result of crime, as well as the harm experienced by the community or communities of which victims and perpetrators are part. Crime is also presumed as an outgrowth of prior violence, a symptom of already-existing damage in our relational webs.

Restorative justice thus advocates that perpetrators take responsibility to redress the actual harm their deeds cause, rather than being punished. The humanity of victim and perpetrator is emphasized throughout any restorative justice process. Because the assumption is that violence begets violence and that most perpetrators' harmful behavior is a result of prior cycles of violence and damage, restorative justice is deeply interested in breaking such cycles — cycles that punishment in prison usually makes worse.

Requiring perpetrators to respond to and redress actual harms done (which, in addition to paying back what one stole, might also mean sitting and listening to victims and community members speak about what it's like to no longer feel safe in their own homes) is the concrete, material work needed to knit back together the webs of relationships in which human life exists — making our relationships again possible. For those interested in reconciliation work and theory this model, which emphasizes healing human relationships by pursuing repair of harm, is presumed applicable beyond the interpersonal situation of crime to situations of systemic and structural harm, violence, and domination by one group (for example, a racial group) of and toward other groups.

A second area out of which reconciliation studies emerge is the historic accomplishments of the Truth and Reconciliation Commission (TRC) in South Africa. In the challenge of coming out of apartheid and birthing a new civic society, (a) it was not feasible to imagine one could prosecute and punish all of the perpetrators for their gross participation in human rights violations; (b) layers of secrecy and lies made getting to the truth of the past virtually impossible without significant cooperation from perpetrators; (c) learning such truth was perceived as one of the most important needs of victims if they were to become full participants in a new civic community; and (d) the possibility of massive social violence (civil war even) threatened at every turn in the transition to a "new South Africa" such that some type of honest, collective, and public contending with the past had to take place if nationhood was to have any hope of success.

That the TRC managed to enable a kind of collective lament and public remembering, as well as civic forgiveness (in the sense that perpetrators who disclosed the full truth were eligible for amnesty, *not* in the sense that individual victims were required to forgive — a point Desmond Tutu emphasizes more than once in *No Future Without Forgiveness*), following such a bloody and brutal history stunned the world.

For those pursuing reconciliation in response to an astute and clear-eyed analysis of the violence, structural dimensions, and historical legacies that cause inter-group alienation today, the TRC has stirred the imagination: can this model be brought to other situations in which historical legacies of group violence remain a source of alienation and ongoing suffering and harm?

A relatively recent, outstanding example of such work then articulates an understanding of reconciliation far more robust than that which I have been critiquing to this point. In volume 1 of *Ambassadors of Reconciliation,* Elaine Enns and Ched Myers engage New Testament teachings on peacemaking and reconciliation in the context of enmity and strife, and they explore in a subsequent volume the contours of real-life incidents of harm in which reconciliation — or, at least, work for it — indeed emerges from difficult, concrete responses to "injustice, violation, and/or violence."[33]

Enns and Myers study actual cases of victims who refuse to succumb to a desire for retribution and who instead value the healing possibilities that accrue to themselves when a response to violence interrupts its cycles rather than continuing to create more harm through retribution.

The cases of reconciliation the authors study are themselves diverse. They include everything from more traditional restorative justice responses — as seen in the work of Murder Victim Families for Human Rights, through which victims of horrific crimes determine to work for the rehabilitation of offenders and abolition of the death penalty — to the formation of September Eleventh Families for Peaceful Tomorrows — composed of persons who lost loved ones in the September 11, 2001, attacks and who organized early to advocate a peaceful "no war" response and, in subsequent years, have participated in trips intended to cultivate peace in the Middle East.

The most relevant organization for our purposes is the Greensboro Truth and Community Reconciliation Project. This project is a response

---

33. Elaine Enns and Ched Myers, *Ambassadors of Reconciliation,* vol. 1: *New Testament Reflections on Restorative Justice and Peacemaking* (Maryknoll, N.Y.: Orbis, 2009), and Elaine Enns and Ched Myers, *Ambassadors of Reconciliation,* vol. 2: *Diverse Christian Practices of Restorative Justice and Peacemaking* (Maryknoll, N.Y.: Orbis, 2009).

to the 1979 politically motivated massacre of anti-racist activists in Greensboro, North Carolina, by the Klan. Keenly identifying the myriad ways the entire city has been negatively impacted in the long term by this unredressed violence (no one was ever convicted despite the killings being caught on tape by four television crews),[34] African American Christians initiated the project and since 2001 have been leading the entire Greensboro community in a process of healing.

Their work includes attention to the needs of victims, including emotional healing but also symbolic restitution to victims' families: those involved in the shootings contribute financially to a public monument commemorating the history and/or to groups working on social justice. It includes supporting the rehabilitation of offenders by advocating restorative rather than retributive justice: working with offenders and their families to enable them to admit their participation in the violence, take action to set things right, and when possible, sit down face-to-face in a facilitated engagement with victims.[35]

This project assumes that deep racial alienation in Greensboro requires naming and claiming this history, specifying the harm and its long-term impact, and engaging in processes and actions that repair the damage done as work intrinsic to any hope of healing.

The frameworks and analysis just presented give perhaps the best examples of work toward and conceptions of reconciliation that make deeply particular structural and material mechanisms central to a vision of authentic, mutual beloved community. In any of its related but distinct guises, reconciliation or restorative justice in this context presumes that healed relationships can only be an outgrowth of serious and detailed contentions with history that bring to light specific harms done — material, emotional, and spiritual. For it to be feasible, reconciliation or restoration must attend to the long-term legacies of these harms and to repentance, repair, and redress by those responsible.

This body of work does advocate a model of reconciliation that values coming together across lines of difference and alienation these histories have created. But it does so without succumbing to the temptation of downplaying actual harm done or inappropriately emphasizing that the needed

---

34. The settlement was $351,000. It was discovered that the Greensboro Police Department was aware of the Klan's plans ahead of time yet failed to prevent the killings. Enns and Myers, vol. 2, 139.

35. Enns and Myers, vol. 2, 156.

work is simply to learn to embrace each other. It does not render concrete, systemic realities of harm done as of secondary importance to the work of healing or forgiveness. So, for example, Donald L. Shriver argues that hope for the "renewal of . . . fractured relationship[s]" can only exist if preceded by unequivocal "moral judgment" wielded through a concerted naming and remembering of the past.[36] Robert J. Schreiter emphasizes the need for a theology of reconciliation that rests on the "urgent need to rebuild ravaged societies and human relationships, to heal memories of horror and degradation." The healing of victims' humanity and restoration of justice in a broken society destroyed by violence and oppression are basic characteristics of what Schreiter calls the "horizontal" dimension of reconciliation.[37]

In short, rather than de-emphasizing the lines of division that mark real and true differences, this work emphasizes the lines by explaining them and responding to them through honoring them and seeking to repair the conditions that created them.

I have not intended here to give a comprehensive reading of this field of work and theory in which there are many active scholars and practitioners worthy of attention. Rather, my intention is to simply make visible articulations of reconciliation that do not — in order to accomplish a vision of "coming together" — soft-pedal the actual, material realities that mediate our relationships (including the historical atrocities and violence of which we are inheritors), or misconstrue the nature of difference.

Quite the contrary, specific and careful documentation, naming, hearing, and responding to as many dimensions of such atrocity and violence as possible (the source of our difference if we take the construction of race seriously) are seen as precisely the work required to humanize relationships between perpetrators or unjust beneficiaries and victims. Only on this basis is reconciliation remotely possible. This understanding of reconciliation is far more robust, adequate, and closer to the reparations paradigm for which I am preparing to argue explicitly than it is to the pervasive use and embrace of reconciliation found among either mainline Protestants or prophetic evangelicals.

36. Donald W. Shriver Jr., "What Is Forgiveness in a Secular Political Form?" in *Forgiveness and Reconciliation: Religion, Public Policy, and Conflict Transformation,* ed. Raymond G. Helmick, S.J., and Rodney L. Petersen (Philadelphia: Templeton Foundation Press, 2001), 154-155.

37. Robert J. Schreiter, "Reconciliation and Healing as a Paradigm for Mission," *International Review of Mission* 94, no. 372 (January 2005): 79-80.

Moving toward a Reparations Paradigm

There are problems still even in the best work on reconciliation and aside from the white-privilege problem explored in the first half of this chapter. One of these pertains to the difficulty even the most successful reconciliation process (including what took place in South Africa) has in securing the participation of perpetrators — and what less-than-robust participation of perpetrators means for how willing we should be to still use the language of reconciliation. I am rather suspicious and wary on this point.

A second problem is how easily even these stronger versions of reconciliation give way to merely symbolic forms of repair of harm, as opposed to specific, structural redistribution of resources unjustly acquired through harm done. (Precisely this issue came up in South Africa's TRC, which gave amnesty to perpetrators who told the truth, but virtually no reparations to victims whose lives were devastated by acts of perpetration as well as by the relentless and systemic nature of apartheid.) This symbolic tendency may be related to the difficulty of securing the participation of perpetrators (unless they are already caught up in the criminal justice system, in which case there is more clear incentive to participate).

Another problem is the tendency in these models — even as they name harm done and expect apology, repentance, and repair by perpetrators — to assume or imply that forgiveness must be the work of victims. While reconciliation work initiated by victims often does name the importance for their own purposes of coming to a place of forgiveness, models or assumptions that impose such expectations on victims are a different matter altogether.

Philosopher J. Angelo Corlett has much to add to our understanding of the particular dynamics we risk reproducing even in robust notions of reconciliation. His work is especially germane as we think about ways to move into different forms of relationship across racial lines in the United States.

Corlett's premise is that both descendants of victims and of oppressors need to be seen as "heirs of oppression." His analysis challenges responses to the crises of relationship that exist among heirs of oppression in the United States (African Americans, Native peoples, and white Americans in particular) that uncritically presume a "moral duty to reconcile matters between surviving victims of oppression and their oppressors."[38] Corlett is concerned

---

38. J. Angelo Corlett, *Heirs of Oppression* (Lanham, Md.: Rowman & Littlefield, 2010), 187.

about the degree to which a discourse of forgiveness shows up in reconciliation models — and though he doesn't speak directly about the authors or activists described above, his concerns would pertain to them.

Corlett is blunt. On the matter of forgiveness: if reconciliation requires, expects, or obligates victims to forgive their oppressors, then achieving reconciliation is literally impossible. Forgiveness in this use becomes "an unthinking ideology," because whether or not forgiveness might benefit victims is irrelevant to the question at hand.[39] The only moral question that matters is the question of oppressors' responsibilities for rectification given the actual nature of relationships existing among heirs of oppression. Further, it is for the oppressed and the oppressed alone to decide, based on an assessment of their own needs and their actual experiences of the oppressors' repentance, when or *if* forgiveness will ever be pursued.

The prominence and logic of forgiveness within reconciliation theory, according to Corlett, inevitably places an undue and thus immoral burden on the victim. This is ironic because if our concern is the caliber of our interracial relationships, this burden is placed on victims' shoulders at the precise moment victims' needs and the debt owed to them should be the entirety of our focus.

In fact, Corlett goes even further to question why it is we would not demand an adequate explanation of "why reconciliation between offenders and their victims is always a good thing, that is, *from the perspective of the victims.*" He continues, "There is little doubt that reconciliation between such parties is sometimes good, especially for the offenders." But the same has not been demonstrated to be true for victims, especially if "rectification" has not taken place in response to the oppressor/oppressed relationships.

In these cases, imposing reconciliation actually further oppresses the already oppressed.[40] In short, an ideological commitment to forgiveness as a necessary part of reconciliation mystifies and muddies moral analysis.

Corlett goes on to argue that the only legitimate way to even begin to bring the notion of forgiveness to the table, therefore, is in the context of a "rectification" instead of a "reconciliation model." What he has to say on this point may be less surprising than his denouncement of forgiveness as an ideology: perpetrators have to make a genuine apology to the victims before the word "forgiveness" should even be uttered. And apologies must meet a set of conditions. Perpetrators must:

39. Corlett, *Heirs of Oppression*, 190.
40. Corlett, 189.

(1) communicate effectively to the victim *what* she did that was wrong; (2) communicate effectively to the victim *why* what she did to the victim was wrong; (3) communicate effectively to the victim *that and in what particular ways* she is actively committed to rectifying the wrong; and (4) offer to the victim *good reasons* why she will not harm the victim again.[41]

It's worth repeating here that even if such an apology actually takes place, forgiveness is still not a moral obligation for victims.

And, says Corlett, even if victims choose to forgive, they still might not necessarily want to integrate or reconcile with their perpetrators! The legitimacy of such a desire (or lack thereof) must be honored. Such a suggestion flies in the face of the deep-seated assumption Christian communities hold that interracial community is obviously a good. But when we view this claim in the context of crime, it is not at all difficult to understand that a victim might make the move to forgive but then choose *not* to become a deep, great friend with her perpetrator.

If we take Corlett seriously, we must conclude that we are only unable to understand how the same might be true for victims of U.S. legacies of white supremacy and racial oppression if we mute and take less seriously the depth of violence and subjugation African Americans and Native peoples have experienced.

Christians longing for reconciliation might argue that the theological premises on which we base our emphasis on reconciliation give it different contours than that of which Corlett speaks. For example, we might be willing to continue to stand on the theological claim that God desires unity and community as evidence of the instantiation of the body of Christ. Corlett would be correct were he to respond to such a claim by suggesting that theological premises deserve the same level of scrutiny and suspicion as do the non-theological.

But even if we persist in the belief that there are good theological reasons for viewing reconciliation as ultimately having some sort of ontological imperative (and thus disagree with Corlett's willingness to suggest that reconciliation might not be innately "good"), Corlett's work is deeply instructive still. The extent to which Christian notions of reconciliation tend to quickly partner with other theologically inflected concepts such as "forgiveness" or

41. Corlett, *Heirs of Oppression*, 190.

"repentance" (which we might link to apology) means we should take his analysis to heart.

So, imagine if we were to insist in any of our curricula or resources on reconciliation or diversity that, before any talk of beloved community could commence, white Christians need first to issue an apology for ongoing complicity in white supremacist structures that continue to harm African Americans. And imagine that we insist this apology must meet the conditions specified above: from clarity and specificity about what is being apologized for, to what white Christians intend to do to rectify the harm and actively refuse to oppress again.

Clearly our use of a reconciliation paradigm has not been able to garner this level of accounting for ourselves and the nature of our relationships to Black Christians or other Christians of color. Yet such specificity would immediately begin to locate us on the very ground on which we need to stand. Concrete material responses to and repair of the actual structures and histories through which we come to be in such alienated relationship to one another would be a foregone conclusion in this move.

While the notion of apology is not radical for white Christians who ostensibly value theological commitments to repentance, the actual embrace of the work of repentance would cause our understanding and response to these matters to shift radically indeed.

Conclusion

Even if we continue to stand by a vision that emphasizes reconciliation as a hoped-for outcome — if not by a reconciliation paradigm which overlays and flattens attempts to get at particular responsibility of whites for damage done — the work of this chapter suggests we might gain a great deal of traction for progress in our interracial relationality and collective responsiveness to racial injustice if we put a moratorium on any reconciliation-speak (talk of trust and invocations of forgiveness for guilt) until we have secured a genuine apology and the clarity of repair, rectification, and ongoing strategy for disrupting complicity with structural oppression that such apology would necessitate.

There is better work and more adequate analysis happening in some versions of reconciliation than that which reconciliation most often procures among Christians longing for it. But at the end of the day reconciliation does more to cloak and make difficult attention to particularities and the deep, specific, and sustained work required of whites before we can have any business talking about reconciled relationships in a collective manner.

When couched carefully with attention to structures, such as some of the work explored here does, a reconciliation paradigm has some promise. But that promise comes not from the paradigm, but from the attention to structures that manages to emerge despite the paradigm.

Thus, in light of all these things — Corlett's clarity and analysis, the insidious tendency to privilege a white perspective on reconciliation, the prevalent practice of overemphasizing the need to better embrace difference *per se,* the willingness whites show to subordinate structural anti-racist work to interracial relationship building, and generally speaking, the pervasive grip of a paltry and less-than-adequate notion of reconciliation in Christian contexts — I am left firm in my conviction that the reconciliation paradigm *undermines* our ability to do (or to enable and activate white people to take particular kinds of responsibility for) the very work necessary to realize truly transformed racial realities and relationships.

A reconciliation paradigm simply is not the most efficacious way to move forward. Its problems are too deep.

We need a paradigm that instead insists on and enables the conundrums of whiteness and the relationship of white people both to white supremacy and to people of color to be dealt with directly, deeply, and without equivocation.

Such recognition need not send us into despair. There is a paradigm for race that already exists that meets these very criteria and avoids most of the problems inherent to reconciliation. This other paradigm also has important theological and historical precedents. It is a paradigm less well known by whites, because in the historical moment it was introduced whites generally and white Christians in particular fled from it. But it is a paradigm in which powerful hope for real transformative justice exists in equal measure to a relentlessly particularist ethic for understanding race and a willingness to call out whiteness in all its specificity.

The Black Power movement lifted up an important corrective to, or disruption of, the reconciliation paradigm of the civil rights movement. And that corrective came in the form of a reparations paradigm. In the next two chapters, therefore, we will explore the historical and theological emergence of this paradigm, the way it engaged whiteness, and the hopeful challenge it posed for Christians and Protestant communities in the late 1960s. (In chapter 6 we will envision what a reparations paradigm might look like for an array of justice work in Christian communities today.)

Reconciliation simply is not the answer. Reparations might be. At the very least, at a certain point of success in challenging the structures and repairing the histories — work toward which reparations relentlessly directs us — those of us who are white and who long for reconciliation might find ourselves working side-by-side, but from our own particular ground, with brothers and sisters of color who are already and always working in these terms.

Perhaps at a certain point we might discover that inclusion and diversity do not even begin to capture the actual reality for which we truly long. We might find ourselves experiencing in such partnered, sustained work far more organic, meaningful, and authentic relationships than any of us can think of and project in the abstract from the alienated and still unredressed ground on which we currently stand.

It remains to be seen whether that might be case. But if we long for reconciliation as deeply as we say we do, we must be willing to embrace a different trajectory — a different, but not new path — one that has already been revealed in our own history. Taking another look at that path is the work to which we now turn.

PART TWO

Reparations! Going Backward before Going Forward

CHAPTER FOUR

The Black Manifesto

White Christians today are much less familiar with the Black Power movement than they are with civil rights. This lack of familiarity is not a historical accident. While many northern, white Christians eventually converted to the cause and vision of the civil rights movement, they overwhelmingly rejected Black Power. Yet remembering this history is critical to our work on racial justice among Christian communities today.

For one thing, the way we remember the civil rights movement, which typically involves telling a triumphant tale of successful social transformation, is deeply inaccurate. By the end of the 1960s many Black Americans — including Black Christians — were not hailing civil rights as the success we hail it today. In contrast, the end of the 1960s found many African Americans in a state of despair and outrage. Such despair and outrage was less a response to innate weaknesses of the movement itself than to the persistence of white intransigence and the ongoing Black suffering such intransigence ensured despite the brilliance, longevity, and human cost of the movement.

When we misremember civil rights we forget and ignore the analysis of the movement that African Americans rendered at the time. We forget and ignore the festering and deepening racial alienation — including between those who had been allies during the movement's heyday — that marked its end. Simply put, neither within nor outside the church did we leave the civil rights movement a relatively unified collective needing merely to complete the unfinished vision articulated by Martin Luther King Jr. and so many others.

We left the movement with Blacks increasingly persuaded that key assumptions of the movement were not viable: that, at their core, liberal

whites were not interested in a deeply transformed social and economic order despite what they claimed; that the witness of nonviolent suffering would
not ultimately trigger a humane response among more recalcitrant whites
despite the power of nonviolent civil disobedience; that the primary analysis,
interpretations, and responses of the civil rights movement had not put us
on essentially the right national path for realizing racial justice. In short,
though one might not know it when we listen to our public recollections
today, we did not come to the end of civil rights with most Black Americans
embracing the movement as a widely realized success.

Several years ago I heard a prominent womanist ethicist describe what
happened at the seminary at which she was a student when the community
there received word that King had been assassinated.

Upon hearing the devastating news, older African American students
literally locked the doors and barred younger African American students
from leaving the chapel that day. As fresh tears of grief and rage overcame
many in the audience, she explained how they stayed there together, locked
in all night, so older students could ensure the younger students did not leave
the campus and "get themselves killed" by pouring into the streets to express
the rage that consumed them in the wake of this atrocity. Her story and the
immediacy with which it evoked unhealed pain among those gathered fits
not at all into the official tales we tell today about civil rights in the church.

Besides the innate importance of historical accuracy, there are many
reasons to revisit and acknowledge the changed ethos that actually came to
exist in the United States, and among Christians, toward the end of the civil
rights era.

First, by not remembering this more complete account, we lose touch
not only with how much work was deemed remaining, but with *the kind of
work* Black Christians increasingly made clear still needed to be done. Our
ongoing deployment of a reconciliation paradigm today flies in the face of
what Black Christians and other Black Americans demanded we begin to
take more seriously in this period. Christians serious about reconciliation
need to remember this history and root our work in it.

In addition, remembering Black Power not only further helps explain
why we should not be surprised that reconciliation has evaded us. More than
forty years ago African Americans, many of whom had been deeply active in
civil rights, concluded and declared reconciliation an inadequate vision for
the actual state of U.S. racial problems. Nothing has so dramatically changed
in those forty years that we should have been led to conclude reconciliation
would be radically more efficacious today.

More important, we must remember this history because when we persist in a reconciliation paradigm, we continue to actively repudiate much of the analysis of African Americans *today* in precisely the same ways whites repudiated and looked away from it and from African American rage and despair *then*. We can be sure that racial alienation deepened because of white responses to the analysis and rage that emerged widely among African Americans in this period.

Thus, it is not only important that Christians longing for racial reconciliation return to this history because of what it offers in terms of more adequate understanding of the challenge of race. It is also important because Black Christians laid down a kind of a gauntlet in the late 1960s that white Christians *have yet to pick up*. This era thus haunts us — even more so in our forgetting of it.

A reconciliation paradigm has failed us, therefore, not only because it is theoretically unsound. It has failed us also because its ongoing use reveals how deaf white Christians remain to the significant, transformative claims Black Christians began making by the middle of the 1960s.

Thus it is to the analysis proffered largely by those affiliated with Black Power that we must return. When we do so, we discover the clear articulation of a different paradigm — a reparations paradigm. And while white Christians at the time refused to seriously take heed, it is precisely this paradigm that needs to be heeded and embraced still by white Christians as we admit the impasse to which reconciliation has continued to bring us.

This chapter thus engages in a selective remembrance of Black Power, focused specifically and narrowly on one of the most important moments it directly challenged white Christians: namely in the events leading to and following the Black Manifesto. Remembering this under-remembered church history provides us a much more deeply informed perspective on where racial relations in the church actually are today. It allows us to step into a part of our history in which a reparations paradigm made a rich and promising, if brief, intervention into Christians' racial analysis and foci — one that remains powerful and promising.

Indeed, it is almost eerie the degree to which the analysis of Black Power and the kinds of interventions it generated (such as the Black Manifesto) presumed and predicted precisely the kinds of gaps, inadequacies, and frustrating results to which our work on race has come in our ongoing use of a reconciliation paradigm. It would be more eerie, however, if we continue on our way in such work without remembering and honoring this history. For this history remains our present, and it speaks directly to our hoped-for future.

Setting the Context

Black Power articulated its claims with increasing urgency during the mid- to late 1960s — at the same time increasing numbers of participants in the civil rights movement began to realize that many of the movement's dreams and visions were going to remain woefully incomplete. As the movement waned and hope for achieving beloved community faded, Black Power brought a different, persuasive vision: the problem was not separation. The problem was power.

Building power through an embrace of identity, culture, and political and social solidarity among Black people was the necessary response to systemic white exploitation. Black Power responded to the integrity, intentions, and potential "redemption" of whites — including those who had presented themselves as sympathetic allies to civil rights — with much greater suspicion than had civil rights activists early in the movement. In the face of ongoing white violence, Black Power called into question the philosophy of nonviolence, arguing that African Americans had the right to defend themselves — that self-respect demanded as much. Given how progressive evangelicals and mainline Protestants frame our understanding of reconciliation — in regard to which multiracial demography is considered a key measure of success or failure — the suspicion of integration as a goal in Black Power's analysis is acutely relevant to our query.

Integration was deemed inadequate to the task of achieving Black liberation and full justice at best, and at worst as impeding such empowerment. Integration could not admit, for example, the important role that racial separation often played for communities of color. And achieving integration without transforming power relations between whites and Blacks could only have deleterious effects on Blacks.

As with the civil rights movement, Black Power had theological expressions, and many Black clergy and laypeople were leading voices in it. In the 1960s Black Christians formed, for example, the National Committee of Black Churchmen (NCBC), Black Methodists for Church Renewal, the Black Unitarian Universalist Caucus, and other groups.[1]

White Protestants' most dramatic encounter with Black Power began with James Forman's 1969 disruption of worship at New York City's River-

---

1. See James Findlay Jr., *Church People in the Struggle: The National Council of Churches and the Black Freedom Movement, 1950-1970* (New York and Oxford: Oxford University Press, 1993), chapter 6.

side Church to present the Black Manifesto. In the months that followed, Black clergy publicly endorsed the Manifesto, which declared that white Christians owed reparations for centuries of complicity in the exploitation of Black people.

If King's beloved community built on a universal vision of shared humanity, Black Power built on an unabashed embrace of particularity. Black Power was clear that the differences human beings embody are not to be ignored, nor seen as moral equivalents. It recognized that racial identities are living embodiments of histories and material realities. And, thus, while Black Power focused on celebrating Blackness and cultivating solidarity among Black people, it also made clear that white folks were to be named and acknowledged as *white* folks, with all the historical and material baggage such naming revealed.[2]

In fact, if white folks were truly to be allies for racial justice, taking responsibility for that history and material baggage was not negotiable. Further, it is from the framework articulated by Black Power that it became possible to say, for example, that white people who claimed to be committed to anti-racism should go work with and among other white people — where the racial problem was actually rooted. And, in many ways, whites' willingness (or not) to take up distinct roles and responsibilities was considered a measure of the adequacy of their understanding of the actual racial situation.

Careful inquiry into the events surrounding the Black Manifesto provides an opportunity to engage an important history with which most white Christians are unfamiliar. It also offers the opportunity to engage a reparations paradigm for understanding race. For, by starting with particularity, Black Power introduced a reparations paradigm for interpreting the meaning of race and the problem of racism. This paradigm presented a deeply challenging vision of the path white Christians needed to follow in order to participate in realizing justice and interracial reconciliation. (It is important that I be clear that these are my words and my way of framing one impact of this paradigm. Black Power as a movement had no interest in talking about reconciliation; it also did not use the concept of "reparations paradigm," which is mine.)

It is my view that the authenticity of the hope for transformation offered by the Black Manifesto and its talk of reparations existed in equal

---

2. Recall, for example, James Cone's repeated use of the word "Whitey" in 1969 in *Black Theology and Black Power* (Maryknoll, N.Y.: Orbis, 1997).

measure to the depth of the challenge it laid down to white Christians. I believe this close relationship between hope and challenge continues to exist.

In many ways this is a painful history to revisit. As will become clear, white intransigence asserts itself at every turn. But bearing witness to this history is a critical next step after the critique of the reconciliation paradigm provided in part one of this book. For if white Christians can become able and willing to hear, understand, and respond to what African Americans said to us in this era — *and in many ways have continued saying since* — perhaps we will be able to chart a more effective, meaningful, and transformative path toward interracial solidarity.

A reparations paradigm generates the possibility for white Christians to take this different journey in regard to racial justice — a journey much more likely than the one on which we now tread to result in the transformations the church desperately needs. But that possibility can only be realized if whites accept the challenge of responding to the particularity of whiteness in ways that we refused to do more than four decades ago.

From Civil Rights to Black Power

On May 4, 1969, James Forman interrupted Sunday worship at the historic Riverside Church and read a statement titled the "Black Manifesto." The manifesto demanded that "white Christian churches and Jewish synagogues . . . begin to pay reparations to black people in this country."[3] It proceeded to call for the sum of $500 million and to detail how the funds were to be spent.

Forman's action rocked the worlds of white Christians and sent shockwaves through mainline Protestant denominations. Two scholars of the period claim "Manifesto-related events caused greater vibrations in the U.S. religious world than any other single human rights development in a decade of monumental happenings."[4] But when the dust settled, what actually resulted from these vibrations was far less consequential then what did not result.

Robust financial commitments to eradicate racial inequity and bolster Black empowerment did not come. Repentance for racism and repair of

---

3. James Forman, "The Black Manifesto," in *Black Manifesto: Religion, Racism, and Reparations,* ed. Robert S. Lecky and H. Elliot Wright (New York: Sheed and Ward, 1969), 120.

4. Robert S. Lecky and H. Elliot Wright, "Reparations Now? An Introduction," in *Black Manifesto,* 3.

racial harm on the part of white churches was not to be found. An era of improved regard between white and Black Christians did not break through. If anything, quite the opposite came to be true.

Given the resistance and, sometimes, hostility that the very word "reparations" evokes among whites, these results may not seem surprising to us today. But the fact is that things could have turned out otherwise.

Some Christians at the time actually believed the churches might "get it" and do other than they eventually did. Some claimed the manifesto was precisely what was needed in order for a new era of race relations in the church to unfold.

After all, mainline Protestant denominations had had a significant awakening during the civil rights movement. They had come to recognize racism as sin and to be troubled by racial injustice. And as urban neighborhoods burned in response to King's assassination in April 1968, religious bodies had pledged nearly $50 million for "social action and racial justice."[5]

Moreover, some Christians publicly reasoned that, in the large scheme of things, even $500 million was not an overwhelming figure.[6] The manifesto demanded only "fifteen dollars for every black brother and sister in the United States." One white theologian at the time wrote of his surprise the demand was "so modest." He pointed out that churches could raise $500 million in a mere month of Sunday collections. He went on to state that if $500 million was unobtainable, then the appropriate interpretation was "not that the demand is excessive, but that organized religion in America is anti-Christian."[7] His interpretation of what the Black Manifesto meant or might mean for the church was by no means the dominant one. But the fact that he — along with numerous African American Christians — insisted this to be true is significant.

Last, and perhaps most important for understanding where we are today in regard to race and the church, several denominations and major institutions did initiate new programs in response to the Black Manifesto.[8]

---

5. Arnold Schuchter, *Reparations: The Black Manifesto and Its Challenge to White America* (Philadelphia: J. B. Lippincott Co., 1970), 3.

6. Forman, "The Black Manifesto," in *Black Manifesto*, 120.

7. Ronald Goetz, "Black Manifesto: The Great White Hope," *The Christian Century* 86 (June 18, 1969): 833.

8. This group included the Riverside Church, the United Methodist Board of Missions, the General Assembly of the United Presbyterian Church, the General Synod of the Reformed Church in America, the General Assembly of the Unitarian Universalist Association, the National Council of Churches, Union Theological Seminary in the city of New York, the United Church of Christ, and the World Council of Churches. Lecky and Wright, *Black Manifesto*, 21.

They did not do so without loud protest and resistance from within their ranks. They did not do so in the manner for which the manifesto called. But the fact they responded at all suggests the manifesto struck a chord that resonated. In some way, shape, or form many white Protestant Christians recognized themselves in the charges delivered that morning at Riverside Church.

The origins of the Black Manifesto lay in work that had been initiated by many of the same communities that would eventually reject the manifesto's demands. In 1967 a number of religious organizations had come together to create the Interreligious Foundation for Community Organization (IFCO).[9] IFCO's charge was to fund organizations cultivating self-determination and empowerment in poor communities. This charge necessarily included urban areas with predominantly Black populations and was a response to the urgent and impoverished conditions in which Blacks in the United States continued to live despite all the legal victories of civil rights.

Historian James F. Findlay writes that IFCO was created, in part, to serve as "interlocutor between whites and blacks who were less and less able to speak and act directly together."[10] As African Americans who had been committed to civil rights came to believe that the movement was failing in significant ways, many began to embrace different analyses as to what was required to achieve justice.

These analyses differently diagnosed both the problem and the solutions to racial oppression (which in civil rights' analysis had been legal equity and a focus on segregation and integration). Those increasingly persuaded by Black Power rooted their analysis in language that took seriously the material histories out of which race and racial relationships emerged, spoke clearly about the distinct meanings of blackness and whiteness in the United States, and emphasized the economic, political, and social manifestations of racism (the complex manifestation of racism, which framing the primary problem as "legalized segregation" could not capture). These analyses — endorsing an ethic of racial particularity — distinguished Black Power starkly from the universal ethic of the civil rights movement. They also were met with great

---

9. The founding members included the American Baptist Home Mission Societies, two bodies within the United Methodist Church, the Executive Council of the Protestant Episcopal Church, two bodies within the Presbyterian Church in the U.S.A., the Board for Homeland Missions of the United Church of Christ, the Board of American Missions of the Lutheran Church in America, the American Jewish Committee, and the National Catholic Conference for Interracial Justice. Schuchter, *Reparations*, 2.

10. Findlay, *Church People in the Struggle*, 188.

resistance from whites, whose disparagement of Black Power generated the racial polarization to which Findlay refers in explaining IFCO's 1967 origins.

Public critiques of the adequacy of civil rights' analyses had begun as early as 1964. Organizers in Rochester, New York, said it was not the right to vote but access to jobs that was needed to transform the racial landscape, and they created a campaign challenging Rochester-based Eastman Kodak to hire unemployed young African Americans (after three years of tensions and difficult negotiations this finally happened).[11]

While these activists obviously endorsed the notion that all U.S. Americans should have legal equality, they were clear that equal rights on paper were no panacea for the diverse, complex, and specific ways oppression and subjugation impacted Black life. Integration came under fire too. For, much like the priests in the Episcopal Church who realized integration actually eroded the few arenas in which African Americans had established some measure of autonomy and empowerment, those persuaded by Black Power argued that integration actually exacerbated subjugation because it did not deal with the power differences.

This particular analysis of the problem of racism deserves further scrutiny because it remains relevant today. Consider this example: It is one thing to insist Black and white children should sit together in classrooms and even to create mechanisms to ensure that this happens (for example, busing). That's what integration does. But it is a different matter altogether to ask who runs the schools. Who are the teachers? Who are the principals? Who sits on the school board? Who has decision-making power over the lives of these students? These are questions integration does not necessarily (nor is necessarily prepared to) ask.

Meanwhile, to integrate Black children into white schools, where all the decision makers are white, without addressing such power issues can have very negative results. Or, to state it from the opposite direction, imagine what can happen when Black children learn in classrooms where they are taught and mentored by Black teachers and where Black principals are empowered to make decisions about what is best for them educationally. Imagine Black children facing no risk of encountering anti-black bias in even its most subtle forms from those who have direct and authoritative contact with them day-to-day (teachers), nor of being seen by their white classmates as token minorities or targeted for more overtly hostile racial aggressions.

Malcolm X's description of his experience in a white school is illus-

11. Findlay, 171-172.

trative here. He writes of being treated by fellow white students as more of a mascot or a pet than a peer. And he relays the effect on his psyche when he told a white teacher he wanted to become a lawyer: the teacher smiled and told him that becoming a carpenter would be much more realistic for "a n-----." Malcolm X describes this experience as "the first major turning point in my life."[12]

To say all of this is certainly in no way to make a case in support of segregation. Such a case is certainly not what Black Power was making. Segregation is imposed by a dominant racial group in order to deny access. It is always immoral and, as a larger system, deleterious. To recognize the dangers of integration is not to sanction segregation, then, but to acknowledge that — to the extent segregation removed them from contexts in which they would have to be around white people — one result of segregation was relative insulation of children in their day-to-day lives from the nefarious behavior of whites (something to which they become more exposed in integration models).

Segregation is also distinct from the self-chosen and empowered decision to separate and to create Black-only environments where Blacks — rather than whites — are ultimately the decision makers. Thus, to engage Black Power's critique of integration is to return to the nuances that exist in the difference between segregation and separation, and to emphasize the significance of power and its impact even in contexts where legalized segregation is taken off the books. It is to insist that an over-focus on integration (or, in our day, diversity and inclusion) cannot address all the ways we see the actual racial impact of white supremacy play out in those subjugated by it — and sometimes might make it worse.

Emphasizing power and attempting to transform racial relations by building Black power generated tensions between younger, more militant voices within the activist Black community and older activists more devoutly committed to the goals of integration and the centrality of nonviolence.

These tensions are perhaps captured best in the strains that developed between the Student Nonviolent Coordinating Committee (SNCC) and the Southern Christian Leadership Conference (SCLC), which became public and marked by 1966 when Stokely Carmichael was elected chairman of the SNCC. The tensions between the SNCC and the SCLC are part of a longer and layered history that has been well-documented and need not be re-

12. Malcolm X, *The Autobiography of Malcolm X: As told to Alex Haley* (New York: Ballantine Books, 1964), 43.

hearsed here.[13] They pertained to socioeconomic class issues that emerged more obviously as King took his organizing north, only to discover his vision of integration and beloved community was perceived as less relevant to urban Black communities, to the centrality of nonviolence (which younger Blacks began to call into greater question as more and more activists were murdered with impunity), and even to Christianity as younger Black activists became suspicious that Christianity itself might be too deeply inflected with white visions of reality to be viable for Blacks.

Yet if tensions were significant within the Black activist community, those that developed between African Americans and white liberals were even more so. In *A Promise and a Way of Life: White Antiracist Activism,* Becky Thompson traces the ways in which white SNCC members overwhelmingly rejected the influence Black Power and its framework assumed among Black SNCC members. She describes the impact this rejection had on the work of the SNCC.[14]

For example, Black leaders in the SNCC began to urge whites in the organization to focus their efforts on educating, challenging, and organizing the *white* community in support of civil rights, rather than working primarily in the Black community.

These leaders were recognizing the different work that was required among Black and white communities, the different ways in which whites and Blacks tended to be equipped for such work, and the extent to which white allies, despite their professed good intentions, continued to exhibit racism in their dealings with both the communities they were organizing and their fellow SNCC workers. Their racism looked more like paternalism than outright bigotry, and more like presumptions about their right to be in charge than formal endorsements of Black inferiority, but they were deeply harmful nonetheless. Integration certainly did not interrupt them.

African American leaders in the SNCC began to insist that a true vision of racial liberation and justice meant Blacks should set the agenda for the work and how to go about it, rather than being expected to defer to white liberal expectations, perceptions, and comfort. These leaders did so without

13. Among the many excellent and detailed accounts of the many challenges and fissures among civil rights activists through the 1960s, Taylor Branch's trilogy is particularly thorough. See *Parting the Waters: America in the King Years 1954-63* (New York: Simon and Schuster, 1989), *Pillar of Fire: America in the King Years 1963-65* (New York: Simon and Schuster, 1999), and *At Canaan's Edge: America in the King Years 1965-68* (New York: Simon and Schuster, 2007).

14. Becky Thompson, *A Promise and a Way of Life: White Antiracist Activism* (Minneapolis: University of Minnesota Press, 2001), chapter 3.

apology and were clear that deferring to whites not only failed to honor what Blacks knew (and what whites could not) about the experience of racial injustice, but also perpetuated older patterns of racism in Black-white relations.

To use the language I have introduced here, these leaders increasingly adopted a particularist approach to race. Race was coming to be seen not as a surface-level or skin-only difference underneath which lay our more important human sameness. Whiteness was coming to be seen not as a parallel, equally meaningful (or beautiful) kind of difference to blackness.

The work required, then, of persons with vastly different experiences because of their identity and vastly different actual relationships to white supremacist structures was, as a result, simply different: whether this came to the kinds of education needed or the educative work of which one was perceived capable, whether it pertained to the efficacy of organizing in different communities, or whether it came to the moral work required to actually come into a reconciled state.

What was being unapologetically insisted upon was that the problem of race was not a problem of general or generic brokenness. It was a problem of oppressor and oppressed. And empowering the oppressed — beginning by naming oppression and oppressors in unflinching terms — was essential to actually transforming the fundamental nature of those relationships.

The SNCC transition was by no means an isolated phenomenon. Findlay captures this when he writes,

> Reflecting the increasing frustration of African Americans nationwide that alliances with liberal groups outside their community were no longer moving the nation toward elimination of poverty and an end to discrimination, the black power slogan caught on everywhere.[15]

The impact of the introduction of the language and analyses of Black Power on interracial relations was real. If measured by the ability of whites to sustain their commitment to the movement in light of this new framework for understanding the racial problem and the path toward justice, the transition did not go well.

Chasms began to open throughout the broader movement between offended white liberals and frustrated Black activists. Relationships and alliances between Blacks and whites who had begun civil rights with so much hope, working side-by-side, came to a disrupted halt.

15. Findlay, *Church People in the Struggle*, 183.

These chasms impacted the churches too. Even though it is true, for example, that mainline Protestant denominations had increased their social justice programming significantly during the civil rights years, it is also true that Black leaders had articulated frustrations relatively early about how paternalistic and white-directed these efforts usually were.

Such frustrations were directed publicly at the National Council of Churches' (NCC) Commission on Religion and Race in 1965. In its first two years the commission had generally been perceived as effective and powerful. It had mobilized successfully at the grassroots level, engaging many laypeople in letter-writing campaigns on behalf of the Civil Rights Act and working in partnership with organizations like the NAACP to help the act pass.[16] Black and white Christians had been active together in the commission.

But ending discrimination in public accommodations did not require much sacrifice from middle-class whites, writes Findlay. As it became clear that the justice issues were more and more about jobs, housing, and the distribution of national resources, more came to be on the line for whites. In response, whites became much more ambivalent, and their support waned.[17] By 1965, Findlay writes, the commission had "lost steam." It had also become caught up in church bureaucracies, which are notorious for moving slowly.

Black Christians who had been part of the commission's work began to express their frustration more publicly with how white-led the commission was and how often it had failed to fully include Blacks in its decision-making processes.[18]

When Benjamin Payton was named the first African American director of the Commission on Religion and Race in 1965, he began his tenure by telling the NCC assembly, "The *rights* which have been *couched in law are now being sought in life as practical social and economic matters* [emphasis in original]."[19] This language signaled a move toward Black Power among mainline Protestantism. Here equality on paper was deemed insufficient (thus the language of "economics"), and relations between Blacks and integration-committed whites needed to be freed from racist dynamics and power imbalances (thus the language of "practical"). Such shifts could be sought only through Blacks empowering themselves.

By 1966 "Black Power" had been uttered loudly in the civic sphere and,

16. Findlay, *Church People in the Struggle*, 58.
17. Findlay, 64.
18. Findlay, 173, 177.
19. Findlay, 178.

consistent with the larger shift in racial analyses this utterance represented, Payton called the African American members of the commission to form the National Committee of Negro Churchmen (which was soon changed to the National Committee of Black Churchmen [NCBC]).

In July 1966, the NCBC published a statement in *The New York Times* and the *Chicago Tribune* explaining and endorsing Black Power.[20] The statement disparaged white Christians' hysteria over Black Power as "the same old problem over power and race which has faced our beloved country since 1619."[21] It described riots among Blacks in urban centers as eruptions caused by the "silent and covert violence that middle-class Americans inflict upon the inner city." And it decried American leaders for having "tie[d] a white noose of suburbia" around the necks of Blacks — all while smiling; leaving them with no jobs and dilapidated education systems, and having failed miserably to use their power to "create equal opportunity *in life as well as in law* [emphasis in the original]."[22]

The statement raised questions about King's strategies and the depth of his white Christian supporters' commitment to the full liberation of Blacks. It also made a theological case for the legitimacy and importance of power in the lives of Blacks. Findlay describes the NCBC's work as evidence of how early there existed "blunt and painful public criticism" of mainstream Protestant churches who had presented themselves as allies to civil rights.[23]

Despite the clarity of Black explanations, white Christians continued to be thoroughly unable to accept the analyses of Black Power. And like the anger of Black leaders in SNCC when white activists rejected their embrace of power, within a very short period of time white Christian rejection generated unmuted anger among Black Christians as well. In October 1968 the NCBC passionately condemned white Christians' repudiation of Black Power when a speaker at an NCBC gathering announced: "Let the church see that the Black Power Movement is assuming power and consolidating power, then the white church seeks to coopt it by funding its community organization programs and then coopting its leaders. The whites are always in control. They dictate what must be done."[24] He was met with loud applause.

20. See National Conference of Black Churchmen, "'Black Power' Statement, July 31, 1966," in *African American Religious History: A Documentary Witness*, 2nd ed., ed. Milton C. Sernett (Durham, N.C.: Duke University Press, 1999), 555-564.

21. "'Black Power' Statement," 555.

22. "'Black Power' Statement," 557.

23. Findlay, *Church People in the Struggle*, 187.

24. Quoted in Lecky and Wright, *Black Manifesto*, 7. The NCBC was made up pri-

Historian Arnold Schuchter writes that by 1968, "Racial polarization was no longer a threat but an accomplished fact."[25] We should tarry with this surprising diagnosis for more than a moment.

Schuchter's diagnosis is precisely the opposite of what we expect to have been the case as the civil rights movement came to a close. This diagnosis is a complete inversion of the story we white Christians generally tell today about the civil rights movement and what it achieved: besides the end of segregation, greater racial harmony, more racial understanding, and deeper appreciation of racial difference. Given how sacred that version of the story is to so many of us (for some good reasons), it becomes even more important that we attempt to deeply absorb Schuchter's claim and allow it to really shake us.

If it is accurate — which histories of this period suggest it is — this claim adds urgency to our attempt to become constructively suspicious about the reconciliation paradigm we use to frame our racial justice work. Given what this history reveals, it is no small matter if we still today take our racial paradigm largely out of the civil rights movement's playbook without nuancing or altering it relative to the critiques of Black Power and the racial polarization that resulted when white Christians could not hear these critiques.

It is no small matter if our collective white Christian memory of the civil rights movement and the stories we pass down about it contain significant omissions. For it is only if we are committed to understanding today what we failed to understand then that we can presume to attempt more adequate work today. Thus a closer look at the Black Manifesto and the different reactions whites and Blacks had to it, in the interest of developing such understanding, is warranted.

The Black Manifesto

In the year after the founding of the Interreligious Foundation for Community Organization (IFCO), the Kerner Commission released its report stating that "'white racism' [remained] the major cause of black disorders and urban

---

marily of Black caucuses in the American Baptist Convention, the United Church of Christ, the United Methodist Church, the United Presbyterian Church in the U.S.A., the Unitarian Universalists, as well as various bodies from among the Lutheran churches and the Protestant Episcopal Church. Schuchter, *Reparations*, 3.

25. Schuchter, 3.

problems." King was assassinated. The Poor People's Campaign — developed to broaden and make more substantive the social transformations sought by the movement through emphasizing economic empowerment and not just legal equality — had received only token recognition from the government. Prospects for serious federal funding for Black economic development were increasingly on the wane.[26]

It was in this context that Lucius Walker, executive director of IFCO, decided to host the National Black Economic Development Conference (NBEDC). The plan was for a grassroots, Black-only event in which diverse leaders would come together to envision the "what next" in economic and community development strategies for the Black community. The NBEDC met April 25-27, 1969, at Wayne State University in Detroit.

James Forman, who at the time was director of international affairs for SNCC, was in attendance. On the last night of the conference, he took the stage and introduced the Black Manifesto. A vote was held, and the manifesto was endorsed 187 to 63.[27] On Sunday morning, Walker announced that the manifesto had been approved as an official statement of the NBEDC.

Nearly 1,000 delegates had attended the NBEDC. Thus a vote by only 250 people was later cited by white critics as evidence that the manifesto did not really have the support of the Black community. However, the vote had taken place on Saturday, the last night of the conference, when many delegates were not in attendance. Schuchter emphasizes that the next morning, when more delegates had returned, Walker announced the manifesto as an official statement of the NBEDC, and at that point no rescinding action was taken or attempted. Thus the Black Manifesto should be understood as representative of the will of the constituents.

Four days later Forman, Walker, and 25 members of the NBEDC met with leaders of the Episcopal Church to introduce the manifesto's demands. This would be the first of many meetings between NBEDC participants and denominational leaders. But no meeting would garner the attention that came after the disruption of worship at Riverside Church only a week later.

On the following Sunday, as the minister, choir, and two-thirds of the congregation walked out in protest, Forman began:

> We the black people assembled in Detroit, Michigan, for the National
> Black Economic Development Conference are fully aware that we have

---

26. Schuchter, *Reparations*, 3.
27. Schuchter, *Reparations*, 2-4.

been forced to come together because racist white America has exploited our resources, our minds, our bodies, our labor. . . . We are demanding $500,000,000 from the Christian white churches and the Jewish synagogues. This . . . is not a large sum of money, and we know that the churches and synagogues have a tremendous wealth and its membership, white America, has profited and still exploits black people. We are also not unaware that the exploitation of colored peoples around the world is aided and abetted by the white Christian churches and synagogues. . . . Fifteen dollars for every black brother and sister in the United States is only a beginning of the reparations due us as people who have been exploited and degraded, brutalized, killed and persecuted.[28]

Wrapped in revolutionary rhetoric, endorsements of Black power, and repudiations of capitalism, the Black Manifesto went on to specify to what the $500 million would be allocated: a southern land bank, publishing and printing industries, audio-visual networks, a research skills center, a training center, assistance to the National Welfare Rights Organization, a National Black Labor and Defense Fund, the establishment of an International Black Appeal to raise money for cooperative businesses in the United States and the African motherland, and a Black university in the South.[29] The demands were specific and clear.

Right away we should notice from our vantage point that the Black Manifesto put racial relations on starkly material grounds — the very realities that generate and make difference meaningful and recognizable when we understand race as something constructed through social structures and systems. Furthermore, these demands were constructive responses to the precise gaps that had been revealed as persistent despite civil rights victories — constructive responses to the ways the movement had not achieved the deep, material transformation of the situation of African Americans that civil rights activists had hoped it would. These demands were also precisely the realities through which white and Black relationships were (and in many ways continue to be) mediated.

In the weeks that followed, Forman read the manifesto at numerous denominational headquarters and Protestant institutions. Church officials

28. Forman, "The Black Manifesto," 120.

29. That morning at Riverside, Forman articulated additional demands specific to Riverside Church because of its Rockefeller-endowed wealth: family and corporate interests he deemed to be actively engaged in the ongoing economic exploitation of Harlem. "The Black Manifesto," 121-122.

held their breath, anticipating when the "violence-prone black revolutionary [who] seemed as unforgettable as Satan himself" would show up at their door.[30]

One image stands out as particularly poignant. Forman, evoking Martin Luther's ninety-five theses, nailed a copy of the manifesto to the doors of the national headquarters of the Lutheran Church in America.[31]

Religious furor followed, and it manifested primarily as three different institutional responses. First, white evangelical Christians overwhelmingly were outraged. The editors of *Christianity Today* described Forman as having "invaded" Riverside, his actions as having encouraged "blackmail or extortion."[32] He was identified "as a key formulator of the new anti-church revolution."[33]

But evangelicals were also rather smug. They claimed that liberal Protestants were reaping what they had sown when they confused the work of the gospel with social issues.[34] *Christianity Today* also blamed the rise of Forman on the "implicit repudiation of biblical revelation in today's seminaries."[35] Reflecting on manifesto-related actions at Union Theological Seminary (UTS), one commentator declared that the UTS president's "socialistic eggs" were finally hatching.[36]

A second group of institutions — including several Catholic archdioceses and mainline Protestant groups — also flatly rejected the Black Manifesto. They denounced Forman's tactics and legitimacy. In many cases they went on either to publicly cite their "already existing initiatives" to address poverty or to reiterate a general "concern over poverty."[37] They were clear and unshaken in their confidence that they stood on firm moral ground and did not need to take the manifesto seriously.

30. Schuchter, *Reparations*, 6.

31. Here Forman specifically demanded $50 million cash and 60 percent of the revenues from the church's assets. Schuchter, 5.

32. Editors, "Union Seminary: An Ethical Dilemma," *Christianity Today* 13 (June 6, 1969): 27.

33. "Manifest(o) Destiny: IFCO and the Churches," *Christianity Today* 13 (June 6, 1969): 42.

34. Lecky and Wright, *Black Manifesto*, 17.

35. "Union Seminary," 27.

36. "Manifest(o) Destiny," 42.

37. These included the American Baptist Convention, the American Lutheran Church, several dioceses in both the Catholic and Episcopal Churches, the American Jewish Committee, the National Jewish Community Relations Advisory Council, and the Synagogue Council of America, among others. Lecky and Wright, *Black Manifesto*, 18-21.

It is a third group that is most interesting here because this group best reveals the pitfalls of continuing to insist on a reconciliation paradigm for race when a reparations paradigm is being demanded. This revelation comes because members of this group did *not* fully repudiate the Black Manifesto's underlying assumptions. They rejected the strategy of the manifesto, often excoriated Forman in the process and/or questioned whether he was a legitimate leader of the Black community; but ultimately they *did* initiate some new program(s) in response to the manifesto.

In fits and starts the institutions within this group eventually carved out tens of thousands of dollars for initiatives geared toward the well-being of Black Americans. They did so out of an acknowledgment of the reality of racial inequity and Black suffering. Sometimes they even expressed gratitude for the wake-up call the manifesto provided for the sin of racism — and for the chance to be renewed and made newly relevant in society. However, with one partial exception they made certain to carefully separate their new programs from the language of reparations and to avoid the manifesto's actual demands.[38]

This avoidance was made manifest most clearly in relation to the role of the Black Economic Development Conference (BEDC). At the close of the NBEDC, a freestanding steering committee had been formed to continue the work of the conference. (The name of this committee was soon changed from the NBEDC to the BEDC.)[39] The Black Manifesto specified that reparations monies were to be directly allocated to the BEDC, which would have exclusive control over how funds were used. This meant that those who endorsed the manifesto also explicitly authorized the BEDC as their representatives.

But the institutional bodies that responded in a partially affirmative, but deeply ambivalent, posture to the manifesto consistently did end runs around the BEDC. Any funds they earmarked post-manifesto were allocated to some other group. With that evasion and what it represented in terms of whites' equivocation over actually relinquishing white power and admitting the justice of the demands history made clear, they thoroughly alienated Black clergy, leaders, and laypeople who were part of that institution — a

---

38. The Presbyterians did not use the term "reparations," but unlike other institutions they did give funds directly to IFCO, "supporting program possibilities 'including those which develop as a result of the National Black Economic Development Conference.'" Lecky and Wright, *Black Manifesto*, 24.

39. "National" was dropped on July 11, 1969. For the sake of simplicity, I subsequently use the acronym BEDC to refer to the committee/organization post-NBEDC and NBEDC to refer to the conference as a whole.

visible and vocal cohort of whom had gone on public record in support of both the BEDC and reparations.[40]

At UTS, for example, a group of Black and white students shut down an administrative wing for twenty-four hours until they were allowed to speak to the board of directors on behalf of the manifesto. After finally giving the students an audience, the board voted to invest $500,000 of endowment monies in Black enterprises in neighboring Harlem, to try to raise $1 million to finance the seminary's involvement in community projects in the neighborhood, and to ask each board member to contribute to a special fund. According to the board, the use of both the special fund and the $1 million would be allocated "under policies to be determined by the black community of the seminary, through a committee composed entirely of black students, faculty, alumni, and Directors."[41]

These responses may seem laudable. These were not small amounts of money. But students rejected the board's response. From their perspective it did not address the unequal power balance between Black communities and white churches. They also claimed it created a power faction within the Black community at UTS and divided Black and white communities within the seminary "in a manner not sought."[42] White and Black students had stood together in their address of the board in unified support of the BEDC.

Forman, too, denounced this circumvention of the BEDC. He noted particularly, in reference to the board's intention to invest in Black businesses in Harlem, that the point of the Black Manifesto was not to make more Black capitalists.[43] The demands of the manifesto were specific and clear. In the face of such specificity, the actual decisions of the UTS board were not, therefore, genuine responses to the manifesto itself.

40. The Rev. Dr. Ernest Campbell of Riverside Church did use the word "reparations" in his initial response, though Riverside specifically prohibited funding the BEDC. Lecky and Wright, 22.

41. Board of Directors, "Resolution Passed by the Board of Directors," Special Meeting (May 15, 1969). Courtesy of the Burke Library Archives, Series 4B, Box 2, Union Theological Seminary, New York. With thanks to Drake University's Center for the Humanities for funding provided to research the archives of Union Theological Seminary.

42. Roy Birchard and Jon DeVries, "Theology Students Support Black Manifesto," in packet of information prepared by the students of UTS and the Mobile Resource Team (May 1969). Courtesy of the Burke Library Archives, Series 4B, Box 2, Union Theological Seminary, New York.

43. James Forman, "Control, Conflict and Change," in *Black Manifesto: Religion, Racism and Reparations,* ed. Robert S. Lecky and H. Elliot Wright (New York: Sheed and Ward, 1969), 50.

The Black Unitarian Universalist Caucus, which was formally aligned with the BEDC, pressured the Unitarians (UU) to invest $5 million in manifesto projects. The denomination responded by offering, instead, "a *substitute* motion investing $1.6 million in projects with *'high social value'* [emphasis added]."[44] The caucus protested this response. Refusing to confer upon it any dignity, the caucus withdrew its demands entirely.

In the United Methodist Church (UMC), Black Methodists for Church Renewal formally endorsed reparations in mid-May. The caucus created a list of demands, which included $750,000 for the BEDC, and submitted these to the Methodist Board of Missions. The executive committee of the board established a $1.3 million fund for "economic empowerment" in response. Like the UTS board and the UU decision makers, the UMC, too, circumvented the BEDC. Instead they specified that Black Methodist bishops would administer the fund.

The bitterness this decision created was reflected in one bishop's sarcastic response that "perhaps" the United Methodist Church had other structures through which it might administer such resources (namely the BEDC — which those same bishops had commended to the UMC) without "coopting black bishops." The bishop went on to note that very likely Black bishops already had as much to do as did white bishops without being given more work they had not requested.

Here too, Black Methodist bishops were clear that they had already authorized the BEDC as their representatives and that their denomination's response effectively rebuffed their demands. It was an evasive, nonresponsive response. Acting on behalf of the caucus, director Cain Felder refused the $1.3 million in protest.[45]

In just these three examples, it becomes easy to see precisely the kind of behaviors the NCBC denounced so passionately in 1968. White moves to stay in control were everywhere. These moves were especially insidious, moreover, because they were repeatedly couched in terms that suggested whites wanted to respond to their Black colleagues. They responded, but consistently on their own white terms.

With excruciating irony, another way in which white Protestants evaded the BEDC was to make the NCBC the target of funds. Given the NCBC's early, clear, and unified support of the BEDC as legitimately representing Black interests — and the fact that many members of the NCBC were

44. Quoted in Lecky and Wright, *Black Manifesto*, 22.
45. Lecky and Wright, *Black Manifesto*, 23.

also members of the BEDC — whites' targeting of the NCBC was particularly infuriating to Black churchmen (to the NCBC itself!).

Only four days after Forman's foray into Riverside Church, the NCBC issued a statement in which they described the effects of the Black Manifesto as a necessary shaking of the foundations of the church. They claimed the manifesto represented "the cleansing and healing work of Christ." Calling the churches the "moral cement of the structure of racism in this nation," the NCBC insisted that reparations would demonstrate "the authenticity of [the church's] frequently verbalized contrition of their faith in the justice of God."[46]

The NCBC unequivocally supported the demands of the BEDC and called for Black Christians to develop strategies within their respective denominations and institutions to obtain the demanded funds. It described Forman as a modern-day prophet.[47]

Despite these endorsements from Black churchmen who were long-time members of the mainline denominational fold and often allies with whites in the civil rights movement, the National Council of Churches (NCC) responded to the manifesto not by engaging the BEDC but by taking it upon themselves to appoint a sixteen-member committee of Black leaders — many of whom were NCBC members — to "negotiate" with the BEDC. This committee was to be charged with bringing program recommendations to the NCC. This response belied the reality that the Black Manifesto already contained an explicit and comprehensive program (and thus it actually ignored the manifesto).

The NCBC responded to the president of the NCC with outrage. It accused the NCC of trying to walk both sides of the fence. It charged the NCC with trying not to alienate their white constituents by actually acknowledging the manifesto, while hoping to still placate their Black constituents who stood unapologetically behind it. "White churchmen [sic] have a problem," the NCBC wrote on June 26, 1969.

> They have been confronted by an adversary whom they choose not to recognize but whose message wreaks havoc with their consciences. . . .

46. National Committee of Black Churchmen, "Statement of the Board of Directors of the National Committee of Black Churchmen" (May 6, 1969). Courtesy of the Burke Library Archives, Series 4B, Box 2, Union Theological Seminary, New York.

47. Bruce Younkin, "Clergymen Confounded About Reparations," in packet of information prepared by the students of UTS and the Mobile Resource Team (May 1969). Courtesy of the Burke Library Archives, Series 4B, Box 2, Union Theological Seminary, New York.

[W]hite churchmen persistently voiced the plea that they be advised by black churchmen as to what they ought to do. Black churchmen have not ignored this plea. At every turn we have spoken to you on this point. We have spoken independently; we have spoken through many of the several black caucuses; and, finally, we have spoken through the powerful instrumentality of the National Committee of Black Churchmen. In each of these instances our message has been simple and unambiguous. We have advised white churchmen formally to recognize the NBEDC.

They continued,

In view of the foregoing, and in light of the fact that we recognize your demonstrated indifference to our opinions as a totally unacceptable insult, we advise you that no black churchmen shall sit with either eight or eighty of you to discuss anything with the NBEDC. . . . Unmistakably, our position is one of recognition of and support for the NBEDC. You have rejected this position out of hand. In so doing, we are constrained to communicate to you our strongly held belief that you have chosen to reject us.[48]

It is almost impossible from our vantage point today to fathom what the NCC chose to do next. After such a clear, passionate, insistent public address, *the NCC pushed the negotiation forward anyway.* They simply did it without the participation of NCBC members. It cannot be understated what a morally convoluted and racially offensive and alienating choice that was.

In 1969, William Stringfellow, an Episcopalian and one of only a few white voices who argued that white people were guilty as charged, watched white Protestants' actions in response to the manifesto and described the white Christian psyche. He wrote, "Meanwhile it does not take a psychiatrist to discern that the denial of inherited, corporate guilt is a symptom of it. That, of course, points further still to the fact that corporate guilt is a pathological state, a condition of profound disorientation, and even a kind of moral insanity."[49] As they encountered the manifesto's demands, white Prot-

48. National Committee of Black Churchmen, "White Churchmen Have a Problem," in *Black Manifesto: Religion, Racism and Reparations,* ed. Robert S. Lecky and H. Elliot Wright (New York: Sheed and Ward), 148-149.
49. William Stringfellow, "Reparations: Repentance as a Necessity to Reconciliation," in Lecky and Wright, *Black Manifesto,* 59.

estants repeatedly did precisely what their Black colleagues demanded they not do, and refused to do what their Black colleagues demanded they do.

Resistant behavior is not necessarily perplexing in and of itself. Had white Protestants simply said they believed their Black colleagues were wrong or admitted they did not care how Black Christians felt about their decisions, their actions would have been quite consistent and coherent — perhaps even more honest (as were the evangelical and Catholic responses in this sense). What is perplexing is that white Protestants pled their good intentions all the while, pled their desire to do the right thing, pled with their Black colleagues to advise them (thus implying they were interested in actually responding to what they heard), and pled their longing for authentic Black-white relationships.

It's hard to imagine a more convoluted stance. Stringfellow's words are not a stretch. Such convoluted and contradictory behavior does seem symptomatic of, at least, a kind of moral disorientation.

Perhaps the strongest public example of disorientation took place in the Episcopal Church. The EC initially rejected the manifesto, but then reconsidered it at a Special General Convention in September 1969. At the first plenary session of this weeklong meeting, several Black participants interrupted the proceedings and insisted the convention immediately allocate $200,000 to the BEDC as a first installment toward reparations. Schuchter describes the discussion that followed as "an emotional debate ranging from violent condemnations of the Manifesto to [white] humble admissions of personal guilt."

In the subsequent vote the assembly decided to recognize the BEDC "as a legitimate movement" on paper. *But they simultaneously voted not to fund it.* Instead, the BEDC was invited to apply for funds through an already-existing antipoverty and minority group fund.[50]

At this point the Rev. Junius Carter, a Black priest from Philadelphia, confronted the convention:

> You've talked about black brotherhood, but forget it, Joe. You don't mean it. . . . It's nothing but a damned lie. You don't trust me, you don't trust black priests and you don't trust black people. You keep saying "Be calm, be patient," but the waiting is over. . . . I'm sick, I'm sick of you. . . . To hell with love.[51]

50. Schuchter, *Reparations*, 14.
51. Quoted in Schuchter, *Reparations*, 14.

Presumably in response to this debate and to Carter's stinging charges, the convention changed the resolution the next day to state they would give "not less than $200,000" and it would be earmarked for the BEDC. They specifically described this decision as an expression of trust in Black leadership within the church.[52]

However, the resolution went on to make another unfathomable move. It included a provision that the money not be channeled directly to the BEDC. Instead, it would go to the NCBC to be disbursed. This was a full four months after the NCBC had written its letter emphatically stating its solidarity with the BEDC, and three months after publicly repudiating the NCC's attempts to use it as a go-between.

The EC's actions (ignoring their Black colleagues by evading the BEDC) having already contradicted their stated intentions (to demonstrate trust in their Black colleagues) once, the Episcopal leadership went on to insist in its press release, "This fund should not be considered a response to the Black Manifesto, nor an acceptance of the concept of reparations."[53] Thus the denomination ultimately doubled down on their white rejection of the demands made by Black clergy — the very colleagues they simultaneously and repeatedly professed to trust and with whom they claimed to long to be in a reconciled state. Whether perceived as moral disorientation or insanity — however strongly one wants to describe this behavior — the white intransigence in this history could not be more painfully evident.

A Reparations Paradigm

The troubled journey of the Black Manifesto and the failure of our denominations to collectively remember this history are important. Remembering calls us back to events in white Christians' understanding of racial justice and our relationships with Black Christians that remain deeply unresolved, despite the four decades that have since passed.

More will be said in the next chapter about the ways in which the racial alienation characterizing Christian relationships at the close of the 1960s should be seen by those of us longing for racial reconciliation today.

52. Merle Longwood, "Justice and Reparations: The Black Manifesto Reconsidered," *The Lutheran Quarterly* 27, no. 3 (August 1975): 206.
53. Quoted in Longwood, 206.

And it needs to be stated explicitly that evangelical responses to this history go largely unnoted here, because white evangelicals began and ended their response to the Black Manifesto with the rejection described earlier in this chapter.

But despite this troubled history and in addition to understanding why a return to it is critical for us today, we should pause here to be very clear about the way in which the Black Manifesto offered to Christians in the United States a reparations paradigm for understanding and responding to the challenge of race. This paradigm goes beyond the important and clear call the Black Manifesto made for reparations for slavery; though that dimension of its call is worthy of attention and will be taken up explicitly in the final part of this book.

Like the Black Power movement out of which it emerged, the Black Manifesto offered a fundamentally different set of assumptions (than did the reconciliation paradigm) out of which to make sense of race and our various relationships to it. And, as a paradigm, it thus, necessarily led to different kinds of conclusions about what constitutes an appropriate and efficacious response. (Question: "I see your sweater. What color is it?" Response: "Why, yes, it is a sweater. It's blue.")

A reparations paradigm is marked by several characteristics in terms of how it understands and responds to the challenge of race. We can identify these contours by looking at what the Black Manifesto did, bearing in mind the contrast it represented to the prevailing paradigm of the day.

The Black Manifesto assumed with clarity that difference and the rejection of difference was more a cosmetic than substantive aspect of the problem of race in the United States and among Christians. To that end, coming to know each other more deeply and living into beloved community through a shared recognition of one another's humanity on just and mutual terms was simply not a solution.

The Black Manifesto articulated in no uncertain terms the specific nature of our differences and located these as our racial problem: the histories through which we came into relationship — the history of the Middle Passage, imperialism, slavery, and colonialism. It insisted on making visible histories largely unacknowledged by white Christians. It insisted on identifying the legacies of harm and structural subjugation those histories continue to bequeath Black and white Christians — legacies largely unacknowledged by white Christians. It set limited terms on which any sort of mutuality could thus begin to be realized — only with full Black empowerment and no indulgence of deluded white notions of patronage, charity, or good will;

and only with the massive transfer of wealth that remains embedded not only in our differential relationships to contemporary social structures, but also in the deepest recesses of our radically inequitable relationships to each other across racial lines.

A reparations paradigm thus assumes deeply that beloved community without redistribution is not only a fantasy; it can only reproduce the same or similar results to which we have already come in our connections to one another.

Each of these dimensions marks the contours of a reparations paradigm because the diagnosis is historical and material, and there is a prioritizing and centering of the need to rigorously and robustly redress the alienated conditions in which we relate to one another and to the history we share.

Indeed, given its rootedness in understanding the constructed nature of race (though it did not use this language) and the nature of that construct, it's fair to say that a reparations paradigm would experience or view reconciliation en masse without redress of such conditions as so much babble, abstraction, and absurdity.

In addition, the Black Manifesto spoke from a deeply particularist ethic. It gave not even the slightest nod to the notion that we might have similar work to do to heal our historic alienation from each other or to respond to our shared history. The particular differences we embody are clear: oppressor and oppressed, white and Black. The Black Manifesto unequivocally recognized that, given their constitution, Black and white should never be seen as moral, political, or spiritual parallels (again, to speak in such terms is so much babble).

The fundamental hinge on which the analysis turns, then, is the assumption that — and an assessment of what — whites in particular owe to Blacks.

A reparations paradigm indeed assumes and acknowledges relationship and a shared history. But it insists on a clear-eyed recognition that the conditions and the nature of those relationships *are* the racial work: transformation means dramatically transformed ground on which we stand. The vexed attempt to speak of "white" as beautiful or unique that persists in a reconciliation paradigm disappears. Whiteness and its nature and constitution become something to be addressed, redressed, challenged — including and especially by those who are white and have a moral sensibility that allows and requires us to admit and face this history. In a reparations paradigm, repentance replaces cultivation of multicultural sensitivity. Repair and redress of harm done replace learning to better embrace difference.

Conclusion

The chaos and crisis into which the Black Manifesto threw white Protestants at the time has largely been forgotten. Along with that has been forgotten the painful truth about interracial relationships at the end of the civil rights movement, especially what happened to visions of beloved community as the southern civil rights vision revealed its inadequacy for addressing the northern situation, the commitments of white allies waned, and King was assassinated.

This history is best perceived as part of the civil rights story, not as an addendum to or departure from it. And it is in precisely this history that we are offered a reparations paradigm that speaks aptly and responsively to the ways reconciliation has continued to fail us to this day.

In the history of the Black Manifesto we see a call for reparations for slavery. There is much still today, forty years later, to commend this specific call. Significant evidence exists (alongside the compelling moral demand reparations points to) that the structures, violence, and marginalization that began with the origins of European/African relations on this land base continue to structure our lives together.

But in addition to this particular reparative work, the Black Manifesto offers a more viable and promising, if challenging, way to understand race and respond to it. It generates a paradigm more fundamental to understanding and more applicable to a range of contexts than only — though it would include this — reparations to African Americans for slavery in particular.

A reparations paradigm presumes that the particular ground on which we stand and meet one another and the painful wounds to which that ground bears witness must be spoken of. It calls whites to repentance, meaning that apologies are due; and if a vision of a different future is to be part of that, it knows that apology is only real when accompanied by concrete rectification and a clear strategy for ceasing to harm again.

It is not too late for us to return to this moment. Indeed, I am convinced that doing so is our best hope for racial progress among Christians. A return allows us to face the added harm and alienation that came to be when white Christians refused to take heed and thus better understand who we are today. And a return allows us to retrieve a reparations paradigm for our engagement of race today. The analytically sound and deeply moral vision that was lifted up in this history need not remain a relic of the past.

To embrace this past and a reparations paradigm for today, there is more we need to do. We need to be clear about what it was that made it so very difficult for white Christians to hear and respond to the Black Manifesto.

Thus, before beginning to envision concrete possibilities and moves that embrace of a reparations paradigm might open for those of us longing for reconciliation, and before serious talk about reparations for slavery and one hundred fifty subsequent years of structural dominance and violence might look like, we must scrutinize carefully and specifically how the phenomenon of "whiteness" made it impossible for white Christians to give the Black Manifesto a real hearing.

Such scrutiny can equip us to identify and resist making the same excuses, overlays, end runs, and evasions that so easily emerged from white U.S.-Americans generally and white Christians specifically — and that emerge even today amid the painful realization of the degree to which our racial past remains our racial present.

To state it again, the purpose of any such painful work is in the interest of allowing us to live a real hope that we might have a different future.

CHAPTER FIVE

The Particular Problem of Whiteness

In the months following May 4, 1969, official white responses to the Black Manifesto rejected the notion of reparations as an "appropriate moral justification for remedies to combat racism or the poverty afflicting black people."[1]

As with white evasion of the Black Economic Development Conference (BEDC), something powerful was at work and something profound was at stake for institutional bodies to put various programs in place and to engage with angry Black clergy, but then to dance so intensely around the issue of reparations themselves — to dismiss reparations so completely without even presuming the need to explain why.

It seems especially clear that something powerful and profound was present given the evidence that white Christians *realized* the same Black clergy to whom they claimed to be showing regard were slipping into deeper despair, anger, and alienation. What was so powerful that it would cause white institutions to imperil so much of what they claimed to stand for and so many of the relationships with folks with whom they insisted they wanted to stand? What was so profoundly at stake that less alienating choices were somehow unthinkable for most white Christians?

With distance, can we look carefully at this white behavior with the hope of avoiding similar behaviors and think in the radically different terms a reparations paradigm requires?

The Black Manifesto insisted unequivocally and unapologetically on a

---

1. Merle Longwood, "Justice and Reparations: The Black Manifesto Reconsidered," *The Lutheran Quarterly* 27, no. 3 (August 1975): 206.

reparations paradigm for pursuing racial justice. Consistent with the Black Power movement out of which it came, the manifesto moved away from analyses in which race is primarily a matter of surface-level differences, and away from the diagnosis of racism as the disparagement of and division resulting from such differences.

Instead, the manifesto assumed race to be a reality most meaningfully understood in relation to the structural and material conditions made real in the lives of differently racialized communities — and out of which difference actually emerges. It focused on the economic, political, and social manifestations of racial oppression in the lives of Black U.S.-Americans. It located contemporary racial oppression in specific historical legacies of imperial conquest and enslavement initiated and sustained by white/European people and white institutions. Thus it unequivocally understood Black-white relations through a historical perspective.

To place Black-white relations in this historical view is to render a universal ethic for viewing race — an ethic in which it is assumed that we humans are *all* essentially the same underneath our differences or that our differences are *all* uniquely beautiful — rather irrelevant. A deep historical reading of race (of which just a glimpse was provided in chapter 2) disrupts and renders incomprehensible an understanding of race relations that implies we all need to engage in similar and shared work to realize the goal of coming together in community.

Instead, history — and the atrocities, wealth transfers, and endless effects of subjugation to which history directs our attention — makes clear that a particularist ethic is the only way of approaching race in the United States that makes sense. If concrete, material structures created race and continue to give race a lion's share of its actual meaning, taking history seriously makes it impossible to avoid speaking about perpetrators and victims, about the persons who benefited and continue to benefit unjustly from these legacies, and about the persons who were and continue to be harmed.

History makes clear that whiteness is a racial identity unlike the racial identities of communities of color and that the moral work thus required of white people is of a different sort than that required of communities of color.

In this view it becomes almost impossible to argue anything other than that redress and repair of the historical and contemporary structures through which we are in racial relationship to one another are the means through which we must engage these relationships. In this view we can simply cease speaking about difference *per se* and center the assumption fully on the work of redress and repair — which, of course, demands distinct responses from differentially racialized communities. Thus, a particularist ethic and a reparations paradigm go hand in hand.

Given what a reparations paradigm assumes and argues — to the extent it accurately interprets the actual racial situation in the United States — white Christians could not, therefore, respond to the Black Manifesto with integrity without taking up the issue of whiteness; without engaging the particular problem of white people's unique relationship as perpetrators and beneficiaries to supremacist racial structures.

Indeed, the Black Manifesto threw down a gauntlet that made any other response than that of picking up that gauntlet an act of evasion and rejection — not only of the realities of Black experience and analysis, but also of white experience and participation in our shared history. Yet despite the fact that northern white Christians' conversion during the civil rights movement prepared them to speak with concern about and to condemn the harmful experience of Blacks in U.S. racial structures, these same Christians were unwilling or unable to talk about and critique the experience of whites in U.S. racial structures — let alone respond in ways that would have revealed the clarity and efficacy of the moral and political logic of a reparations paradigm.

The failure to address what the manifesto made impossible to avoid goes a long way toward explaining the maddening incoherence of white Christians' dance around the manifesto, reparations, and their Black colleagues who stood behind both. The moral disorientation observed in the prior chapter was the result of whiteness powerfully at work in Protestantism in the summer of 1969 and beyond.

Whiteness motivated the specific ways white Protestants responded to the manifesto. Ironically, one of the most powerful forms this response took was in urgent, panicked moves to ensure that whiteness itself — brought to light so visibly by the manifesto — would go unnamed and unacknowledged. And here lies one of the most important lessons for our work on these matters today.

For the sake of clarity, it is worth making explicit here what is signaled in my use of "whiteness." This concept can be difficult for whites to grasp deeply — in part because the language of reconciliation does not demand (or, in some ways, even allow) a specific discussion of "whiteness." Being challenged to think or talk about being "white" throws us into moral confusion and distress, in part because our experience of white racial hierarchy and privilege makes it possible for whites to let whiteness go unnoticed.

"Whiteness" as I use it here is a phenomenon — a powerful one. It is a phenomenon that can exist only with the direct involvement and complicit participation of white people. At the same time, it is also larger and more powerful than the individual white person, having taken on a life of its own. In other words, regardless of one's beliefs, commitments, and even one's actions, white people cannot simply "opt out" of whiteness.

To speak of whiteness is to name the reality that the light-skinned among us (people categorized as "white") are implicated in perpetrating and perpetuating white supremacy, however actively or passively. To speak of whiteness is to explicitly name the reality that white people live out real *agency-filled* choices in relation to racism and racial issues and to state that white people have a particular and active relationship to white supremacy and racial injustice (as suggested in chapter 2).

It is worth noting that being implicated in very real ways impacts every dimension of the lives and living of the light-skinned. It impacts us spiritually, morally, psychologically, and otherwise. While it is beyond my purposes to explore these here, much good work has been done elsewhere to bring the powerful effects of whiteness on the lives and living of white people into view, in the hopes that better understanding these impacts will enable us to more effectively challenge it.[2] These effects are also what are indicated when we speak of "whiteness."

Lastly, my use of "whiteness" in this chapter relates directly to the two chaos-producing exercises we explored in chapter 2. To realize that race is a social construct and, as a result, has material and structural meanings is to understand that in a social landscape characterized by white supremacy, the relationship of the light-skinned to those structures is deeply, deeply vexed. Perhaps it is most vexed among those of us who perceive ourselves as valuing justice and equality. Such realizations necessarily admit the existence of a distinct, complex phenomenon we can call whiteness.

---

2. There are many works that dig into this phenomenon in powerful and provocative ways and from a diverse array of scholarly fields. A select few include Toni Morrison, *Playing in the Dark: Whiteness and the Literary Imagination* (New York: Vintage, 1993); Ruth Frankenberg, *White Women, Race Matters: The Social Construction of Whiteness* (Minneapolis: University of Minnesota Press, 1993); Shelly Tochluk, *Witnessing Whiteness: The Need to Talk About Race and How to Do It* (Lanham, Md.: Rowman & Littlefield Education, 2008); Wendell Berry, *The Hidden Wound* (New York: North Point Press, 1989); Tim Wise, *White Like Me: Reflections on Race from a Privileged Son* (Brooklyn: Soft Skull Press, 2011); David Roediger, *Black on White: Black Writers on What It Means to Be White* (New York: Schocken, 1999); and Janet Helms, *A Race Is a Nice Thing to Have*, 2nd ed. (Microtraining Associates, 2007).

And yet, for many reasons, whiteness is something we typically avoid and do not acknowledge. The actual, specific relationships of those of us who are "white" to white supremacy is rarely given careful and specific attention — even by those of us who are white and who decry racism and care deeply about justice. This silence and lack of attention undermines our justice work.

Ironically, it is when white people avoid, ignore, and deny an honest naming and contending with it that whiteness is most powerfully at work. Whiteness covers up the very connections we must see and disrupt if we are to make genuine progress toward racial justice. The silence, therefore, that whiteness both coerces and on which it depends is so powerful that a particularist ethic — which insists that the distinct experience of white people be seen, named, and called to account — is imperative.

We have already seen the institutional rejection of the Black Manifesto by Protestants. A careful look at the specific choices made and postures taken by white Christians to avoid addressing the problem of whiteness and acknowledging their agency in sustaining racially supremacist structures is now warranted.

Such a look is important not so we may unduly criticize these actors from afar and, in the process, distance ourselves from them. Rather, it is critically important because from a distance it is easier to see clearly the absurdity that results from attempts to avoid whiteness in the context of a paradigm that makes naming whiteness unavoidable. The need to engage whiteness might be more obvious from this vantage point in ways that are helpful for our contexts today. It is also important because it remains inordinately difficult for white people to look directly at our whiteness and our racial agency that is so deeply indicted within it.

In other words, we are no less likely to engage in such postures of avoidance today, and attempts to argue for or engage a reparations paradigm today could easily lead to the same results.

A careful inventory of one past example in which white postures of avoidance are so evident can be critically helpful, therefore, in enabling us to understand and be more alert to the temptations we will face today — even if and when we try with open hearts to embrace the invitation issued by a reparations paradigm. The way a reparations paradigm might manifest and shape our racial justice work today will be the work of chapter 6. But before exploring the possibilities reparations invite, let us take more difficult stock of what one refusal of such a transformative invitation looked like.

White Moral Agency

A first way we see white Protestants' turning away from the work of ac-knowledging white moral agency was in their hyper-focus on the scandalous nature of Forman's methods for presenting the Black Manifesto.

It may not be surprising that white Protestants found Forman's meth-ods offensive and shocking, but their obsession with them is nonetheless important. For several months following the disruption at Riverside, "liberal" Christian publications such as the *Christian Century* printed a range of op-eds responding to the manifesto.

These included columns written by whites and Blacks who were sym-pathetic to the manifesto's demands. But the editors of the *Christian Century* immediately focused on the "threat" Forman posed to the freedom of wor-ship and, thus, ostensibly to civil liberties: "Disruption of worship is a mean game," they warned, "which any number can play, including segregationists and fascists."[3] This sentiment was echoed by others, including the Rev. Dr. Ernest Campbell, the senior pastor of Riverside Church.

Campbell issued what was characterized in several reports at the time as one of the most sympathetic responses to the manifesto. This character-ization is rather surprising given the fact that he had walked out during Forman's presentation. Six days after the disruption at Riverside, Campbell delivered a radio address. But despite being described as sympathetic, during the portion of his address focused on "The Church's Response" the vast ma-jority of Campbell's words were devoted to addressing not how the church should respond to the manifesto's demands, but how the church would pro-tect itself from future disruptions.

In fact, Riverside Church had immediately obtained a civil restraining order against Forman, and Campbell made clear the church would not hesi-tate to involve the New York Police Department if "necessary" in the future.[4] This response captured the overwhelming sentiment of churches in the area. Sixty religious leaders in New York City met with the mayor and were given a hotline that would dispense police protection if called.

This collection of related responses is troubling for many reasons. First, the *Christian Century*'s claims suggest there exists moral equivalency be-

3. Editors, "Will the Black Manifesto Help Blacks?" *Christian Century* 86 (May 21, 1969): 1.

4. Ernest Campbell, "What Shall Our Response Be? Riverside Speaks First," in *Black Manifesto: Religion, Racism and Reparations*, ed. Robert S. Lecky and H. Elliot Wright (New York: Sheed and Ward, 1969), 129.

tween Black Power advocates and fascists and segregationists. Second, the volumes of prose devoted to criticizing Forman's methods imply that if he had only chosen a different approach, whites would have taken the manifesto seriously. Yet we know from the explorations of the previous chapter the falsity of that insinuation.

A third perilous dynamic can be seen in these responses. There was no reason to assume Forman or anyone else associated with the manifesto represented a physical threat to any white Christian. Moreover, given their allegiance to King, white Protestants were presumably convinced of the moral and theological legitimacy of civil disobedience and disruptive protest. In the face of this, it is stunning how quickly and with what ease white Protestants turned to long-standing images of Black people as threatening and scary (white supremacy–produced images we still contend with today) to shape their response.

We do well to remember here again how many of the folks involved with the manifesto were integral members of the institutions being addressed, folks who had worked alongside whites in the civil rights struggle. Such a quick move to involve the police in the context of such relationships is beyond troubling. It speaks volumes about the perceptions and biases white people brought to these relationships.

Meanwhile these initial responses stand out as a first clear example of whites' unwillingness to look at and take seriously their own moral agency.

It would have been eminently reasonable to begin with the question of the facticity of the manifesto's charges, which were hardly open to historical debate. As indicated in my previous description of what happens when Black-white relations are historicized, doing so would have made addressing white agency unavoidable. Every other move or response by white Protestants could have flowed from that reasonable starting point. (And, again, the same remains true today.)

Instead, white Protestants focused not on the historical facticity of the charges, but on Black people and Black activity. Instead of starting with history and reality, they started with the danger manifesto supporters posed to the church's business-as-usual.

Such a starting point was morally vacuous. Beyond this, such unwillingness to engage and grapple with the historical roots of U.S. racial oppression, how it continues to function, and its material impact not only on Blacks but on whites allowed whites to rhetorically hide from their roles in perpetration of, perpetuation of, and complicity in oppression. This hiding made it possible for them to describe the existence of oppression as merely "unfortunate" or "tragic." Those are not benign adjectives in such a context.

If a problem is "oppression" or "exploitation," the active behavior of oppressors is an unavoidable phenomenon about which to be concerned, a problem of equal or greater urgency than the behavior of the victims as they respond to such oppression. In contrast, an "unfortunate" situation does not necessarily demand that one speak to causes. Tragedies are often unavoidable flukes of misfortune. By almost never acknowledging that their own moral agency and choices were the originating causes of Forman's disruptions in the first place, whites remained rhetorically comfortable obsessing about, focusing on, and judging the behavior of Black folks instead of their own oppression. Given the lens the manifesto brought to bear on whiteness, this was a significant diversion.

Fixation on Forman's methods reveals another dimension of whites' inability to bring themselves into view. As the previous chapter showed, the collective behavior of white Protestants in the third group indicated they did recognize that racial realities needed to be addressed. But this recognition co-existed with a more entrenched perception: that worship space was somehow separate or sacrosanct from the demands of such realities.

If we assume worship is supposed to concern itself with one's existential status and moral nature, this is a rather peculiar perception. But it seems that in the white Protestant mind racial realities could legitimately be held distinct from the existential status and moral nature of white people; and that the existence of profound Black suffering — *caused* suffering — did not have theological implications for who white people were or for their relationship to the Divine.

Had whites perceived the nature of worship (or oppression) differently, it would have been obvious to those debating and denouncing Forman's tactics that the question of whether it was immoral to disrupt worship was meaningless without first asking whether the manifesto's charges were true. Here again, we might expect that white Protestants' affinity for King would have prepared them to think through these two questions in reverse order. King had made clear that the morality of "breaking the law" (thus behaving "immorally") was irrelevant if the law itself was unjust. The first question always pertained to that of the morality of the law in question. Thus, if Forman's charges were true — and few among this group overtly argued they were not — how could one *not* accept the right of such urgency to be named in the context of worship?

How could one not agree that the moral stakes in this problem were of such urgency that concerns about violating the right to expect orderly worship had no weight? How could one not conclude that the whiteness of the worship space itself and the wealth in which it was ensconced (this was Riverside Church, after all, which had been built with Rockefeller money) was evidence of sin given the history that undergirded such wealth? Again, white Protestant responses, focusing on the morality of disrupting worship, functioned to radically absent the implicated white racial self from the framework.

Whites' understanding on this matter was fundamentally different from that of Black Christians, who made clear in their array of responses that race and worship, material realities and the moral nature of the self, could not be disconnected. One account from the period illustrates particularly well the difference between how deeply Blacks related the existential, worshiping self to issues of race in contrast to how whites did.

Several weeks after the Black Manifesto was issued, at the annual National Workshop on Christian Unity, Muhammad Kenyatta, a member of the BEDC, rose to speak at a Quaker service that was closing out the workshop. He began by saying, "Our witness is not to an abstract God. Our witness should be to flesh and blood. We feel moved to say as Gandhi said — that God has no right to appear to the hungry other than as bread." Kenyatta went on to condemn a reference that a worship convener had made to Philadelphia, the site of the workshop, as the birthplace of liberty:

> That's a sacrilege to my people. To us this is the burial place of the Indian nation. We have no love or historical respect for anyone — Quaker, Jew, Episcopal, Roman Catholic — whose history is with those who helped con the Indians out of what was theirs.

At this point, the convener rose and asked Kenyatta to conclude so that the group could "continue with worship."

"Mr. Kenyatta replied, '*I am worshipping* [emphasis mine].'"[5] In Kenyatta's terms, addressing one's moral status as it is determined through social and material relations was not only an appropriate focus for worship, it was the very substance of worship itself.

In addition to making Forman's methods their focus, a second way white Christians refused to take white moral agency seriously can be seen in

---

5. Quoted in Religious News Service, "I Hear My Brother," in Lecky and Wright, *Black Manifesto*, 153-154.

their use of language expressing regret that such a poor state of things existed that Forman felt the need to act as he did. This collection of responses was related to the phenomenon described above of calling that which was the result of exploitation an unfortunate or tragic situation.

Language that transformed specific charges of white Christian complicity in the exploitation of Blacks into more generic language of poverty and disadvantage proliferated. The Interchurch Center of New York, for example, issued a statement saying they were "deeply sympathetic to the causes of [the] poor but cannot tolerate occupations."[6] Bishop Hines of the Episcopal Church called for the establishment of a $10 million fund to address the "needs of suffering and oppressed people."[7]

We saw other examples of this language in the previous chapter — the Unitarian Universalists' fund for "high social value" projects or the UMC's "economic empowerment." Recall as well that the second group of institutions which rejected the manifesto without apology emphasized their existing "poverty" initiatives as evidence of why their consciences were clear in the face of the manifesto's charges.

These responses were particularly powerful because such silence around race was layered on top of an unwillingness to name the factors, actions, or people who caused or benefited from such "poverty" and "suffering." To turn racial exploitation into poverty, suffering, and disadvantage is to make these categories states of being that somehow naturally exist. Agency is erased.

More important, *white racial* exploitation is thickly camouflaged, and along with it the active choices that are implicit to such exploitation. One white observer recognized this phenomenon with bold dismay. Dean Gordon E. Gillette of the Episcopal Church confessed, "We're not ready to face up to the fact that the real problem is white racism, not just poverty and injustice."[8]

Other rhetoric that obscured white agency permeated the commentary of the day. One editorial spoke of church leaders meeting "to struggle with the most difficult problem confronting the churches and the nation."[9] Note here that the agency lies not with the white folks who have created the problem, but with "the problem" itself. The problem is active and confronts

6. See "Chronology," in Lecky and Wright, 168.

7. Quoted in Arnold Schuchter, *Reparations: The Black Manifesto and Its Challenge to White America* (Philadelphia: J. B. Lippincott Company, 1970), 12.

8. Quoted in Schuchter, *Reparations*, 13-14.

9. J. Robert Nelson, "Preparation for Separation and Reparations: The Churches' Response to Racism?" *Christian Century* 86 (June 25, 1969): 862.

the churches. How it came into existence is given no attention; it somehow just showed up at the church's door. There is no suggestion in this piece that the problem was created and caused, in part, by the church.[10] There is no indication that white church leaders have helped perpetuate the problem.

In fact, the problem is never described as having any close or intrinsic relationship at all with the white church leaders who were wrestling with it. (And, notably, "the church" in this editorial is not specifically described as white members of the church, despite being clearly to whom the author is referring. As we know, Black Christians were taking active and passionate roles in insisting this problem be dealt with, a reality the editorial also obscures in the way it speaks of "the problem.")

In short, throughout this era the crisis of the Black Manifesto was rarely attributed to the actual actions of real people — other than, perhaps, dissatisfied Blacks — let alone to the specific people or institutions being called out by Black Christians. It was regularly characterized as a problem of suffering and disadvantage with no racial perpetrator or beneficiary in sight.

A third way the inability or unwillingness to engage the problem of white moral agency manifested itself had a more absurd character. Yet this manifestation is perhaps the one most likely to tempt us today — thus it is a tendency of which we should be particularly aware. Some white respondents publicly expressed agreement with the manifesto while going on to dismiss it on any other number of other more practical grounds.

"While professing 'essential agreement' with the justice of the manifesto's cause, Howard Schomer [NCC] . . . questioned the document's strategy as based upon an exaggeration of the power of ecumenical and denominational officers over the assets of the churches."[11] In other words, from Schomer's perspective, the NCC had no way to garner the funds. This response is absurd not because the challenge of garnering funds might not have been real. It is absurd because nowhere did this official then proceed to offer a different strategy through which a response might be attempted.

One would expect "essential agreement" to translate into some sort of attempt to generate a different proposal — one more in line with the power the NCC did have. Otherwise, the claim of essential agreement is radically doubtful. (This is not to mention that, as we saw in the previous chapter, the NCC *did* have some funds and went to great lengths to garner these but avoid the BEDC and reparations talk.)

---

10. The rest of the editorial goes on to describe the issue similarly.
11. Alan Geyer, "May Day in Manhattan," *Christian Century* 86 (May 14, 1969): 671.

The following week a different editorial in the same magazine read, "The real problem is not the *idea* of reparations: it is in effective implementation of the idea."[12] Here again, the direct insinuation is that reparations are potentially legitimate. As such, it is difficult to explain why the author feels no need to explain the failure to this point of folks who ostensibly embraced such an idea to seek out some sort of implementation.

Even more saliently, the author does not go on to suggest a different implementation proposal or to call others to try to create such a plan, as difficult as effective implementation might continue to be. This, too, is a glaring and suspicious omission in the face of suggesting that the idea of reparations has some merit. It is extremely unsatisfying to perceive the problem of effective implementation as sufficient reason to simply end the discussion.

Similar objections were cast in theological terms. According to one perspective, agreeing to reparations might give whites the incorrect idea that "one can buy one's way out of sin."[13] This was judged repeatedly to be a dangerous course of action. Here the concern is (supposedly) that white folks not be let off the hook too easily. From this perspective, the danger was so great that it was considered better to do nothing at all and to leave the moral debt unpaid — despite the fact that Black folks would continue to suffer as a result.

The likelihood that those actually suffering the effects of white racial oppression might not see this risk as serious enough to stymy attempts toward a repentance and repair process goes unmentioned. Meanwhile, those articulating this perspective presume to admit the existence of white sin but give no indication of how whites intend to stop sinning — let alone of how they will repent from such sin so they might legitimately be forgiven.

The list of diversions made on presumably pragmatic grounds is long. Concerns and accusations were also repeatedly raised (almost always by whites) as to whether Forman had the full backing of the NBEDC, had forced his way into the conference, or represented a real constituency, among others. Such concerns were accompanied by stated suspicions about how the reparations money would be spent and who in the Black community was capable of spending it. Here again the moral complicity of whites was not the overriding concern; the focus remained on just what Black folks were up to.

The overall effect of this third type of diversion was to create a distant and non-implicated perspective — a voice that presumed to render an au-

12. "Will the Black Manifesto Help Blacks?" 1.
13. Quoted in Schuchter, *Reparations,* 11.

thoritative judgment of "yes" or "no" on the "issue" of reparations. This perspective was not acknowledged as coming from the same folks who were in the actual, embodied position of being accused and implicated, from those who were living the very relationships deemed exploitative and oppressive (with evidence having been provided to back up such charges). The effect of these diversions was, again, to remove the white racial community from view as the active, agency-filled community of subjects that a reparations paradigm insists they are.

With their various entrée points, white responses to the Black Manifesto worked together to evade the moral demand of seriously engaging with the manifesto's charges — without ever having to admit that was precisely what they were doing. As we will see in the next section, even as they simultaneously enacted white moral agency yet refused to take it seriously, white Christians assumed the privilege of dictating the where, when, how, and to whom any kind of response would be made. The paternalism of these assumptions was not lost on Black Christians.

The Moral Logic of Reparations

As already suggested, the moves white Protestants made to avoid whiteness were a response to the Black Manifesto's call for reparations — a call that explicitly highlights whiteness because it historicizes our racial identities and relationships. To successfully dodge the issue of white moral agency and accountability, reparations talk must be avoided at all costs.

Reparations as a paradigm necessarily and immediately invokes a perpetrator and a victim, an unjust beneficiary and an aggrieved party in ways that reconciliation simply does not. Recognizing this truth, one student at Union Theological Seminary put it this way: reparations are not "a guilt offering or stewardship. . . . [Reparations are] a simple call to begin paying back what has been stolen, what is justly owed to those stolen from."[14]

In other words, the moral logic of reparations is justice. A debt has been incurred, it remains owed, and repayment of that debt is (morally) due. The moral logic of reparations is *decidedly not* charity or compassion.

A reparations paradigm assumes that unjust material conditions struc-

14. Mark Sellers, "Tomorrow Belongs to God But It Also Belongs to Us," in packet of information prepared by the students of UTS and the Mobile Resource Team (May 1969). Courtesy of the Burke Library Archives, Series 4B, Box 2, Union Theological Seminary, New York.

ture the relationship between perpetrators and victims, and as a result it calls for bi-party participation in a process seeking justice. It insists that healing the relationship between perpetrators and victims requires restructuring the material conditions through which the parties relate to one another (repairing and redressing the specific conditions that caused and continue to cause harm). Such healing work is particularly incumbent upon the harm-creators.

Indeed, given that our reconciliation-based attempts at authentic interracial relationships have failed — by most meaningful standards of assessment — this is the very reason a reparations paradigm is so hopeful and inviting. It focuses our attention unflinchingly on structural relationships to which we can and must attend, rather than on vague calls to appreciate difference or recognize essential sameness while assuming the good will or intentions of the offending party.

Finally, in the context of U.S. racial history, a reparations paradigm makes it impossible to obscure the painful truth of race today. Black Americans are not simply disadvantaged in some natural, pre-existing manner. They have been systematically oppressed and suppressed by white people, and the effects of that subjugation remain pervasive in our life together, both within and beyond Christian communities.

Accepting the legitimacy of a reparations paradigm, therefore, means fundamentally recognizing that the offending party has no grounds on which to dictate or influence how the victimized party uses the redress.

In fact, any attempt on the part of the perpetrator to do so serves as evidence that the party has already rejected the moral logic of reparations as a justice response. For any attempt to exert control or presume the right to have some say is to step away from full admission of guilt and acceptance of responsibility. (At this point it is helpful to recall J. Angelo Corlett's focus on oppressors' responsibility and his clarity that anything less or other than this unduly burdens victims and diverts into irrelevancies.)

Precisely this tendency toward control permeated the response of the third group of institutions. Speaking about that group, Stringfellow addressed precisely such issues:

> The white religious institutions which have so far seemed most receptive to the demand [of the Black Manifesto] . . . have charged that the National Black Economic Development Conference . . . is unrepresentative of what whites call "the mainstream" of the American black community, and have accused the conference of being too indefinite about how any monies paid would be utilized. . . . [I]n reparations[,] control of the utili-

zation of payments lies exclusively with the injured claimant, and for the party who had committed the wrong to exercise such control is a contradiction and in the instance of payments by the white churches it would be a preposterous extension of the very paternalism of those churches which is a prominent feature of the harm they have done to blacks.[15]

Here, of course, Stringfellow was decrying precisely what white Protestants did in word and deed as they positioned themselves as sympathetic to Black suffering without actually taking the manifesto's charges seriously.

"[C]ontrol of the utilization of payments lies exclusively with the injured claimant": the justice logic of the manifesto required whites to relinquish all rights to control the use of the funds demanded and owed. Instead, they responded with charity and pity, maintaining control in the process. Recognizing the moral logic assumed in a reparations paradigm helps interpret the effects of white Protestants' nonresponsive responses to the manifesto: rage and alienation among Black Christians.

Though white Protestants took action, which in some cases involved significant funds, they did not actually see, honor, or acknowledge the injured claimants. Their attempts to maintain control over use of the funds revealed a basic rejection of the justice logic of the reparations paradigm on which the Black Manifesto was based.

Their failure to grasp or refusal to accept the basic justice logic of the manifesto was evident by their unwillingness to give up control, even in cases where they made some concessions to the charges raised by the manifesto or expressed appreciation for or partial agreement with it. For example, unlike the other national bodies, the World Council of Churches (WCC) claimed to endorse the legitimacy of the concepts of "recompense and restitution." In so doing the WCC came closer to endorsing reparations language than did any other institution.

But reporting on the WCC consultation at which that endorsement was made, J. Robert Nelson went on to describe the questions that emerged when the WCC discussed the implications of its action:

To endorse the principle of reparation, however, is not necessarily to support every means of implementation. Must the churches sign every blank check shoved before them? Is the first group of black instructors

15. William Stringfellow, "Reparations: Repentance as a Necessity to Reconciliation," in Lecky and Wright, *Black Manifesto,* 62.

to arrive on the scene the one capable of representing it? If, as the consultation agreed, money should be given without any strings attached, does this mean it must be given with no questions asked?[16]

On their own those questions may seem reasonable. But in the historical context they belie a completely different agenda. No Protestant response had come anywhere close to signing blank checks. Nor were there multiple groups of "black instructors" lining up to ask for funds. Rather, there was a relatively well-organized, prominent group of Black activists, clergy, and church leaders who had a clear, defined platform and set of program priorities. Not all, but most, prominent Black church leaders who weighed in on the issue had expressed their solidarity and support for this group. And the funds demanded were not exorbitant relative to the historical realities being addressed or to the available resources in the white Protestant community.

So we must take notice. *Where* is white moral agency primarily located in the way Nelson reported on these white questions? Not primarily in the cause of oppression, but in arbitrating the "solution." *Who* are white people here? Not persons desiring to repair and heal the "moral insanity" resulting from being implicated in a system of white supremacy, but morally neutral characters helping the oppressed and presuming their right to do so, at least partially, on their own terms.

Where is Black agency in these questions? Not self-determined and acknowledged by those they had addressed with moral precision and clarity, but delineated and objectified by white attempts to continue to maintain control.

The tenor and logic of the WCC questions secure a quick retreat from the reality that a genuine embrace of reparations requires white people be moved from the center of power even as our active agency in racial exploitation is admitted (confessed? repented?). These questions make it impossible for whites to step utterly into the role of responsive participants in a relationship, for whites to take authentic responsibility for the ongoing effects of legacies of oppression, and, in the process, for whites to acknowledge the actual nature of that interracial relationship and demonstrate a desire for its radical transformation. Thus, while the WCC came closest to a reparations paradigm, it too ultimately rejected it.

The actions white Protestant institutions took in regard to the Black Manifesto and the rhetoric whites used to inveigh against it demonstrate

---

16. Nelson, "Preparation for Separation and Reparations," 865.

how powerful white racial agency actually was and remains in regard to racial justice and interracial relationships. However disoriented they might have been, time and again white Protestants chose with determination and resilience to ignore their Black colleagues.

Despite their professed concern to heal the racial divide in the church, we cannot attribute their choices to a misunderstanding of what Black Christians were demanding. Black Christians were clear. The Black Manifesto was clear. And Black Christians repeated themselves with ongoing clarity as it became obvious over the ensuing months that white Protestants would refuse to listen. White Protestants chose to insist that white power be left intact in the churches.

As white Christians displayed their strident inability to engage in mutual, equitable relationships with their Black colleagues, the possibilities Black Christians saw for the end of white power and for the real transformation of racial oppression and interracial relationships were subverted. The NCBC diagnosed this failure in painfully simple terms: "you have failed to open the door to the opportunity to give black churchmen equal respect with yourselves."[17]

Despite how complicated whites continually asserted the issues to be, a relatively straightforward response was, in fact, available and would have prevented the alienation exacerbated in this history: white Christians needed to acknowledge the historical accuracy of the manifesto's charges and that their Black siblings' analysis of what was needed for repair and justice was sound; subsequently, they needed to agree that a lens of repair was therefore a logical and appropriate way through which to understand Black/white relations, and to fund the BEDC in light of the sensible, clear, and specific programs it advocated.

Instead, white Protestants allocated funds to any number of groups of Black Christians other than the BEDC (despite being repeatedly directed not to), set aside resources for the "disadvantaged" (using the language of poverty more often than that of race), and disparaged or avoided the basic concept of reparations (without any clear explanation as to why churches should reject reparations as a legitimate, moral paradigm given the historical evidence of the nature of white-Black relations).

The former path, while relatively straightforward, would have been hard and humbling. It would have allowed and required whites to acknowl-

---

17. National Committee of Black Churchmen, "White Churchmen Have a Problem," in Lecky and Wright, *Black Manifesto*, 149.

edge and draw attention to white perpetration, to white agency, to the white self in the racial relationship, and to the structural and material relationship between whites and Blacks. This path would have seen white Christians acknowledge the meaning of race as it is described in chapter 2.

If white Christians' inability to seriously entertain the first set of potential responses reveals the powerful presence of whiteness, naming these responses reveals what was at stake in taking the Black Manifesto seriously — and the real transformative possibilities that would exist for our relationships if we had located them on such different ground. Such a radically different moral equation and set of outcomes resulting from a willingness to step into a reparations paradigm would have directly and powerfully challenged whiteness itself. It still could!

But humility is difficult. And the steps required to walk that path are difficult to take when one's vision of race is formed primarily through a reconciliation paradigm, which grants whiteness undeserved cover. Thus, the latter path allowed the white churches to make Blacks the object of white charity, to focus on the needs of Black folks but not on their moral due, on their suffering but not on its causes.

As Schuchter puts it, the NCC and all other "white churches"

> . . . predictably approached the Black Manifesto from the perspective of philanthropy, charity and antipoverty activities, with the usual embroidering of moralism and out-of-context Biblical quotations. No one at the Convention had the audacity or sense to insist that participants address themselves to the issues of economic and social justice reflected in the Manifesto and, in particular, to the past, present and future role of the church in relation to white racism and oppression.[18]

This path resulted from their insistence on absenting themselves as implicated parties in a material relationship with African Americans, one that was in desperate need of being reconstructed according to a norm of justice. It allowed the churches to ignore and even deny the reality of whiteness and the power it has in white lives, Black lives, and the constitution of white-Black relationships.

The era of the Black Manifesto left Black and white Christians more obviously alienated from one another than they had been prior, especially during the hopeful years of the civil rights movement. James Findlay Jr.

18. Schuchter, *Reparations*, 16.

writes that by the early 1970s outreach across racial lines had dried up: "Everywhere there were signs of disruption and decline in the old coalitions and friendships between whites and blacks in the churches."[19] It was the end, he claims, of a *kairos* moment, a moment in which real change had been possible in race relations in Protestant Christianity.

The analysis of Black Power made clear that racial justice requires addressing the structures and material realities that create a breach in interracial relationships, one that is already so deep that the universalist, integration, reconciliation vision is simply inadequate as a response. By focusing on the conditions that created and continue to create the breach and calling white Christians to attend to those structures in concrete ways, the Black Manifesto could have therefore been understood as having called upon white Christians to redress the very processes through which they became white in the first place.

In so doing the invitation could have been understood as one that offered white Christians the chance to join in true siblinghood with their African American brothers and sisters by revealing a path toward making their racial identities as distinguishable from, subversive to, and disruptive of white supremacy — as African Americans had (and have) been doing in their living out of Black racial identity since the beginning of race's origins on this land base.

But such a transformation was not to be.

Implications and Invitation for Today

What might have happened if white Christians had responded differently than they did to the manifesto? What if they had taken Black Christians at their word and seriously engaged the demands presented to them? Would the nature of racial relations in Protestant Christianity today be different? Would we be at a point where an emphasis on diversity and vision of reconciliation would actually make more sense?

The purpose of asking such questions is not to pretend we can alter the course of a history that has long since been written. But such questions bear directly on real choices white Christians still face today.

19. James Findlay Jr., *Church People in the Struggle: The National Council of Churches and the Black Freedom Movement, 1950-1970* (New York and Oxford: Oxford University Press, 1993), 220.

Hope for racial transformation in the church resides in this history as part of the legacy and learning of the civil rights movement. It is only if we can acknowledge the viability still of such questions that we will be prepared to take up challenges that continue to exist in relationships between Black and white Christians and to entertain the idea of making radically different choices than we ever have to this point. For such questions presume that the manifesto, its analysis and demands, and its supporters not only deserved to be taken seriously, but that they deserved such because they offered a real, life-giving moral option for the church. If we cannot imagine that this history could have unfolded differently, we are less than ready to imagine a different course for ourselves today.

The power of whiteness notwithstanding, this history indeed could have unfolded differently. Though the number of white Christians who pushed for a real hearing for the Black Manifesto was small, Stringfellow was not alone in calling for a Protestant reformation. Other whites similarly called their community to take the manifesto seriously. As one white minister put it:

> The Black Manifesto's demand . . . should be taken literally and should be allowed to do its traumatizing but necessary work on the white body of the established church. . . . Here is a chance for the white church to become Christian in the New Testament sense — a chance that may never come again.[20]

The existence of even a few white Christians who recognized and affirmed the moral logic of the Black Manifesto indicates that it was possible for the majority of white Christians to do so.

Some supporters argued that the manifesto and the events it provoked actually offered an opportunity for the church to finally make clear to the world that it would no longer be complicit in the blood-soaked history of white racial oppression in the United States — that it would no longer sanction white supremacy and exploitation as consistent with Christian truth. Some claimed the manifesto offered a saving moment for the church, a chance to finally open up white Christianity's heart and soul, an invitation to disrupt the ways it had been of a piece with the oppression so deeply embedded in U.S. racial culture and history.

---

20. Ronald Goetz, "Black Manifesto: The Great White Hope," *Christian Century* 86 (June 18, 1969): 833.

If the churches would simply and truthfully repent, this theological perspective continued, a widespread and radical transformation might become a reality. As Stephen Rose wrote, "[T]he demand is just; the time is right; and a proper response by the white churches would be the painful prelude to something like an appropriate commencement of something new in America."[21]

Given the centrality of Christianity as a moral voice in U.S. society — particularly in the 1960s — it stands to reason that Rose may have been right. A different response might have had powerful repercussions for race in U.S. society as a whole.

Put succinctly, here is the case for the salience of a reparations paradigm for us today: if white failure meant Christians closed the era more racially alienated from one another than we had been prior, we are hard-pressed to find a moment when this alienation healed.

White Christians have never apologized for the intransigence of our institutional responses to the manifesto. We have not since had a conversion moment in which we took the initiative to show we have changed our minds and opened our hearts to a different understanding of what is required to achieve racial justice for African Americans and to pursue racial healing between Blacks and whites.

Yes, there have many important shifts and much progress in white Protestant perceptions of race and racial justice. Yes, evangelicals too are demonstrating different understandings of the call to racial justice today than they did in 1969. I do not discount the significance of these any more than I discount the brilliant, courageous achievements of the civil rights movement.

But we know that separation between racial groups remains more normative in our churches as a whole than does reconciliation. More important, we know that the suffering and marginalization of Black communities in the United States remain, according to virtually every measure of social well-being, stark and abysmal relative to that of their white counterparts. While the contours of the gulf might be slightly different today than they were in 1969, the gulf so powerfully and painfully described by the Rev. Junius Carter remains present nonetheless.

Furthermore, as most of us know from our own interpersonal relationships, alienation does not simply go away. Even if two parties who have been seriously alienated eventually, out of necessity, begin to work together and/or

---

21. Stephen C. Rose, "The Manifesto and Renewal," *Christianity and Crisis* 29 (May 26, 1969): 142.

speak to each other again (after a period of acute confrontation and anger), if left unresolved the issues that caused the hurt and separation remain present in a real way. They continue to affect the quality of the relationship. On top of that, if or when these parties experience any subsequent relational strain — even if for reasons unrelated to the original alienation — the wounds and anger created in the original alienation usually make themselves known once again, quickly and powerfully.

What we know from interpersonal experience is not so different from what remains the case between whites and Blacks. The alienation that existed at the close of the Black Manifesto era did not and will not simply go away. Healing requires attending to the causes of alienation. In the case of white-Black relations, this means not only attending to the events related specifically to the manifesto itself, but taking up in a serious manner the unrepaired structural harms to which the manifesto spoke and from which whites retreated.

At this point, then, we need to state this vision in positive terms. The invitation made in 1969 — issued by way of African Americans' unapologetic, historically accurate, and morally courageous advocacy of a reparations paradigm for understanding race and their relationship to white folks — remains open, outstanding, and available to white Christians today. While the moment in which the Black Manifesto served as the specific platform on which Black Christians stood together to articulate their demands has passed, the way in which the manifesto framed the issues of racial justice and the analysis through which it described the structures and material relationship that mediate white and Black relationships remain applicable.

It thus remains for white Christians today to deal with this history and respond to the challenge of taking up the reparations paradigm introduced by Black Power in a way we have, with a few exceptions, heretofore refused. Given the profound hurt and anger that white behavior caused at the end of the civil rights era, and given the ongoing failure of our reconciliation paradigm to realize robust, diverse Christian communities today, how can those of us who long for reconciliation not find ourselves compelled to focus on and take up this other paradigm so passionately and insistently revealed?

Meanwhile, let us also be clear — if and when we begin to seriously entertain the notion of a reparations paradigm — that the very powerful presence of whiteness and the way it shaped white behavior in 1969 has not retreated. So if and when we get serious, several lessons from this era must attend our dialogue about what the embrace of a reparations paradigm might mean.

Besides the understanding of and response to race this paradigm ensures, embracing it also means we attend to white behavior and responsibility. We must be explicit that the suffering and disadvantage of African Americans is not simply unfortunate and tragic. It is not a fluke or an accident. It is caused by the active choices real live people have made and/or passively tolerated — and which must be identified.

Moreover, we must not make the oh-so-tempting mistake of concluding that the difficulties of crafting effective reparative strategies or creating deeply pragmatic responses render the demand itself less imperative or legitimate. Difficulty is not a moral argument.

The legacy of the Black Manifesto is with us. It beckons still, calling for a genuine anti-oppression, anti-racist, *particular* white response — a response that takes white moral agency and the specific relationship of white people to U.S. legacies of racial oppression seriously. It beckons us still to truly demonstrate by our actions that we desire our own repentance and a mutual, responsive relationship with our African American brothers and sisters — a relationship that can only come into being if we admit the actual conditions that have characterized that relationship to this point.

Conclusion

The radical differences between a reconciliation paradigm and a reparations paradigm remain urgently relevant to understanding the challenge and invitation Christians continue to face today.

The reconciliation paradigm attempts to challenge white supremacy through a universalist ethic that emphasizes the humanity we all share and need to honor more deeply. Interracial togetherness becomes the solution to the problem of division. And while we may admit the need to attend to the power imbalances, white privilege, and unjust structures that make such togetherness more difficult, the primary understanding revolves around the pursuit of deep, mutual, authentic togetherness across the lines of division that have kept us apart. This is work for which we are all responsible.

Yet to the extent that reconciliation models see racial relationships as constituted primarily by a universal shared humanity, the embrace of which is needed to overcome division, they fail. The reconciliation paradigm holds out a beautiful vision, but it too easily ignores the actual reality of racial relationships.

The reparations paradigm insists on a particularist ethic for approaching race. This ethic acknowledges our real differences as the only places from and through which we can and must begin to understand and reconfigure our relationships to one another. It insists that our differences are a result of a history we share, one that puts us in intimate relationship with one another. But this is the intimacy of oppressor and oppressed, a relationship of deep alienation. Unredressed histories and social structures continue to mediate our lives, leaving us with violent, alienated, harmful (to Blacks), and unjustly enriching (to whites) relationships.

Reconciliation thus is not and cannot be the first goal or work required. Repairing those structures and attending to those living histories is the first work. And it is work for which we are differently responsible, work that insists a repentant posture of repair and redress is incumbent on the oppressor. It is work that we have no right or ability to morally "see beyond" unless and until we have done it with all our might, because this work should fill the entirety of the lens through which we see ourselves and our actual situation for now.

Because the reparations paradigm recognizes that brokenness comes from specific harms done, whiteness comes plainly into view. We must embark on a journey in which we contend with the actual history out of which our racial identities and relationships emerged, and with the way this history lives on in the present.

In a reparations paradigm, authentic pursuit of racial justice as *a whole though broken and alienated community* demands that the perpetrator(s) come forward and participate in concrete redress. The focus is not on dialogue with the victim, nor on abstract hopes to heal relationships with the victim. The focus required is on the harm done (and continuing to be done) to the victim and unequivocally ceasing that harm and violence.

Like reconciliation, all parties have a stake in a reparations process. This is work that belongs to all of us. But rather than learning how to embrace our oneness, we need to describe with unrelenting clarity — and with all particularity and specificity — the moral realities embodied in the differences that constitute our relations.

It is precisely in this painful and, perhaps, counterintuitive attentiveness to harm and alienation that a reparations paradigm is most likely to succeed where reconciliation has failed. Rather than spinning off into beautiful but abstract and idyllic visions for which we have not yet collectively prepared ourselves, it addresses the actual reality of our interracial relationships — just as they are. And it is in its ability to begin from the actual reality of race and interracial relations that a reparations paradigm becomes so (potentially) hopeful.

A reparations paradigm provides no cover for those of us who are white. Perhaps the greatest contrast between reconciliation and reparations is that the reparations paradigm insists on specifically naming and calling out the relationship of white people to racial justice. Given the ways it highlights the material and structural meanings of race and roots itself in a deep understanding of U.S. racial history and the specific causes of Black oppression, it must.

A reparations paradigm does not emphasize the relationship of white people to racial injustice as human beings who are, underneath their skin, the same as African Americans. Nor does it valorize or exempt from moral scrutiny goodwilled white people (who genuinely care about the well-being of all) in regard to the realities of racial injustice. Such visions are abstract truth-claims at best, false at worst.

Instead, a reparations paradigm enables us to see clearly and offers us the chance to actively mourn, grieve, and thus challenge in shared outrage the particular relationship of white people to racial injustice. It allows us to see ourselves *as white people,* as people racialized in a thoroughly supremacist and subjugating social and political landscape.

This is no easy paradigm for whites.

It is relatively easy, in our post–civil rights era, for white Christians to speak with passion about the sin of racism and to morally condemn the ways structural injustice in U.S. society continues to impact communities of color. But it is very difficult for white people to sit still, tarry with, and look squarely at the issue of white moral agency in the face of racial injustice.

It is difficult for us to name what it is that white Americans, Christians included, have done and to acknowledge how white Christians have benefited unjustly from a history of racial violence and oppression. It is difficult for us to make explicit connections between our nation's origins and the trajectories that exist from those origins to the experiences of poverty, political marginalization, inadequate access to quality education, criminalization, and a myriad other experiences of subjugation that continue to dominate collective experiences of Black communities.

It is difficult for us not only to own the reality that these same trajectories continue to insulate and (over)privilege white communities, but to admit the saturating presence and impact of whiteness in our lives. It is difficult for us to recognize that to the degree we do not actively protest and interrupt these trajectories, we tolerate and accept them (regardless of whether we disagree with them in our minds and hearts).

A reparations paradigm thus opens precisely this most unwelcome, but truthful and potentially cleansing view of the constitution of our racial lives in the United States.

Until we take in that view and determine just what it is we want to do in response to it, I feel sure that racial alienation will continue to be the most salient characteristic of the relationship between whites and communities of color, both in the church and in the nation beyond.

Yet the inverse is also true. It is my deepest conviction that by doing precisely the work to which a reparations paradigm points, we may stand a chance of undertaking the slow and arduous journey toward authentic reconciliation.

CHAPTER SIX

A Reparations Paradigm

The word "reparations" connotes the era of slavery for a number of reasons, and the Black Manifesto specifically rooted its call in this history. The final chapters of this book will consider contemporary reparations movements unfolding in Protestant denominations and what these might contribute to the way we pursue racial justice work. These movements focus specifically on slavery and its legacies. However, while there are morally persuasive and compelling reasons for honing our attention to that particular history, the work of this chapter is of a slightly different nature.

Although I have emphasized the particular history of slavery here by choosing to lift up the Black Manifesto and its aftermath — a moment in the life of U.S. Christianity that deserves particular regard given the extent to which the narrative of the civil rights era shapes the church's self-understanding today — the paradigm that came to life in the era of Black Power has broad relevance and utility. This chapter thus lays out the theoretical scaffolding that constitutes the reparations paradigm.

The key components of this scaffolding are relevant for analyzing racial realities and making constructive, justice-seeking judgments about what is required in any situation and social relationship in which race is relevant. Thus, while I have a particular commitment to advocate reparations for slavery in the United States as one response to addressing the actual racial situation and relationship between white and Black Americans, in this chapter I highlight the scaffolding of a reparations paradigm to offer insights about ways diverse Christians longing for reconciliation in varied geographical, confessional, and activist contexts might choose to deploy and apply it in response to the racial justice issues they deem most salient.

In a certain sense, then, this chapter revisits insights that have been made available in the preceding chapters. But in this chapter I name these more directly and systematically.

Identifying elements of a reparations paradigm that emerged in the manifesto history — but which are not limited to the specific history the manifesto addressed — may help us envision more broadly what a shift away from the reconciliation paradigm and toward a reparations paradigm might actually look like, along with what kinds of justice pursuits it might commend us to focus on. Such a shift is sorely needed to enable the church to engage in more just, successful, and robust paths toward racial justice.

To this point we have taken several steps to bring into view the scaffolding of the reparations paradigm. These steps included, first, an analysis of why the reconciliation paradigm fails. That analysis involved observing the chaos into which a reconciliation paradigm is thrown when whiteness is brought to bear on it, and then engaging the notion that "race is a social construction" as a way to explain that chaos.

A second set of steps included observing the ways a reconciliation paradigm and the universalist ethic it assumes came under fire in the waning days of the civil rights movement. A look at this recent history made it possible to understand the precedents for a reparations paradigm; the reasons a reparations paradigm began to make more sense to many African Americans; and the ways the alienation that resulted from this era remains instructive for how we think about race, interracial relationships, and racial justice today.

Contained within both sets of steps was insistence on the need to always historicize race. Here, rooting our understanding of race in the specific histories through which material structures have both constructed race and structured interracial relationships makes clear that repair of harm done must be a central aspect of justice-focused attention to racial relationships. We must address the harm that has been caused by perpetrators and that continues to materially benefit those same perpetrators, even as it continues to negatively impact victims.

Taking stock of these three dimensions — *race as a social construct, an emphasis on racial particularity, and a focus on the repair of unjust structures* — will allow us to do two things in this chapter. First, it will allow us to consider more concretely how deploying a reparations paradigm might shape the ways congregations, intentional communities, and even non-faith-based civic groups in specific locales (and as members of a larger nation-state) work on matters of racial justice.

Second, it will allow us to reflect on the ways the moral crisis of being white, which causes chaos in a reconciliation paradigm, can be attended to or, even better, faced with unflinching moral courage by way of explicit and specific focus on it. In other words, we will consider how reparations can truly enable white people to participate in work for racial justice with more integrity, freedom, and clarity.

After emphasizing dimensions of the scaffolding that a reparations paradigm makes available — and that Christians communities might (and should!) use in their attempts to differently configure and respond to their longing for reconciliation — I will give three specific examples of justice issues that a reparations paradigm not only renders particularly urgent, but more critically and adequately frames our conceptions of and approach to (particularly regarding the work of white Christians). Environmental justice issues, immigration and citizenship, and the crisis of mass incarceration are each best perceived through and responded to by way of the historical, material, and particular dimensions on which a reparations paradigm insists.

The Scaffolding of a Reparations Paradigm

In 1975, Vine Deloria Jr., a brilliant and prominent figure in Native American activism and scholarship, asked the following question: "Would it be fair to say reconciliation is what Christians must be about, not reconciling souls to Christ but reconciling themselves to the land?"[1] In framing reconciliation in these terms, Deloria invoked a reparations paradigm in the sense I have articulated here. Unpacking the implications of Deloria's question makes it possible to dig more deeply into the three dimensions that constitute the reparations paradigm.

Not unlike the historical overview provided in chapter 2, which emphasized the ways "white" was constructed in the process of institutionalizing slavery, "white" in the 1600s was also brought into being on this land base

---

1. Vine Deloria Jr., "God Is Also Red: An Interview with Vine Deloria, Jr.," interview by James R. McGraw, *Christianity and Crisis* 35 (September 15, 1975): 206, quoted in "Introduction: An American Critique of Religion," in *For This Land: Writings on Religion in America,* ed. James Treat, by Vine Deloria, Jr. (New York and London: Routledge, 1999), 13.

through imperialist dispossession and acts of genocide against Native peoples — and through the ideologies Europeans deployed to legitimate such.

In other words, just as a historical genealogy exists in relation to white-Black relations, there exists a genealogy through which it is possible to trace the concrete, material meanings that have come to constitute both whiteness (Europeans became white through the course of this history) and white-Native relationships. Such genealogies exist similarly in regard to racial relationships between white U.S.-Americans, who sit at the top of the racial hierarchy here, and any other nondominant racial group.

Thus, there are profound ethical implications to insisting we understand race primarily as a social construction and not as an intrinsic identity of difference. This is not to say racial identities do not represent real differences about which we should care, some of which we need to learn to value and embrace. It is to say that it is possible and — for the sake of the integrity and efficacy of our justice work — necessary to identify how race has been constructed in any historical period (including the present), in any geographic locale, and in relation to any racial identity or interracial relationship.

In turning our attention away from racial difference as the ethically meaningful nodule, race as a social construction turns our attention toward the specific, concrete material and structural realities contained in race; toward what race means in the day-to-day living of those of us who are racialized (which is all of us in this nation). These realities become the primary focus of our racial justice work in ways that disentangle us from the problems and conundrums in which we find ourselves when reconciliation (and inclusion and diversity) is our primary focus.

I sometimes tell my students, for example, that to recognize race is socially constructed is to realize that being Black literally means that one is eight times more likely to be arrested for marijuana use than one's white counterpart.[2] Of course, this is not to say that is the only thing it means to be Black! The agency-filled resistance that communities of African descent have always lived out — agency that transforms "black" to "Black" — is more central. But it is to insist on naming one specific systemic reality that gives blackness powerful meaning in the state of Iowa.[3]

Notice how a social-construction focus invites my white students here

---

2. "ACLU: Iowa Is Worse in U.S. in Disparities for Black Arrests for Marijuana Use," June 4, 2013; accessed at http://blogs.desmoinesregister.com/dmr/index.php/2013/06/04/aclu-iowa-is-worst-in-u-s-in-disparities-for-black-arrests-for-marijuana-use/article.

3. See http://www.sentencingproject.org/crackreform/.

to orient not first or primarily toward learning to better embrace the difference of blackness in the lives of African Americans but first toward the criminal justice system as the morally meaningful focus of racial justice work. Echoing Deloria, we might describe this latter focus as a kind of pursuit of reconciliation. We could ask, "Might we say reconciliation is about reconciling ourselves to incarceration practices in Iowa and the nation more broadly (in which case just reconciliation would have to mean destroying the racial disparities innate to that system)?"

Orienting in this constructionist way also makes it possible for us to meaningfully ask, "What does it mean to be white?" Rather than attempting to explain how and why we must appreciate the difference of whiteness, we learn to speak of the meaning of whiteness in terms of the criminal justice system. We can say that to be white means it is more likely our white children, siblings, or parents will be given the opportunity for substance abuse treatment if they need it or let off with a warning if for some reason they are stopped and found in possession of illegal substances.

When we say this, we bring to the surface the profound intersection between white supremacist structures and our own racialization as white people. But rather than being immobilized and confused by our identity, our lens focuses on the structures that create the moral crisis of being white. It becomes clear, as well, that challenging and disrupting those structures is possible.

Targeting the criminal justice system is possible. Moreover, doing this kind of work actually builds the very ground on which we need to be able to stand more firmly to take increasingly adequate responsibility for the relationships of white people to white supremacy. Acting can actually decrease the level of incoherence and cognitive dissonance we so often experience in regard to our own white racial identities — the kind of chaos that the exercises in chapter 2 induce among "well-meaning white Christians."

Through a constructionist lens, therefore, we can acknowledge the way disparate treatment by systems and structures places a moral crisis at the heart of white racial identity without finding ourselves in absurd discussions of how to become more comfortable with whiteness or learn to embrace it. Only through active work, sustained over a long period of time and pursued not just individually but also collectively, might we have any hope of disrupting and transforming the meaning of "white" as a racial category. We can and should only get "comfortable" — though I am uncertain this is the best word choice — with our whiteness to the extent mobilization of our light-skinned bodies against white supremacy is a substantive part of our identities. The converse is also true: by taking such action against white supremacy we enable ourselves to become more comfortable acknowledging and living with the tensions engendered by being embodied in our own "white" skin making us more likely to show up at the diversity table as whole selves. Constructionist views of race lead us to recognize that challenging such disparities is not only work calibrated to disrupt harm being committed against our brothers and sisters of color, it is also work that directly confronts the moral crisis of our own white racialized lives.

Race as a social construction turns us away from abstract attempts to improve our relationships with people of color and toward concretely engaging the material realities that mediate and alienate our interracial relationships.

To return to Deloria, if race is a social construction, we recognize in the genealogy of its birth that the evils of dispossession and genocide are the very substance of white-Native relations. Deloria's question about being reconciled to the land is, in fact, a call to reconcile to one another across racial lines. But, as his comment insists, we can only do this by literally going through the land, which is the very site and substance of our alienation. As Deloria stated elsewhere, "Morality must begin where immorality began."[4]

To speak in these terms is not to suggest that land rights are the only matter of relevance to Native peoples in their dealings with non-Native U.S.-American Christians (and non-Christians). Nor is it the only area of life in regard to which Native American communities experience marginalization and subjugation. To give just one example, there is a devastating industry of anti-Native images and stereotypes in U.S.-American culture. White U.S. Christians must become more aware of and actively challenge these every time we encounter them — from our children's Disney movies to our NFL football teams. But such disparagement is only one dimension of the relationship between whites and Natives.

Non-Native Christians are remiss if we focus the bulk of our attention on attempting to appreciate and value the diversity and beauty of Native American lives and communities without concretely challenging the structures and systems actively devastating Native communities. Without clear, sustained attention to the actual nature of white-Native relations (of which rights to the land is one of the most ongoing and encompassing issues), rec-

---

4. Vine Deloria Jr., *Custer Died for Your Sins: An Indian Manifesto* (London: Collier-Macmillan Limited, 1969), 52.

onciliatory attempts will ring hollow at best. At worst they will exacerbate the alienation that exists between non-Native people and Native peoples.

We need to focus on the blood-soaked land: the land to which Native peoples still claim rights the U.S. government denies, the land from which white U.S.-Americans experience untold riches and benefit, the land we white U.S.-Americans use to talk about how important it is to "own" something or to "belong" to. The land *is* the relationship. This land is where white racial identity and Native American identity are constructed in relation to one another.

An important caveat must be identified here. Although I cannot take it up in depth, discussing white-Native relations always makes clear the degree to which nationalism and imperial/colonial dynamics are intertwined with white supremacy in the United States. And the category "white" is entangled with "U.S. American," "Christian," and "colonial-settler" as well because of these histories. This is an argument I have made elsewhere and that is as relevant to white-Black relations as it is to white-Native relations (the Middle Passage was an imperial project).[5]

In this sense, the language of race is rather inadequate for what I am pointing at here, not least because "Native American" is not best understood as a racial identity; the same would be true, for example, in relation to "Japanese American."[6] Yet the analytical framework I have built to this point works, nonetheless, if we recognize the analysis that categories of difference are constructed through histories of violence and structural relationships and that a reparations paradigm demands acute response to and redress for these.

I will not this far into the book theoretically reconstruct the terminology basically adequate to engage Black-white relations that has been our primary focus to this point, but which is too mono-dimensional to adequately reflect the complexities of the Native-white experience (something that would have been done differently were this book primarily focused on Native-white relations). But these differences should be noted and must

---

5. See, for example, Jennifer Harvey, *Whiteness and Morality: Pursuing Racial Justice Through Reparations and Sovereignty* (New York: Palgrave Macmillan, 2007). Also Jennifer Harvey, "Dangerous Goods: Seven Reasons Creation Care Movements Must Advocate Reparations," in *Buffalo Shout, Salmon Cry: Conversations on Creation, Land Justice, and Life Together,* ed. Steve Heinrichs (Waterloo, Ont., and Harrisonburg, Va.: Herald Press, 2013).

6. In fact, Native Americans cannot even be appropriately called a "group." Only the fact of imperial/colonial realities on this land base led to the construction of a group called "Native Americans." Native peoples overwhelmingly continue to identify with their nations.

certainly be engaged and understood deeply by communities involved in justice work in regard to white-Native relationships.

In short, a lens of social construction can and must be used to analyze the actual relationship between white U.S.-Americans and any other racial communities historically impacted by white supremacy. It is the first measure by which white Christians can assess the extent to which we are deploying a reparations paradigm to approach our justice work.

Constructionism enables a reparations paradigm to hone in on what our differences mean and enables complex and realistic readings of these meanings. Such readings enable us to make decisions about where to focus our activism and anti-racist challenges, and in regard to which issues. For example, we might ask, How are relationships between white Americans in Northern California constituted in relation to Chinese Americans? What is the history and structural nature of that relationship? What is the relationship between white Americans and Mexican Americans in the Southwest? Which social issues and material realities need to be targeted for transformation as a first step in a journey toward a different, reconstructed interracial relationship?

Constructionism invites specific and concrete answers to these questions. Thus, the material and concrete meanings of constructed racial categories — as opposed to the interesting differences that seem to naturally go along with different phenotypes — is always to be the starting point for how we think about justice. This criterion already shifts us away from the reconciliation paradigm and toward a reparative one.

Second, the reparations paradigm is constituted by an ethic of particularity. Insisting we speak in particular terms about race makes it possible to contend directly with whiteness and to engage in racial justice work that takes seriously the different responsibilities we have in that work. Such work requires moral courage. While a universalist ethic, out of logical necessity, has to posit white American identity as a moral, political, social, or spiritual parallel to Native identity, for example, the work of this book has made clear such parallelism is a dangerous and deceptive myth.

White racial identity is, in our national context, an identity of domination. Particularity, therefore, relieves us from the need to talk about race in such flawed, universalist terms as the morally and politically meaningful differences between whites and Native peoples become the entrée point for addressing our race and our relations. That entrée point will always reveal and demand specific and distinct responses to those material structures relative to our different relationships to them. So, for example, if Deloria is right that reconciliation to the land is the work of Christians, then reconciliation requires radically different work from Native peoples and white people; this is the very essence of particularity.

In this way, an ethic of particularity actually stands poised to liberate white Christians in our justice work, allowing us to honestly and specifically target for disruption the problem of whiteness and its work sustaining complicity between white people and racially supremacist social structures. We become better able to avoid the conundrums that stop us in our tracks when we deploy a racial paradigm that disallows particularity, conundrums that bind those of us who are simultaneously identified with the dominant racial group and yet who long to actively affiliate with racial justice movements.

Particularity also liberates nondominant racial groups from having to focus their energy and attention on the dominant group and on bettering relations with them, a focus implied or explicit in the reconciliation paradigm. Both the dominant and the nondominant are freed to creatively and specifically focus on structures: on their specific, respective relationships to those structures and on what particular justice work is required from white/ Black/Native/Latino/Japanese American communities.

Imagine, for example, what particularity might look like if it had been fully embraced to frame the UCC's "Sacred Conversation on Race" (chapter 2). Instead of employing a universalist ethic that addressed whites and communities of color by naming their responsibilities toward each another in the shared work of building reconciliation, particularity would have *still* meaningfully enabled them to invite differently racialized people into a shared conversation. But that conversation would be understood up front to be about the distinct but powerful relationships we all have to whiteness and white supremacy and about the ways it has shaped all of our racial lives.

This kind of conversation ensures that participants are clear that the *first* work of white people is to get active in regard to structures that harm communities of color and distort the morality of white people. It enables us to say with legitimacy and without apology that there is distinct work communities of color may need to do to continue to challenge and disrupt racial injustice — work that only communities of color can identify, describe, and name, work that sometimes means taking a serious break from being around white people and trying to dialogue with us.

A conversation assuming a particularist ethic would have also been able to frame itself as an invitation to white communities to explore what it looks like to show up as supportive, reliable allies to such work — to show up not in a stance of pity and paternalism, but in a stance of empowered outrage against the harms that continue against communities of color in our (white) names.

The "Sacred Conversation on Race" would not have asked Christians of color to put white people (and trust of them) high on their list of priorities (a focus Black Power would have denounced). It would have instead dived into calling whites to contend with racial injustice and white privilege concretely, regardless of whether we have "realized diversity."

Such framing would relentlessly focus whites more on white supremacy and less on people of color. (It is focusing on the latter that often causes white folks to step away from our own responsibilities, obsess about the choices and behaviors of people of color, and evade the reality that when we talk about racial injustice we are talking about white complicity and agency — all of which we saw in white responses to the Black Manifesto in the prior chapter.)

It is important to note here that what I am describing presumes racial justice work is to be done by all. This different work and these different responsibilities might even be done together and/or side by side. (SNCC leaders envisioned white activists educating the white community and Black activists working with the Black community as engaged in the same project.)

I am not suggesting that whites and Blacks or whites and people of color should organize separately for action. In fact, I am rather wary of white communities working on their own, not least because white participants in any project may very likely benefit from the insights that come from justice work that takes place alongside a differently racialized group (even if the work being done is distinct). Such benefits help us grow into better allies.

Finally, I am certainly not suggesting whites should define their understanding of justice work in isolation from what communities of color name, analyze, and describe as the most urgent matters facing their communities.

What I am issuing a call for is a radically different way of understanding racial justice work. Constructionism allows us to focus first on material structures (which we recognize as constituting the relationship), and particularity allows us to name overtly and live into our distinct and specific relationships to those structures.

Whether the issue is immigration, the criminal justice system, access to quality education — we can and must work in coalition. But "the how" of the work is critical.

Whether or not we begin with a specific recognition of the different impact any of these issues has on us by way of our differently racialized lives makes a huge difference in how we address it. Our different entrée points in regard to concrete, material places where we are in relationship are acknowledged and shape our responses.

At the same time, while there are risks, a particularist ethic for approaching race does mean whites *can* take on the problem of racial injustice even when there are no people of color in the room. Action as whites is not precluded. We do not have to, nor should we wait for, our communities to diversify before racism and racial difference becomes something we worry about and take action on. White supremacist structures are ever-present (in most cases, the effects of which create the very uniracialness that ostensibly offends us).

We who are white have a particular relationship to those structures, and we have a moral obligation to target them for disruption *right now*. Particularity frees us not only from having to wait for people of color to come be with us in order to be about justice; it makes it less likely we will engage in wrong-headed efforts to try to recruit people of color to join us. The ability to be clear about the different *but complementary* work required of us instead honors where our interracial relationships with each other are to begin with — we are deeply related to one another but in a thoroughly alienated intimacy — and frees us from the false hope that we can realize reconciliation before we whites work seriously on disrupting white supremacy.

White people can work on racial injustice now, wherever we are, wherever we live, whoever is or is not a visible part of "our" congregation or community. We should always do so informed and responsive to the ways communities of color are already naming and targeting the injustices we wish to act against, and responsive to what people of color say they need and want from allies. But, we can do that work now.

The following example, which I have shared elsewhere in print, illustrates what particularity can look like. In one of my courses we were wrestling with the challenges of white people's relationship to racial justice. My white students often described feeling stuck and not being sure what to do about their white conundrum. Then one of these students came back after fall break and shared a breakthrough moment.

She had gone to a concert to see one of her favorite bands, which happened to be from Mexico. The club had heavy security, and most of the patrons were Mexican or Mexican American. White bouncers were frisking everyone, but as my white student entered, the bouncers waved her through. She knew this was a moment where her whiteness was manifesting as a specific relationship to a system of oppression. So she stopped, put her arms in the air, and said at the top of her lungs, "If you are looking for weapons on everyone else here, you better frisk me too."

Her response created quite a ruckus. While the guards tried to collect themselves, other patrons in the line started yelling *"Solidaridad!"* in support of her action.

This action disrupted a moment of white supremacy and was rooted clearly in an ethic of particularity. This student did not conceptualize her justice work as cultivating appreciation of Mexican music or as getting to know other patrons in order to either better embrace their unique differences or commiserate with them about the bouncers' behavior.

Now, she has, in fact, cultivated appreciation of Mexican cultures and does have meaningful relationships across lines of racial difference. These practices are important in her life and shape her racial justice understanding and work. But in this moment, she acted from her specific relationship to white supremacy, at the intersection of racial injustice and her white racial-ized self. She did not need permission from the other patrons to call attention to this intersection, nor did she act patronizingly "for them."

She recognized she could target white supremacy and had her own stake in doing so. She chose to say "no" to the moral deformation that would have come if she had walked past those bouncers in quiet complicity. In that sense, her action had nothing to do with the other patrons, even while it had everything to do with her *actual* relationship to the other patrons. This was an act of conscious racial agency that took her whiteness seriously and publicly rejected white supremacy's attempts to coerce her into silence and passivity.

It is not insignificant that the other patrons recognized the meaning of her response. It is also not a stretch to say that very likely in that moment, even if it was just for a moment, this young person transformed the meaning of her own white racial identity. In Deloria's term, we might see this as recon-ciliatory activity. She did this by way of a particular response (a refusal!) to the specific structures creating and constructing whiteness in that moment.

Particularity is thus the second critical dimension of a reparations par-adigm. We must avoid at all costs any approaches to race or racial justice that ignore the conundrum of whiteness by speaking in abstract, universalist platitudes about shared humanity. Obviously we are all human beings. But such discourse fails us in our attempts to sustain critical anti-racist, racially just work that empowers white people to attack white supremacy.

It fails because it cannot account for the particular relationship white people have to white supremacy, in contrast to the relationships communities of color have. Instead, we must root our justice work in particularity and find in that rooting a gift: the gift of being able to admit and own up to whiteness and the deforming power of complicity and moral compromise.

In the clarity and mobilization that particularity makes possible, we can then move against whiteness as white people. Such work is a far more intimate posture of solidarity with communities of color — despite our worship lives remaining racially divided — than attempts to generate intimacy and relationships through talking about our shared humanity underneath our different skin tones or focusing our energy on getting to know one another across lines of difference.

An approach to race and racial justice that centers on repair (rather than tolerance, inclusion, appreciation, etc.) is the third critical dimension of a reparations paradigm.

Repair offers no easy answers, nor any final solutions (most cases of racial atrocity in the United States can never truly be repaired). But repair does generate a clear, compelling standard by which to organize our activism and move from an unflinching, honest look at the differential impact of white supremacy into actions that attempt to address and redress that impact.

And, of course, reparations themselves are a form of rectification that has significant political and legal precedent in response to massive, historic violations of human rights and unjust accumulation of stolen wealth.

Let us return to Deloria. The land was stolen. The land is the site at which harm was and continues to be done to Native communities. It is the place at which death-dealing violence continues to haunt and at which radical alienation continues to characterize white-Native relationships. This alienation exists because white people still unjustly hold the land.

To say this does not admit any easy solutions to such alienation. But in admitting the truth that our racial relationships are structural and material, economic and political, deeply and unequivocally historical, it becomes clear that reconciled relationships between Native Americans and white Americans can come only through work to create justice in those land relations.

Thus, repair is the work. It is a constant and unending work. But while saying so may risk invoking a process that sounds so overwhelming it induces despair, such framing radically reconfigures notions of relationality and justice away from a reconciliation paradigm that has proven endlessly unsatisfying. Such framing moves us from the inefficacious abstract toward concrete possibilities, hopeful possibilities.

Native communities in numerous locales and regions across this land base are already engaged in justice struggles in regard to their land rights and other sovereignty struggles. These struggles are usually rendered invisible. They are also regularly disparaged by those of us who have insufficient understanding of the political and legal history of relations between the United States and Native nations, let alone of the moral call these relations have on those of us who now occupy the land.

Work to repair will always be partial. It will never truly "undo" the material implications of Native-white relations. But vigorous support for the struggle of the Lakota people in the Black Hills region, for example, is a partial, limited example of what justice work as repair must look like.

Or consider this example: in 2001, non-Native evangelical Christians in Eureka, California, decided to engage in partial repair in support of the Wiyot people, who had been struggling to secure the return of 40 acres of their land from the Eureka City Council since the 1970s. After taking part in a reconciliation event, evangelical churches in the area gathered $1,000 worth of donations to enable the Wiyot to purchase 1.5 acres of this land from the city in concrete support of this land struggle.

"The Wiyot claimed that this reconciliation meeting had paved the way for the city council to return the land [the entire 40 acres] in 2004."[7] To my mind, this is a limited, partial, but real example of what repair looks like. Rather than leaving the relationship at an abstract invocation of reconciliation that might have been invoked in a worship service, or even at the level of verbal apology for the past with no redress activity attached to it, this small community engaged in reparative action that changed the actual relationship that Native peoples and whites respectively had to the land in this region.

We might point to any number of examples as models of what it might look like to embrace a reparations paradigm for understanding race and racial justice. Deloria's analysis here illustrates the larger theoretical approach a reparations paradigm makes possible.

Whatever the history and the concrete, structural nature of the interracial relationship being considered, attending to structures for repair and redress — the same structures through which race is constructed, the same structures to which we have different relationships — is the path we need to pursue to live into the reconstructed interracial relationships for which we long.

In short, a reparations paradigm makes possible a repentance- and repair-based, structural response to the conditions that shape and form our racial lives in relationship to one another, with a serious and unflinching en-

7. Andrea Smith, *Native Americans and the Christian Right: The Gendered Politics of Unlikely Alliances* (Durham, N.C.: Duke University Press, 2008), 74.

gagement of the shared histories and contemporary conditions out of which those relationships emerge.

A reparations paradigm made real in the lives of our faith communities will continually return us to three touchstones to assess our work: race as a social construction; a particularist ethic that insists we respond to (and frees us to respond to) our distinct relationships to injustice; and repair as the living, breathing work of reconstructing our interracial relationships through redressing the structures that mediate those relationships and differently harm and deform our racial lives.

My advocacy for the employment of a reparations paradigm, made up of these basic dimensions, has three major implications. First, I want to challenge our faith communities to step away from our ongoing emphasis on a reconciliation paradigm and, instead, adopt a reparations paradigm for the larger ways we engage, interpret, and respond to race. It should be clear at this point that so doing enables the churches to take the problem of whiteness more seriously and more directly — and that our ability to become racially transformed communities stands or falls on our ability to do precisely this.

Second, individual congregations and regional bodies can and should engage in racial justice work that is most salient in their locale, and a reparations paradigm can be used to come to informed, nuanced assessments of what these efforts should look like. Racial injustice in Iowa manifests in potentially different terms than racial justice work in Florida. A reparations paradigm, with the three dimensions described above, should be used by justice-committed congregations to orient and engage in activism in their particular geographical locale.

Third, broader, salient matters of racial justice do exist that transcend geography and bind us together in our distinct racial identities as members of this civic body known as the United States. In these cases a reparations paradigm directs us in more overarching terms to the work Protestants and prophetic evangelicals should be about in the larger public, civic context. Here, I am thinking specifically about the degree to which white-Native-African relations, the original relations out of which race emerged as a recognizable reality on this land base, remain our nation's "original sins" in regard to which repentance has yet to take place.[8]

Not only do these sins remain unredressed by the nation and by the

8. A phrase invoked by ethicist Larry Rasmussen at the 2002 Dietrich Bonhoeffer Lectures in Public Ethics, "Costly Grace: Race and Reparations, Theological and Ethical Readings of Communities."

white Christians who inherit a faith tradition complicit and implicated in white/European subjugation of Native and African Americans and the material wealth that attends these legacies. But the depth and encompassing nature of these sins places the unresolved racial, imperial, and religious violence they represent at the heart of this nation's identity. Thus, there is a case to be made that these historic relations deserve particular, acute focus and attention from white Protestant Christians and prophetic evangelicals who continue to long for reconciliation.

To make the implications of my argument for a reparations paradigm as concrete and constructive as possible, for the remainder of this chapter, then, I will briefly explore three specific examples of what it might look like to apply the paradigm for thinking about racial justice and our role in seeking justice as members of faith communities and activist groups.

My hope is to challenge white Christians to engage or think about engaging differently on these issues because of a reparations paradigm. I also hope to stir the imaginations of discrete communities about what a reparations paradigm might look like in action on issues with which they are already active or hope to become so.

Regarding my third point of advocacy — the attention our "original sins" demand — we will take up one of these specific examples in greater detail as we close this book by exploring moves Christians are making to take up reparations for slavery.

Making It Real: The Environmental Crisis and Creation Care

In the wake of widespread recognition of the global environmental crisis, Christian communities have taken steps to articulate a theological vision of care for creation. As early as the 1990s the World Council of Churches initiated a conciliar process called "Justice, Peace, and the Integrity of Creation," intended to respond to these crises.[9] A comprehensive resource compiled by a Christian environmental organization reveals an impressive list of statements and resolutions issued by nearly every mainline Protestant denomination, the U.S. Conference of Catholic Bishops, and evangelical communities.[10]

---

9. George E. "Tink" Tinker, *American Indian Liberation: A Theology of Sovereignty* (Maryknoll, N.Y.: Orbis, 2008), chapter 2.

10. EarthCare, Inc., "Creation Care Websites and Statements," accessed at http://earth-careonline.org/creation_care_websites.pdf.

These initiatives share a commitment to undermining traditions that have taken God's direction in Genesis to "have dominion and subdue the earth" as a "license to dominate and exploit."[11] "Stewardship" is re-conceived as special human responsibility for the earth: "As stewards of the natural environment we are called to preserve and restore the air, water, and land on which life depends."[12]

These works also emphasize the need for Christians to recognize that humanity and nature are interdependent; indeed, that we humans are formed of earth itself.[13]

Recognizing the devastation human communities are wreaking on the globe and seeking radical changes in our behaviors and social structures — as well as in our theological, economic, and other forms of thinking — is urgent. Yet here is a perfect example of how important it is to root such work in its larger historical context and examine it through a reparations paradigm.

First, the *specific* lands on which we stand when we advocate for care of the earth are not ours. While it is beyond difficult for those of us who take the existence of this nation-state for granted to absorb this political and legal reality, it is a fact of history (and morality) that the numerous treaties signed between Europeans and Native peoples — and later between the U.S. government and Native nations — were often signed only after Native numbers and power were first systematically decimated by a variety of colonial/imperial mechanisms.

Coercive conditions and illegal practices accurately describe the environment in which most treaties were signed. After that many were repeatedly violated. For example, after "agreement" was reached that determined certain areas would be left "in perpetuity" for Native peoples, the discovery of some desirable resource would make treaty violation irresistible to Europeans/U.S. Americans.[14]

In an expanding nation-state the "desirable resource" might simply be the land itself, and the government would look the other way while white U.S.-Americans encroached on land that a prior treaty had marked as inviolable.

---

11. See Evangelical Lutheran Churches in America, 2, accessed at http://earthcareonline.org/creation_care_websites.pdf.

12. See United Methodist Churches, 4, accessed at http://earthcareonline.org/creation_care_websites.pdf.

13. ELCA, 2.

14. For an outstanding resource on these specific histories, see *A Companion to American Indian History*, ed. Philip J. Deloria and Neal Salisbury (Oxford: Blackwell Publishers, 2002).

There are many specific histories that deserve and have been given attention elsewhere, but here this first point is simply that if we advocate "stewardship" of this land without responding explicitly to the history out of which our contemporary land occupation continues to unfold, we do so *as imperialists*. We assume by fiat something in regard to which we have no coherent legal, political, or moral claim. Creation care for white U.S.-American Christians must mean robust support for indigenous land-rights struggles.

Second, the knowledge postures and belief systems that led people of European descent to wreak havoc on the environment were and remain the same as those enabling displacement and genocide. When Puritan lawyer John Winthrop was still on the boat coming to this land base, he drafted the legal justification for dispossession. He wrote that Native peoples might have a natural right to the land, but they did not have a civic right to it. The reasons? They had not "subdued," "possessed," or "improved" it.[15]

Creation care movements may already recognize the death-dealing power of these concepts. But what bears emphasis is that the same sleight of hand by which Winthrop endorsed a commodified earth established the basis for European colonials' (who became white U.S.-Americans) relations with Native peoples.

To treat the land as commodity required viewing the people who were on the land similarly. Thus, ecocide and genocide always go hand in hand.[16]

When the breast milk of nursing Mohawk women is found to contain 200 percent more PCBs because the women have eaten fish from the St. Lawrence River (Great Lakes region) — which a variety of industries have polluted with toxins — we are observing the relationship between ecocide and genocide.[17]

When as many as 75,000 cases of thyroid cancer are documented among the Western Shoshone between 1951 and 1992 because Shoshone land has been made the site of massive nuclear weapons testing by the United States and Great Britain, we are observing the relationship between ecocide and genocide.[18]

The atrocities and devastations our white U.S.-American ancestors and we, their descendants, have visited on the land and on Native peoples are one

15. Jonathan Winthrop, quoted in David Stannard, *American Holocaust: The Conquest of the New World* (New York: Oxford University Press, 1992), 235.

16. Tinker, *American Indian Liberation*, 57.

17. Winona LaDuke, *All Our Relations: Native Struggles for Land and Life* (Cambridge, Mass.: South End Press, 1999), 18-19.

18. LaDuke, 98, 99.

seamless tapestry. We cannot, therefore, fundamentally redo our approach to creation without simultaneously redoing our relations to Native peoples.

Third, there exists a long legacy, still present today, of white-created images and symbols depicting Native peoples as "savages" — for example, when whites perform the "tomahawk chop" at sporting events. This image pertains to creation care because Europeans and U.S. Americans portray(ed) themselves as civilizers who had/have a divine mandate to tame not only the landscape but the uncivilized savages who were part of it.

While justice-seeking Christians may recognize and reject such disparaging images, Philip J. Deloria has demonstrated the degree to which the "savage" is inseparable from romanticized images of Native people as "sage" in the white U.S.-American mind — an image that seems to turns up whenever Euro-Americans take up environmental issues.[19]

On the one hand, there are good reasons creation care movements may find themselves tempted to lift up Native communities as examples to be learned from, or as embodying ways of being we need to emulate.

Euro-Americans did devastate a continent that Native peoples had lived in sustainable relationship with for millions of years. As Jace Weaver writes, given their population prior to the encounter with European peoples, "Native peoples could have wrought much more environmental damage than was the case." Instead, Native peoples "learned to practice reciprocity and natural conservation techniques in order to ensure ample resources for themselves and their progeny."[20]

On the other hand, Weaver also insists that Native relationships to the environment were themselves complex (like all people, he writes, Native peoples were and are neither saints nor sinners). His point is that whites always see Native peoples "in some distorted funhouse mirror . . . seeing whatever they most desire," he writes. Even the "sage," thus, erases the actual existence of Native peoples as real people, in ways that enable Native peoples and their land to continue to be exploited.[21] White-created images of Native peoples as "natural" environmentalists are a problem.

In 2000, the United Methodist Churches wrote that Native American "religious cultures for centuries have taught them how to care for creation" and that Native peoples have a perspective that insists "environmental prob-

---

19. Philip J. Deloria, *Playing Indian* (New Haven, Conn.: Yale University Press, 1998).

20. Jace Weaver, "Introduction," in *Defending Mother Earth: Native American Perspectives on Environmental Justice,* ed. Jace Weaver (Maryknoll, N.Y.: Orbis, 1996), 7.

21. Weaver, 4.

lems are more spiritual than technological."[22] Such statements may not be untrue, and if (but only if) they generate serious *anti*-colonial/-imperial engagements with Native peoples they may have important potential. But if white Christians seek to "learn from" Native peoples as a means to improve *our* relationship to land, we use Native peoples to our own ends, failing to support the visibility and justice-struggles of the first inhabitants whose land rights have been illegally eviscerated through violence and genocide.[23]

As the authors of *A Native American Theology* put it, "To continue to resist just Native land claims and refuse reparations as compensation for lands illegally taken is to engage in an unhealthy and dangerous psychological denial about the conquest of this continent and the nature of our cohabitation on it."[24] The savage/sage symbolic world is a primary mechanism enabling such denial. To actually *see* Native peoples and radically re-historize the conquest and actual conditions of our cohabitation on this land base is the only way to end such denial — and doing so authentically can only lead to an endorsement of Native land struggles.

Finally, the environmental racism about which creation care movements are often concerned requires endorsements of Native sovereignty. One denomination's statement asserts, "The land and its inhabitants are often disenfranchised by the rich and powerful. The degradation of the environment occurs where people have little or no voice in decisions."[25]

While political exclusion and marginalization mark the experience of all communities of color in the United States, for Native peoples this manifests especially as violations of sovereignty.

Andrea Smith gives an example of what this looks like in terms of reparations. Because most energy resources are located on indigenous lands, U.S. attempts to exert control over such resources means discussions of domestic energy "independence" depend on sovereignty violations.[26]

When nuclear test sites and toxic waste dumps proliferate on Native lands, degrading Native bodies as they destroy the earth, we are witnessing not just environmental racism at its worst but an evisceration of the right to

---

22. UMC, 36.

23. Weaver also discusses this tendency specifically in his introduction to *Defending Mother Earth.*

24. Cara Sue Kidwell, Homer Noley, and George E. "Tink" Tinker, *A Native American Theology* (Maryknoll, N.Y.: Orbis, 2001), 170.

25. ELCA, 7.

26. Andrea Smith, "Reparations and the Question of Land," *Union Seminary Quarterly Review* 56, no. 1-2 (2002): 171.

self-determination through which Native nations would otherwise successfully resist such degradations.

A reparations paradigm requires us to take seriously repair of actual harm done. This paradigm centers white Christian creation care movements on robust support for Native American sovereignty struggles and land rights. Indeed, if we care to not commit more imperial violence, analysis of the urgency and visions of best responses to environmental issues must hold these relationships — our relationship to the land *and* first peoples — in the same seamless tapestry that holds the historical and contemporary context of the United States.

Making It Real: Battles over Immigration

Immigration issues — specifically the public and political battles over "irregular" migration across the southern border[27] — can also be conceptualized through a reparations paradigm. Doing so provides a critical cadence to our analysis of and responses to white-Latino/a relations.

The most recent spate of heightened attention to immigration in U.S. civic discourse might be attributable to the effects of the 1994 passage of the North American Free Trade Agreement (NAFTA). On the one hand, we must always treat U.S. public responses to migration from the south with suspicion. As Linda Chavez (an appointee of President George W. Bush) pointed out, the ruckus surrounding immigration in 2006 was evidence of a kind of "media saturation" because immigration rates were actually lower then than they had been in the late-1990s, when the controversy did not rage in the same way.[28] Such an "out of synch" response should give us pause. There is always something ideological and racial at work in our public discourses on immigration.

On the other hand, NAFTA absolutely did wreak economic havoc on farmers north and south of the border, and the consequences of NAFTA to Mexican workers and the Mexican economy more generally have been acutely devastating. NAFTA restructured the Mexican economy to the detriment of Mexican workers in many ways — for example, small-scale sustain-

27. "Irregular immigration" is the terminology for which Khalid Khoser argues in awareness of the powerful negative effects of the word "illegal." See *International Migration: A Very Short Introduction* (New York: Oxford University Press, 2007).

28. Linda Chavez, "The Realities of Immigration," *Commentary* (July 2006): 34.

able farming became nearly impossible, and 1.5 million farmers had to give up their land in its wake. The below-living-wage jobs in huge factories along the border that replaced such livelihoods have been in no way a replacement.[29]

In essence, NAFTA made it possible for trade and jobs to migrate more freely across borders, but it made no similar provisions for the laborers who would need to follow those jobs.[30] A climate of economic desperation has, thus, pushed would-be migrants north, looking for work — even as northerners (U.S. residents) have become more fixated on and shrill about illegal immigration. Combine these factors with a period of tightened border control that makes crossing the border more perilous than ever, and we have nothing less than a humanitarian crisis unfolding in the desert.[31]

In this layered context, many of the same communities already inclined to work on reconciliation and attentive to the environmental crisis also embrace a worldview that sees immigration and the need for immigration reform as an urgent issue of human compassion. In fact, several evangelical denominations have passed resolutions calling for "gracious attitudes toward immigrants and constructive actions on their behalf."

The National Association of Evangelicals (NAE) has endorsed a statement committing to work for better legislation at the federal level, and leaders affiliated closely with prophetic evangelicalism — Ron Sider and Jim Wallis, for example — have engaged in a variety of efforts to educate non-Latino/a evangelicals about the urgency of immigration reform in order to mobilize them.[32]

Christians have also produced theological reflection on these matters. They have articulated biblically informed perspectives that suggest God's call to those who love God is to provide hospitality to the stranger and safe harbor to the refugee. These include attention to the repeated instructions given to the Israelites to treat the alien or sojourner "like the native-born among you" — especially in light of their own experience in Egypt to the degree to which a fleeing mother, father, and baby Jesus should be seen as refugees escaping to another land to avoid sure death.[33]

---

29. Miguel de la Torre, *Trails of Terror and Hope: Testimonies on Immigration* (Maryknoll, N.Y.: Orbis, 2009), 57.

30. John Fanestil, "Where the Jobs Are: NAFTA and Mexican Immigration," *Christian Century* (September 18, 2007).

31. See de la Torre, *Trails of Terror and Hope*, chapter 1.

32. M. Daniel Carroll R., "An Evangelical Voice," in de la Torre, 150.

33. See Leviticus 19:33-34 and Matthew 2:13-14. Translations in de la Torre, *Trails of Terror and Hope*, 132-133.

The United Church of Christ frames their understanding through God's call to love one's neighbor. Inviting congregations to declare themselves "immigrant welcoming congregations" and to engage in political advocacy on Capitol Hill, the UCC explains:

> The Bible is unambiguous in calling us to welcome aliens and strangers in our land, and to love them as we love ourselves. In these times, let us listen to the voice of the still-speaking God. We will learn how to respond to these new sisters and brothers residing among us.[34]

These theological visions are important and provide critical groundwork for going even beyond advocating immigration reform to more direct resistance to draconian laws that have made the simple act of providing water to someone dying in the desert a crime punishable by incarceration for up to ten years.[35]

But, not unlike theological attention to the environmental crisis, it is important to bring a reparations paradigm into these efforts in an explicit manner. A reparations paradigm pushes white U.S.-American Christians toward a more adequate understanding of the actual realities of immigration and pulls us away from potentially problematic perceptions that unfold as an "us" called to render hospitality to a "them."

While such a perception is not utterly inappropriate (and I reiterate that the stances taken are themselves important), a reparations paradigm insists we center and make visible the unjust and exploitative histories and material relations that actually constitute white-Latino/a encounters in the United States. In so doing we work against the temptation to see immigration reform as "charity" toward those in need — in contrast to work required as we recognize that those who are already part of this civic body and those who continue to cross the border in search of sustenance are people to whom white U.S.-Americans owe a moral debt and to whom repair of harm done (and continuing to be done) is due.

Not so far removed in our national story is the United States having absconded with Mexican land after engaging in bellicose action designed to provoke war. This history is of a piece with that constituting white U.S.-American-Native relations, a history deeply characterized by expansionism and dispossession.

---

34. See http://www.ucc.org/justice/immigration/.
35. Daniel G. Groody, "Testimony on Being a Good Samaritan," in de la Torre, 27.

Andrew Jackson declared U.S. expansionism an extension of the "area of freedom" in 1843; obviously freedom was for whites. John L. O'Sullivan invoked this ideology shortly thereafter to advocate for annexation of Texas and the Oregon Territory, coining the phrase "Manifest Destiny" to describe it.[36]

"Manifest Destiny" was shorthand for U.S. expansionism as a racial-religious (white-Christian supremacist) project. Over and over again this national project was proclaimed to mean the following: God has "reserved America for a special people of Saxon blood."[37]

The larger context of this history makes visible dynamics that have been similarly created in U.S. relations with a number of nations and communities in the global south. As with Native-white history there are specific narratives worthy of attention and relevant to this larger discussion, but which cannot be granted here. But the long-term impact of the Mexican-American War is worth sustained attention to make this case about immigration, citizenship, and repair.

In 1846, President James K. Polk "deployed troops into Mexican territory to provoke the Mexican army to fire first upon U.S. troops." Even at the time some members of Congress denounced this aggression as illegitimate, and General Ulysses S. Grant himself, who served in the war, described it critically in his end-of-life memories as a war forced upon Mexico with the exclusive intent of taking its people's land.[38]

The war and its aftermath hold little space in U.S. civic, public imagination and memory. It was not until my early twenties, for example, despite my long interest in, work on, and study of racial justice, that I noticed that the Colorado heritage of which my family and I are so proud (we were "settlers" after all) was a heritage made possible only because the United States *moved the border.*

When this illegitimate war ended the United States had taken more than half (55 percent) of Mexico's territory. This territory included vast resources: gold, silver, and oil. In addition, while the Treaty of Guadalupe Hidalgo signed at the end of the war obligated the United States to grant citizenship to Mexicans living in the territory ceded to the United States, and

---

36. de la Torre, *Trails of Terror and Hope,* 10. Reginald Horsman, *Race and Manifest Destiny: Origins of American Racial Anglo-Saxonism* (Cambridge, Mass.: Harvard University Press, 1986), 219.

37. Horsman, 209.

38. de la Torre, *Trails of Terror and Hope,* 10-11.

to protect the rights of those individuals to retain their land, both of these provisions were violated in significant measure.

Scholars of this era insist that persistent underdevelopment of Mexico and the longstanding marginalization of Mexican Americans within the United States are indisputable results of the war and its consequences.[39]

The first implication of historicizing U.S.-Mexico relations in the manner a reparations paradigm demands is significant. Massive resources and wealth in the United States — access to wealth that U.S. citizens have — is not only unjust enrichment that resulted from this history; it also fuels the desperate poverty and underdevelopment that contributes to migration across the southern border, legal or not. This structural relation alone justifies understanding our battles over illegal immigration through a reparative lens.

This paradigm asks us to radically rethink the question of what is due to people here or who are seeking to arrive here, regardless of their legal status, because it changes our understanding of what "here" is. As Miguel de la Torre puts it so succinctly, "We didn't cross the border, the border crossed us."[40] *That* border crossing involved unjust appropriation of land and resources to devastating consequence. Reparations and repair of harm done, simply put, are appropriate given this context, and this realization should impact our advocacy.

A second implication of historicizing these relations comes in regard to a need for us to call into question the meaning of "citizenship" in the United States — which is a much-disputed resource in our immigration battles. Namely, do we allow a path to citizenship if we enact immigration reform? Not only does the implicit (white) racial framing of the notion of citizenship commit racial exclusions easily seen as disparaging and problematic (something many Christians active on these matters already critique loudly), but our notions of citizenship and what it means actually rest on so much falsehood.

Citizenship in this nation is as materially and structurally vexed as is whiteness itself. It too can be seen as in a state of moral crisis. "White-only" naturalization laws remained on the books until 1952, formally endorsing the "common sense" belief among white U.S.-Americans that citizens are *white*.[41]

39. See http://www.pbs.org/kera/usmexicanwar/war/wars_end_guadalupe.html.
40. Miguel de la Torre, "For Immigrants," in *To Do Justice: A Guide for Progressive Christians,* ed. Rebecca Todd Peters and Elizabeth Hinson-Hasty (Louisville, Ky.: Westminster John Knox Press, 2008), 75.
41. See Ian Haney López's brilliant *White by Law, Tenth Anniversary Edition: The Legal Construction of Race* (New York: New York University Press, 2006).

But more insidious events are situated here as well. During the Depression, federal officials forcibly deported 500,000 people of Mexican descent to Mexico, more than half of whom were U.S. citizens. In 1954 alone, "Operation Wetback" (in effect through much of the decade) forcibly deported more than one million citizens and noncitizens of Mexican descent to Mexico.[42]

In other words, the active erasure of citizenship of those who are members or promised membership, because race makes them unrecognizable as a citizen, did not begin to end with the Treaty of Guadalupe Hidalgo.

The presumption of illegality based on Latino/a descent identity exists throughout the United States, though it is perhaps particularly suffocating in the Southwest. Latino/a peoples thus live and work in the United States while forced to contend daily with the presumption of illegal status — regardless of actual status — and the invectives, fear, and policing to which such presumptions lead.

The way "whiteness" sits at the center of our notions of "citizen" is yet another good reason to reframe our responses to immigration beyond a "hospitality to strangers" paradigm and through a lens of repair that recognizes we are not, in fact, strangers. We are inextricably interrelated, and some of "us" owe apologies and repair to others of "us."

Some are indeed "new sisters and brothers residing among us" who need particular kinds of support and advocacy.[43] But the implications of the recognition that "many were *already* here; it was the borders that crossed them [emphasis added]" and not the other way around demands that we rethink our understanding of what is as stake in how immigration and citizenship are presented.[44] Those of us who are white need to and can reject the way our white citizen identity is parasitically formed by these realities.

A third reason a reparative paradigm is important for the immigration debate is because of the sheer economic activity within the United States to which it pertains. Estimates vary and scholars do not all agree, but generally there exists consensus that U.S. Americans benefit on the whole from an economy enriched by the labor of the undocumented, who are meanwhile exploited and vulnerable as they go about that work.

Whether in the domestic world, where Latina women serve the tourist and hotel industry or work in homes, or the agricultural economy that literally cannot get its produce harvested without laborers from across the

42. López, *White by Law,* 38.
43. See http://www.ucc.org/justice/immigration/.
44. de la Torre, "For Immigrants," 75.

southern border, we the citizens of the United States directly benefit econom-ically. There is significant evidence that even those here in an undocumented status pay more into Social Security and other social programs than they will ever receive back.

Something is owed because harm has been done. The cadence and resonance of our already-important work on immigration and compassion in justice-seeking Christian communities shifts another critical degree when we engage a reparations paradigm. We become able to hone in on the way re-sponses to immigration and citizenship struggles are invitations (and moral demands) for us to reconfigure the material, structural dimensions and his-tories inherent in the very constitution of *white* U.S. American citizenship.

We are called beyond inviting others in with hospitality; we are called to responsive repair of the history and relations that inhere in our civic bat-tles over immigration and citizenship. As a result, in addition to attempting hospitable, stranger-welcoming work in which we strive to be like Jesus, we see we are more deeply challenged to imitate Zacchaeus.[45] We are called to figure out all the ways we are *in debt* because of having benefited from these racial/imperial realities and to unequivocally come down from the tree and give back to those with whom we have long shared and continue to share a thoroughly interrelated structural life.

Making It Real: Mass Incarceration

Mass incarceration in the United States has garnered increasing attention in recent years. Increasingly we understand it as being at crisis levels. Since the war on drugs was launched more than thirty years ago, U.S. prison popula-tions have skyrocketed. We incarcerate at rates that dwarf those in every other democracy — rates five to ten times those of other similarly situated nations.[46]

Moreover, while it has long been true, it is now increasingly well-recognized that mass incarceration is a racial phenomenon in the United States. African Americans and Latino/as are disproportionately incarcerated relative to their representation in the broader population, at a level surpass-ing the disparities that existed in South Africa during the height of apartheid.

45. Jennifer Harvey, "What Would Zacchaeus Do? The Case for *Disidentifying* with Jesus," in *Christology and Whiteness: What Would Jesus Do?* ed. George Yancy (New York: Routledge, 2012), 84.

46. Alan Elsner, *Gates of Injustice: The Crisis in America's Prisons* (Upper Saddle River, N.J.: Prentice Hall, 2004), 12.

My own state of Iowa has long been at or near the top of the list of U.S. states in this regard. While African Americans make up 2 percent of the Iowan population, they comprise 20 percent of those in prison.[47]

It is not difficult to make a case that Christians should care about this crisis and its many terrifying layers. These layers include the fact that our incarceration boom came alongside a push to privatize prisons. Privatization inserts profit into the imprisonment equation, essentially creating incentives to put more and more people behind bars.

Another layer is the significant evidence that prison is a questionable response to "crime" if our long-term hopes are for a safer society with less of it. Incarceration does nothing to create conditions in which our communities might become more whole, cohesive, and healed. The inverse is true. Incarceration creates damage that extends well beyond the crime itself, with broad, deep, and even intergenerational effects.

Extended families, children, and entire communities are harmed in the rending of familial and other intimate relationships — a rending that has a particularly acute and long-term impact on children: in the loss of a breadwinner in a family system perhaps already on the brink of (or already in) poverty; in the endless hurdles faced by one who has served time in regard to securing legal, living-wage employment; in accessing support networks (federal student loans, for example); and in otherwise knitting or reknitting of a cohesive social, familial, and communal tapestry within which to thrive post-prison.

We should not be surprised recidivism rates are so high. Nothing about incarceration enables the punished to be released as a more whole and healthy human than he or she was at entrance, ready to claim his or her place in the civic body. Not even a society that seems to think retribution is what we want is served by such a system.[48]

47. Elsner, 13.

48. Numerous excellent sources challenging the actual functions of the prison industrial complex, as well as the failed philosophy of retribution, have been written. A particularly excellent one specifically addressing this crisis from a Christian theological perspective is T. Richard Snyder, *The Protestant Ethic and the Spirit of Punishment* (Grand Rapids, Mich.: Eerdmans, 2001). Others that deserve attention include Christian Parenti, *Lockdown America: Police and Prisons in the Age of Crisis* (London: Verso Books, 2000); *Prison Nation: The Warehousing of America's Poor*, ed. Tara Herivel and Paul Wright (New York: Routledge, 2003); and Angela Y. Davis, *Are Prisons Obsolete?* (New York: Seven Stories Press, 2003). In regard to the case for restorative justice as a response to crime, works to consult include Howard Zehr, *The Little Book of Restorative Justice* (Intercourse, Pa.: Good Books, 2002), and *Changing Lenses: A New Focus for Crime and Justice* (Scottdale, Pa.: Herald Press, 1995).

But there is a particular way in which a reparations paradigm directs our attention to mass incarceration because of the manner in which this paradigm makes central the histories, structures, and material realities that construct race and our interracial relationships.

Michelle Alexander's *The New Jim Crow* provides a detailed and terrifying genealogy, tracing how we got to a place in which we systematically send African American youth with no prior record and charged with identical crimes as their white counterparts to prison at six times the rate. Most of these charges are drug related. Such a disparity is staggering on its own, but even more so when we consider that white youth show up in emergency rooms for drug-related problems at three times the rate of Black youth.[49]

The current crisis began in the early 1970s, when race was deployed intentionally and successfully to mobilize white resentment of gains made in the civil rights movement in order to redraw political party lines. It continued through the 1980s, when crime and welfare — represented through a carefully crafted media campaign as "black" — figured centrally in a presidential election cycle that swept Ronald Reagan into the White House. (This is not a Republic sin alone, however; such images were actively deployed through and by Bill Clinton's administration.)

While only 2 percent of the U.S. public named drugs as the most significant national problem during Reagan's administration, Reagan cut white-collar-crime law enforcement in half and shifted the resources to "street crime" enforcement. Budgetary support followed at astronomical levels for the new war on drugs. Local police departments that were at first resistant to being pressured to shift their focus to drugs — they too did not deem drugs the most significant problem — eventually responded to the financial incentives offered in the form of federal grants to departments who could increase their drug arrests. They began to amp up random stop-and-search patrols in the hopes of securing as many of the elusive one-arrest-out-of-one-hundred-stops as possible in order to succeed in securing the federal funds.

Incentives to stop as many people as possible, for whatever reason (failure to use a turn signal, driving too slow, driving while looking too nervous), in other words, led to more aggressive, dragnet-style policing.

Alexander puts it thus: "The ubiquity of illegal drug activity, combined with its consensual nature, requires a far more proactive approach by law

49. Michelle Alexander, *The New Jim Crow: Mass Incarceration in the Age of Colorblindness* (New York: The New Press, 2010), 115 and 97, 98.

186

enforcement than what is required to address ordinary street crime."[50] This proactivity has resulted in rampant policing practices in low-income Black neighborhoods that would never be tolerated in white middle-class neighborhoods with significantly more political capital.

Ask almost any urban-dwelling African American male or his parents: he and they know he will not get through his middle school, high school, or collegiate years without being stopped by the police — probably many times and for no justifiable cause. For even the most innocent of citizens, too many encounters with police is bound at some point to lead to the wrong word said in the wrong tone to the wrong cop in the wrong mood. Disaster results: even an arrest subsequently dismissed without charges filed counts as contact with the criminal justice system and can directly impact one's future in devastating ways.

Meanwhile, the courts have repeatedly granted police wide discretion in these matters. The courts have said that racially disparate outcomes cannot be counted as evidence of discrimination. The only way to prove discrimination is by proving the racist intent. That's a nearly impossible bar to meet.[51] In short, endless statistics and mountains of anecdotal evidence suggest we are not remiss to see our criminal justice system as engaged in a war on communities of color in the United States, one with which our legal and legislative institutions have been utterly complicit.

Despite Alexander's analytical precision in explaining step-by-step with unequivocal clarity exactly how it is that the criminal justice system devastates African American communities in ways that have virtually nothing to do with the guilt or innocence of individuals caught up in it, there is perhaps no paragraph or statistic in her book as powerful as the one that comes on page 1:

> Jarvious Cotton cannot vote. Like his father, grandfather, great-grandfather, and great-great-grandfather, he has been denied the right to participate in our electoral democracy. Cotton's family tree tells the story of several generations of black men who were born in the United States but who were denied the most basic freedom that democracy promises — the freedom to vote for those who will make the rules and laws that govern one's life. Cotton's great-great-grandfather could not vote as a slave. His great-grandfather was beaten to death by the Ku

50. Alexander, *The New Jim Crow*, 100.
51. See Alexander, *The New Jim Crow*, chapter 3.

Klux Klan for attempting to vote. His grandfather was prevented from voting by Klan intimidation. His father was barred from voting by poll taxes and literacy tests. Today Jarvious Cotton cannot vote because he, like many black men in the United States, has been labeled a felon and is currently on parole.[52]

This is where Alexander's harrowing tale begins. She details persuasively, with evidence and with incandescent clarity, the degree to which this system *is an extension of slavery and Jim Crow* in the United States — from racial profiling in neighborhoods, to treatment in the courts, to what any contact with the criminal justice system does to one's life chances, to conditions within prisons, to the impact on communities. It is different in form, but very little is different in kind.

Many urgent justice issues deserve our attention. But the crisis of mass incarceration sits among the most urgent, making a particularly powerful claim on justice-seeking Christians. When we assume that a reparations paradigm is an appropriate way to understand and respond to race in the United States, incarceration commands our attention. It is nothing less than a contemporary manifestation of the origins and long-term effects of this nation's origins — genocide and enslavement — living and breathing among us still.

A host of other epidemic-level manifestations of violence against Black bodies and communities — including systemic white violence against Black communities — are directly relevant to this crisis: from the killing of Trayvon Martin and the subsequent exoneration of his undisputed killer; to the killings of Jonathan Ferrell and Renisha McBride, two different incidents, both killed by whites as they knocked on someone's door, alone and injured after surviving car accidents; to the killing of Jordan Davis and the inability of a jury to convict his undisputed killer of even a lesser charge of manslaughter, let alone first-degree murder.[53] We could go on and on.

To the extent that we can see this system as a literal extension of the control of dark-skinned people that began on this land base in 1619 — a

---

52. Alexander, 1.

53. For more details about these and so many other cases, please see the work of the Malcolm X Grassroots Movement, which is working to draw attention to "extrajudicial killings" of African American men and women (estimated as taking place at a rate of about one killing per 36 hours in the United States). See http://mxgm.org/impunity-in-the-judicial-system-for-extrajudicial-killers/. Also, for more on this see my blog http://livingformations.com. In the trial of Michael Dunn (regarding the killing of Jordan Davis), the jury was hung on the charge of murder; see http://reason.com/archives/2014/02/19/hung-up-on-stand-your-ground.

vision virtually impossible to "unsee" once one encounters Alexander's ter-rifying masterpiece — a reparations paradigm becomes imperative for our response. Mass incarceration and the spate of extrajudicial killings (like those just described) are among the most pervasive and devastating ways race is being constructed in the United States today — as well as being a thick, deadly structure through which whites and Blacks exist in relation to each other.

It is not enough for whites to be outraged by this system, to experience grief and despair when Trayvon Martin's killer goes free — reactions many justice-seeking whites (Christians and otherwise) expressed in the wake of that verdict. A reparations paradigm both enables and demands that we see our stake as white U.S.-American citizens in these issues.

These systems are not merely harming communities of color. They do so in the service of white interests, solidifying white relationships to white supremacy as our children live while the children of others die. We must and need not continue to allow such systems to further the moral crisis of being white.

The particularity that a reparative paradigm demands allows whites to mobilize on these issues from a stance that goes beyond seeing this as a crisis of injustice that harms communities of color. It becomes a crisis of our own to which we respond, "Not in my name!" Such a declaration takes place through vigorous responses to these systems, interrupting them, repenting for them, and actively seeking to repair and redress the harm continuing to be done.

Conclusion

As it clarifies and differently focuses our understanding of and responses to race in the United States, a reparations paradigm indeed demands of white Christians challenging admissions. The particular social, racial crises described above are lament-worthy even before we see them as deeply con-tributing the very formation (moral deformation) of white racial identity in the United States.

Yet when engaged through a reparations paradigm, they register in an even deeper key. They should shake us at our core.

This shaking requires those of us longing for reconciliation to do more — beyond focusing on these issues — to come to terms with and face what it means to be a white U.S.-American in the wake of so much white suprem-acist violence. If naming and acknowledging one's whiteness causes whites disorientation of the sort we saw glimpsed in chapter 2, tarrying with these realities may take us beyond disorientation and into despair. But we need not remain in despair, and we have a responsibility to actively choose to resist remaining there.

Many activists, psychologists, scholars, and religious folk have already dug into the broader experiences and many dimensions and layers that exist when whiteness and our particular relations to it are taken seriously. Those of us who are engaged in these commitments would do well to take these seriously for our own further journeys in regard to the genocidal and epic lie with which whiteness has imbricated our families for generations.[54]

But as we do so, I want to suggest that even as a reparations paradigm enables us to see and face whiteness in a central and particular way (vision that is difficult), it also gives a paradoxical path out of the very conundrum of whiteness. If to be white is to exist in a state of moral crisis, the challenge for those of us who are justice-seeking whites — Christians and otherwise — is to attempt to constantly be white (admit, acknowledge, name, repent, and otherwise own the particularity of our histories and locations) while endlessly and actively refusing to be white (reject, work against, chastise, challenge, disrupt, redress, and repair those same histories and locations).

The cases shared above are only three areas of social life in which such work might begin. The scaffolding of a reparations paradigm presented in the first half of this chapter provides a view of how work might be envisioned and pursued in relation to other, equally urgent issues in our social, racial life. It is for each community, in its own discrete locale, to take up this work, look around for how others are already approaching it, and generate creative, disruptive visions of what a reparations paradigm might mean for the racial relationships in which the community already dwells and seeks to live as part of a collective.

In the final part of this book, then, we turn to one last vision and example. In a few places in recent years, some Christians have finally begun to respond actively to the specific call for remembering, repentance, and repair of our legacies of slavery in the United States that people of African descent (Christian and otherwise) have been issuing for generations. It is in these slow, complex journeys that I find some of the most compelling examples of what it would mean for our interracial relationships were we together (but differently) to advocate a reparations paradigm for racial justice in our faith communities.

---

54. See the sources in this area of work cited in chapter 3.

PART THREE

Stirrings of Hope, Pathways of Transformation

CHAPTER SEVEN

"We Are Called to Remember Our Entire History"[1]

In December 2007, during an oversight hearing of the Congressional Committee on the Judiciary, Bishop M. Thomas Shaw of the Episcopal Church (EC) spoke these words: "With fuller knowledge [of our history] will come true repentance that will then open us to reconciliation and remedies that we believe are yet to be revealed."[2]

Shaw's testimony came as a result of a larger process in the EC that has produced a series of resolutions on racism and reparations. The specific resolution (C011) that led to this testimony was passed by the EC in 2007, titled "Support Legislation for Reparations for Slavery."[3] Shaw's testimony before Congress, thus, came as a formal endorsement of bill H.R. 40, which would create a federal-level commission to study the ongoing effects of slavery and subsequent discrimination on African Africans living today, and consider "appropriate remedies" for such.[4]

1. "Report of the Task Force to Study Reparations," presented to and endorsed by 216th General Assembly of the Presbyterian Churches (USA) (Summer 2004): 9, http://www.pcusa .org/acrec/issues.htm.

2. The Right Reverend M. Thomas Shaw, III, SSJE, "Oversight Hearing on the Legacy of the Trans-Atlantic Slave Trade," transcript from Committee on the Judiciary, Subcommittee on the Constitution, Civil Rights, and Civil Liberties, December 18, 2007, 3, http://www .episcopalchurch.org.

3. Resolution 2006-C011, "Support Legislation for Reparations for Slavery." See "Testimony of the Right Reverend M. Thomas Shaw, III, SSJE, Bishop of the Diocese of Massachusetts; December 18, 2007," at http://www.episcopalchurch.org.

4. See "Govtrack.us: A Civic Project to Track Congress," http://www.govtrack.us/ congress/bill.xpd?bill=h109-40.

The bishop told the committee that researching its own "complicity in the institution of the slave trade will help us, the Episcopal Church, to be transformed." He concluded by stating that H.R. 40 would similarly "aid the nation in its own continued healing."[5]

Shaw's testimony is among the more significant public actions U.S. Protestant denominations have taken on reparations since the start of the new millennium. Since 2000, the EC, PC(USA), United Methodist Churches (UMC), United Church of Christ (UCC), and Unitarian Universalists (UU) have all passed resolutions and/or created commissions that call for a study of the history of slavery, the complicity of white Christianity in slavery, the on-going harms and benefits of that history, and the possibility of reparations.[6]

As the Rev. Dr. Mark A. Lomax, a member of the PC(USA) Task Force to Study Reparations, writes, discussions on reparations are "being raised on Main Streets and Martin Luther King, Jr. Boulevards, in the back alleys and denominational offices and in the halls of the United States Congress."[7]

It would be difficult to say that any of these movements are robust, are certain in their outcome, or have sufficient visibility and support among denomination members as whole. Nonetheless, their existence points to the hopeful possibility that a rethinking of the reconciliation paradigm may be underway, at least in pockets within mainline Protestantism. Further, their existence suggests that in these same pockets a reparations paradigm may be taking substantive root, in this case in the form of specific engagement of the histories and legacies that constitute white-Black relations in the United States.

Given the analysis and perspective offered to this point in this book, the possibility of such emergence is a hopeful one. It is hopeful not only because of the justice possibilities a reparations paradigm opens, but because such movements provide already-existing examples of Christians taking concrete steps to walk a better path toward racial justice. Such examples can inspire and empower other groups to begin similar journeys. They are also invitations for those of us who are justice-seeking to envision ways we might step up and step in to give support to these movements, which have a very long way to go in terms of gaining real momentum.

In this chapter, then, we explore the emergence of two movements,

5. Shaw, 4.

6. Each of these denominations was involved in the controversy surrounding the Black Manifesto.

7. Mark A. Lomax, "Reparations: Getting to the Ground Level," *Horizons* 17, no. 7 (November/December 2004): 19.

in the PC(USA) and EC, advocating for reparations. We will consider three aspects of these movements. First, I will offer an overview of the movements themselves: namely for what have they argued (at least officially) and how have they found themselves engaged in serious discussion of reparations? Second, we will look at theological engagements of history, repentance, and repair (reparations) present in these movements. Third, we will consider the extent to which these movements do and do not make the problem of whiteness visible and open to being addressed — an explicit naming I have argued repeatedly to this point as critical for the success of our racial justice work.

Before turning to this exploration, however, brief attention to the general issue of reparations for slavery is needed.

Overwhelmingly, data suggest that reparations is not only not on the radar as an issue among most white U.S.-Americans, but that a strong majority, when asked, are skeptical or hostile toward the very word "reparations." A variety of polling indicates that only 30 percent of whites believe the government should even apologize for slavery, in contrast to 79 percent of Blacks. Support for reparations among whites is even lower — hovering at around 4 percent, contrasting mightily to the 67 percent of Blacks who say reparations are due.[8] It is likely that these numbers are not much different among white U.S.-American Christians (a survey conducted by the Presbyterians suggests as much; see below).

A number of excellent books engaging in evidenced-based, social-scientific analysis of reparations have been published in the past ten years. These explain carefully and convincingly why there is nothing at all radical about the claim that today's measures indicating the degree to which African Americans are overrepresented in poverty, have worse health outcomes than whites, continue to lag behind in access to quality education, and generally fare poorly compared to equally situated white U.S.-Americans in regard to virtually any indicator of social well-being can be traced to the long-term and intergenerational effects of nearly 250 years of chattel slavery.

The wealth gap that was deeply structured into the national economy in this era, as well as into the actual lives of white and Black U.S.-American communities, is merely one measure. But it alone is significant given that it has never been redressed and that wealth, because of the structure of the U.S. economy, tends to accumulate intergenerationally (through generational transfers, structures of the tax code, wealth generating wealth, etc.).

8. Alfred L. Brophy, *Reparations: Pro and Con* (New York: Oxford University Press, 2006), 5.

Consider this illustration. In 1865, when the Emancipation Proclamation was issued, "African Americans owned 0.5 percent of the total worth of the United States." That is not shocking, writes Dalton Conley. What is shocking, he says, is that in 1990 African Americans owned only 1 percent of the wealth still.[9]

Beyond the reality of wealth disparities — as well as income disparities (between 1968 and 2005, the income gap had only closed between whites and Blacks by three cents per dollar, a rate that will require another 537 years before we reach racial parity)[10] — sits the historical truth that decade after decade after the Civil War and abolition of slavery, the United States formally enacted measure upon measure to ensure these gaps remained pervasive in most areas of social, civic, and political life.

From toleration of lynching, which ensured a pervasive state of racial terror in the South; to endless disparities in educational access that continue to this day; to refusing to hear the 600,000 men and women who survived slavery and organized to lobby Congress for pensions to address death-dealing poverty and malnutrition among elderly Blacks who had been enslaved; to New Deal laws that supported white-only unions, structured Social Security to exclude agricultural and domestic workers (the two main arenas of Black labor in the 1930s), and created housing loans and markets designed to build a white middle class; policy upon policy and practice after practice, in seamless coherence with the logic and aftermath of slavery, have engendered the accumulation of wealth among white U.S.-Americans (including newly arrived European immigrants) while explicitly denying Black Americans access to such possibilities.[11]

Slavery alone is reason to engage in a serious conversation about reparations. But the ongoing, active legacies that have impeded the realization

9. Dalton Conley, *Being Black, Living in the Red: Race, Wealth, and Social Policy in America* (Berkeley and Los Angeles: University of California Press, 1999), 25.

10. Alex Mikulich, "Racial Wealth Inequality and the Myth of a 'Post-Racial' America," *Jesuit Social Research Institute* (Summer 2010): 1.

11. See these outstanding resources, which document the veracity of this list, as well as making clear other dimensions of these legacies: *Should America Pay? Slavery and the Raging Debate on Reparations,* ed. Raymond A. Winbush (New York: Amistad, 2003); *Redress for Historical Injustices in the United States: On Reparations for Slavery, Jim Crow, and Their Legacies,* ed. Michael T. Martin and Marilyn Yaquinto (Durham, N.C.: Duke University Press, 2007); Roy L. Brooks, *Atonement and Forgiveness: A New Model for Black Reparations* (Berkeley and Los Angeles: University of California Press, 2004); Thomas M. Shapiro, *The Hidden Cost of Being African American: How Wealth Perpetuates Inequality* (New York: Oxford University Press, 2004).

of anything approaching equity, let alone justice, make *not* engaging in a serious conversation unconscionable.

It's not just mass incarceration. Virtually all of the racial disparities with which we live today can be shown as originating in or linking back in a substantive way to institutionalized slavery. White resistance to reparations, then, has more to do with an unawareness of the actual impact of this history and subsequent federal and state activity that enabled its devastations to continue unabated, or with a simple but brazen unwillingness to engage in such a discussion for whatever set of reasons, than it does with a reasonable assessment of the evidence. In some cases white resistance may also have something to do with a willingness to allow the pragmatic complexities of reparations for slavery — which do exist — to substitute for a moral argument about what is actually due (as some white respondents to the Black Manifesto did).

The case need not be made here why reparations are due, nor does even the more modest case (which is the substance of H.R. 40) that at least a collective, careful public inquiry into this history and its long-term effects is due. Others have made those cases well already. Others have also constructed clear and careful proposals in regard to the pragmatic questions. Any interested white Christian may inquire into the way the National Coalition of Blacks for Reparations in America (N'COBRA), for example, puts together its reparations platform, as well as how and why it is clear that reparations must be conceived in a redistributive sense.

Namely, much like John Perkins endorsed in the 1970s — in his case, monies to enable educational access in response to one nodule of the "harm done" — most reparations advocates endorse reparations in forms designed to restructure society, redistribute wealth, and build economic and political power among Blacks (not unlike the Black Manifesto's platform).

The goal is that reparations be efficacious structurally for several generations, as opposed to coming in the form of individual redress (which is what was given as a symbol to Japanese American survivors of internment), which is unlikely to disrupt long-term structural harm done to and continuing among African American communities.

In short, there is both a high quality and good quantity of work already underway and available. What needs to be brought home here is merely that a strong basis exists for my assessment that reparations for slavery should be taken seriously and that mainline Protestants engaging these matters and their own histories, however tentatively, stand on solid ground.

So whether white Christians are shocked because we are suspicious or hostile, or shocked simply because we are unaware how much work is being done on these matters, even a cursory glance reveals there is no justification for white, justice-seeking Christians longing for reconciliation to not at least engage in an open-minded, genuinely inquisitive discussion of reparations for slavery.

We do well, on this front, to remember one lesson from the Black Manifesto: the first question we must be willing to ask is whether the charges are true.

While a reparations paradigm has broad applicability and utility, as I have sought to demonstrate, there are compelling reasons to deploy it in particular relation to African American and white U.S.-American relations and in regard to this particular racial era and atrocity.[12] Thus, with this larger context of reparations laid out, we are now better equipped to explore and engage what has been going on in the PC(USA) and the EC.

Toward Reparations: Presbyterian and Episcopal Churches

In 2004, the Presbyterian Church (U.S.A.) Task Force to Study Reparations completed its work and submitted its official report to the 216th General Assembly (GA). The report contained four major components: recommendations, a confession, history, and results of a survey done of laypeople. By an assembly-wide vote, the church formally endorsed the report, accepting all thirteen of the task force's recommendations.

The recommendations ranged from offering general encouragement to Presbyterians to "create opportunities to tell and hear stories of remembering the past and celebrating examples of repair, restoration, reconciliation, and renewal," to specific requests that various denominational offices create study and worship resources on "reparations, reconciliation and renewal."[13] Also included was a recommendation to charge the Washington office of the denomination to "monitor and advocate" for H.R. 40.

In addition, the report contained the text of the Belhar Confession,

---

12. As I also note in the prior chapter, there are equally compelling reasons to do so with Native American history and white-Native relations as well, which need to be given their own full reading because the specific issues and forms of response required are different. My choice to not engage them here is not indicative of my assessment of their urgency, but simply indicative of the chosen focus of this particular book.

13. This included requests to the Peacemaking Program and the Office of Worship and Assembly. "Report of the Task Force," 1. They also ask the Washington office of the denomination to "monitor and advocate" for H.R. 40.

which was written in 1986 by the Dutch Reformed Mission Church in South Africa — a church of Black South Africans — to speak out against apartheid.[14] The report formally commended the Belhar Confession for study in congregations.

Third, the report offered an overview of the history of slavery. Members of the task force framed this history with the biblical exhortation to "remember the days of old, consider the years long past" (Deut. 32:7). They argued that historical memory is a moral imperative for Christians.

Finally, the report presented results from a survey of laypeople on the matter of reparations (to which I made reference above). The survey results indicated that views of reparations among laypeople remain quite negative *even though most respondents recognized that reconciliation remains elusive.* Here the task force noted the irony of these results: specifically, that Christians know we are not racially reconciled and yet are hostile to work to repair and redress the material conditions that are the source of that brokenness. Such irony, the report concluded, is indicative of a need for greater education about the history of slavery and discrimination.[15]

The Episcopal Church's process looks rather different. Instead of one report, the EC has produced a series of related resolutions on racism and reparations. Resolution C011, which prompted Shaw's congressional testimony, passed in 2006. It urged "the Church at every level to call upon Congress and the American people to support legislation initiating study of and dialogue about the history and legacy of slavery in the United States and of proposals for monetary and non-monetary reparations to the descendants of the victims of slavery."[16]

This was the same year the EC passed Resolution A123, which was titled "Study Economic Benefits Derived from Slavery." Resolution A123 was a more substantive document as it pertained to reparations. It formally acknowledged the EC's recognition that the institution of slavery was a sin that "continues to plague our common life in the Church and our culture."[17]

---

14. John W. de Gruchy with Steve de Gruchy, *The Church Struggle in South Africa*, 25th anniversary ed. (Minneapolis: Fortress, 2004), 194.

15. "Report of the Task Force," 10.

16. Resolution 2006-C011, "Support Legislation for Reparations for Slavery." See "Testimony of the Right Reverend M. Thomas Shaw, III, SSJE, Bishop of the Diocese of Massachusetts; December 18, 2007," at http://www.episcopalchurch.org.

17. Resolution 2006-A123, "Study Economic Benefits Derived from Slavery." See "Testimony of the Right Reverend M. Thomas Shaw, III, SSJE, Bishop of the Diocese of Massachusetts; December 18, 2007," at http://www.episcopalchurch.org.

Resolution A123 also apologized and repented for the denomination's participation in slavery. It directed every diocese to begin collecting detailed information about its particular history of complicity in the institution of slavery, along with the economic benefits it derived by way of its participation.[18] This has essentially launched a grassroots effort (chapter 8 will focus on one example of what this process has looked like in one diocese).

While A123 nowhere uses the word "reparations," the stated intention of the diocesan data-gathering was that it be used to determine "how the Church can be 'the repairer of the breach' (Isaiah 58:12), both materially and relationally."[19]

The EC pursued an array of other activities related to reparations as well. Since January 2008, several dioceses have held services commemorating the abolition of the slave trade. The presiding bishop was asked to name a Day of Repentance, and a National Service of Repentance was held in October 2008.[20] A rigorous lay education process has included diocesan showings of *Traces of the Trade*, a film that documents the participation of a northern Episcopalian family in the slave trade.[21]

Rethinking the Reconciliation Paradigm

Given the strength of the reconciliation paradigm in these denominations, how is it then that these initiatives for reparations have emerged?

Among several significant developments in each of these denominations through the 1990s and into the twenty-first century, the most significant has been increasing levels of self-criticism pertaining to their own understanding of racism. This self-criticism has created a context for the more significant shift required to enable a reparations paradigm to emerge: namely a serious engagement with their respective histories.

18. "Resolved, That the 75th General Convention of The Episcopal Church . . . urge every Diocese to collect and document during the next triennium detailed information in its community on (a) the complicity of The Episcopal Church in the institution of slavery and in the subsequent history of segregation and discrimination and (b) the economic benefits to the Episcopal Church derived from the institution of slavery . . ." Resolution 2006-A123.

19. Resolution 2006-A123.

20. The service was held at St. Thomas church in Philadelphia, the parish started by Absalom Jones.

21. *Traces of the Trade: A Story from the Deep North*, directed by Katrina Browne, co-directed by Alla Kovgan and Jude Ray (2008).

When asked about how the EC came to pass Resolutions C011 and A123, the Rev. Jayne Oasin, formerly Social Justice Officer for the Episcopal Church, stated, "The triumphal work was actually getting the issue of racism in front of people's faces. Anything that has been done [in regard to reparations] has been done as a result of that work."[22] She traces that work to 1991, when the Episcopal Church's General Convention was to be held in Arizona — a state that did not recognize Martin Luther King Jr.'s birthday.

Rather than boycott Arizona, the presiding bishop insisted the convention go forward, and "intentionally witness against this thing called racism."[23] At that point, the denomination passed several resolutions. For the first time, it officially named racism as a sin, and it pledged the church to a nine-year commitment of repenting from and struggling against racism.[24]

One of the major documents to result from the 1991 General Convention was *The Sin of Racism: A Pastoral Letter from the House of Bishops of the Episcopal Church,* published in March 1994.[25] Beginning with the bishops' acknowledgment that crafting the letter involved them in a discovery that they have "much to learn, relearn and do,"[26] several surprisingly candid moments of self-criticism give a strong indication that a new understanding of racism was emerging. *The Sin of Racism* states, for example, that in the past many EC resolutions have focused on how to increase the participation of those targeted by discrimination in the prevailing system and that much work has been done attempting to make the system more inclusive. According to the bishops, this has been a flawed approach to racism:

> The unspoken assumption of these resolutions is that victims will adapt and assimilate into the existing system. Their message in essence, has been: "You are welcome to become like us." Such efforts have represented progress in their time, but they are seen by many today as a product of a dominant racial attitude, which is at the heart of institutional racism.[27]

22. Oasin, personal interview, June 25, 2008.
23. Oasin.
24. Oasin.
25. As a pastoral letter, *The Sin of Racism* was to be read from every pulpit in the EC.
26. *The Sin of Racism: A Pastoral Letter from the House of Bishops of the Episcopal Church* (March 1994), 8. See "Testimony of the Right Reverend M. Thomas Shaw, III, SSJE, Bishop of the Diocese of Massachusetts; December 18, 2007," at http://www.episcopalchurch.org/social-justice_57347_ENG_HTM.htm.
27. *The Sin of Racism,* 9.

Of course, Black Christians in the 1960s and beyond have repeatedly pointed out to their denominations that attempts to integrate them into the system are a form of co-optation that does little to disrupt the oppression on which the existing system is built. Nonetheless, this statement comes close to naming whiteness, and it demonstrates the EC as having journeyed quite a distance in its understanding. Moreover, the self-critique challenges the veracity of a strict reconciliation paradigm for the churches' work against racism.

Despite its strong commitment to reconciliation as the theological ideal, challenges to the reconciliation paradigm can also be found in the PC(USA)'s 1999 policy statement *Facing Racism. Facing Racism* includes a historical summary of mainline Protestant involvement in the civil rights movement. Written to demonstrate how prevalent racism remains, this history also includes several moments of self-critique. Describing the denomination's focus during and subsequent to the movement, the statement explains,

> The fundamental principle that informed the churches' advocacy was the belief that racism was a consequence of personal prejudice and ethnic pride. Therefore, the programmatic thrust of churches focused on changing personal attitudes and overcoming bigotry.[28]

This comment directly invokes the reconciliation paradigm to explain that this basic principle was flawed.

Facing Racism goes on to criticize white Protestants' overemphasis on integration and their failure to understand what the Black Power movement did: that by the end of the 1960s it was clear "control and power remained in the hands of White people, demonstrating that integration and racism are quite compatible."[29] Even while this statement is cast as simple historic observation (though one that, they admit, white Protestants failed to observe at the time), to acknowledge this reality is to directly acknowledge the *shortcomings* of the reconciliation paradigm. Given the PC(USA)'s commitment to reconciliation, this becomes a rather radical confession.

Neither *Facing Racism* nor *The Sin of Racism* raises reparations for consideration, nor can either be appropriately understood as endorsing a

---

28. Initiative Team on Racism and Racial Violence, *Facing Racism: A Vision of the Beloved Community* (Louisville, Ky.: Office of the General Assembly of the PC(USA), 1999), 5.
29. *Facing Racism*, 6.

reparations paradigm. Both retain reconciliation as an organizing framework. However, both evidence a more sophisticated understanding of reconciliation — one that acknowledges brokenness as a symptom of a more complex problem.

The self-reflective critiques contained in these early documents are accompanied by a more adequate understanding of racism as well, which also functions to make a move toward reparations possible. *The Sin of Racism* emphasizes the importance of systemic analysis. In its earliest paragraphs, it recognizes there exists a "deeply ingrained" institutionalized preference for white people in the United States.[30] This recognition contributes to the letter's overall tone. Consistent with its observation that previous calls for more inclusion in the system as it currently stands were flawed, *The Sin of Racism* suggests that an overhaul of the system as a whole is required to truly pursue racial justice. In other words, you cannot build beloved community in the system as it is!

The letter goes on to address problems such as segregated public schools and neighborhoods, and an economy that does not provide sufficient opportunities for people of color. The bishops then indicate that a focus on individual attitudes is not enough: "We believe that our mission involves not only changing hearts, but also engaging ourselves in seeking to transform a socio-economic system that drives many into despair."[31]

Because of its institutional nature, the bishops admit, racism "runs on its own momentum." For it to be rooted out, therefore, "requires intentional and deliberate decisions. . . ."[32] The letter repeatedly invokes the particular position of white people in institutions, explicitly naming the problem of white privilege.[33] It directly addresses white people at one point, calling them to take an inventory of places in which they participate in racist structures and to begin to intentionally refuse such participation.[34]

Facing Racism lays out a three-part understanding of what is required to become a community that embodies an anti-racist identity. First, it too identifies the need for social analysis as a priority for challenging racism. There must exist an understanding of racism's manifestations in systems and structures, and the way these structures affect human lives and relationships.

30. *The Sin of Racism*, 9.
31. *The Sin of Racism*, 12.
32. *The Sin of Racism*, 11.
33. *The Sin of Racism*, 10.
34. *The Sin of Racism*, 11.

Second, institutional reconstruction is required. The problem is more than that of welcoming some people while excluding others. While individual healing is eventually named as part of coming to an anti-racist identity, this notion is listed third, and it is made clear it is inseparable from social analysis and institutional reconstruction.[35]

The PC(USA) also actively conducts anti-racism trainings for its members, which specifically focus on "helping people understand the systemic nature of racism."[36] The focus on systemic racism in *Facing Racism* and trainings, according to the Rev. Teresa Chávez Sauceda, formerly the director of the Office for Racial Justice Advocacy, supports the goals of the reparations report. Indeed, when she conducts anti-racism trainings, Sauceda states, "I will take the reparations paper as an example of one way individuals and congregations can get involved."[37]

Both the PC(USA) and EC recognize that there has been no lack of statements against racism, but too little concrete action. *Facing Racism* states that mainline Protestant pronouncements have always been stronger than have their actions.[38] As Oasin puts it, "Episcopalians have a particular thing that we do — though, I suppose it's not just restricted to our denomination. Once we pass these resolutions, we think our work is done."

To counter this tendency, the EC has implemented strategies for working institutionally. One of its primary tools is the curriculum briefly explored in chapter 3, *Seeing the Face of God in Each Other: A Manual for Antiracism Training and Action*. In 2000, the EC mandated this training for all diocesan and lay leaders, at least two other people from every diocese, and all members of national committees and boards. In 2003 the training became a requirement for all ordination candidates.[39]

The PC(USA)'s infrastructure for educating clergy and laity on this front seems to be less developed than is the EC's. Nonetheless, it too understands that adequate challenges to racism require measurable goals. *Facing Racism* proposes a seven-part churchwide strategy that begins with a call to dialogue — phrasing that strongly echoes reconciliation impulses. However, the policy statement is careful to clarify that dialogue must go beyond the issue of interracial dynamics and get to the root causes of racism:

35. *Facing Racism*, 1.
36. The Rev. Teresa Chávez Sauceda, personal interview, July 28, 2008.
37. Sauceda.
38. *Facing Racism*, 5.
39. "So that really put teeth into [it]," states Oasin.

Dialogue must lead to the identification of measurable goals that can be benchmarks of progress. Once benchmarks are established, the more challenging task of identifying obstacles that stand in the way of realizing the vision can begin. Only then can specific strategies be designed that will help us overcome racism.[40]

The seven-part strategy includes initiatives to be pursued at various denominational levels.[41]

A Theology of History

It is a short distance from recognizing the inadequacies of past understandings and inquiry into structures to a serious engagement with history. Self-criticism allows openness to new ways of viewing racism. Focusing on structures creates a more adequate context for understanding it. From this context the question can be asked, "From whence do these injustices come?"

PC(USA) Reparations Task Force member Mark Lomax writes, "There is no question that there is a racial and ethnic breach in the church of God. Repairing that breach will require all of us to wrestle more earnestly with the tough questions that come to us from our collective history."[42] The Report of the Reparations Task Force offers Presbyterians the chance to wrestle with history as it recounts the horrors of slavery and genocide. It then goes further and specifically names the active role Presbyterians played in displacing and slaughtering Native peoples, and holding people of African descent as slaves.

The report does not use the language of race as a social construction, nor does it write of a need for a particularist ethic to understand it. But, we should note here, in specifying the role of white Presbyterians in such atrocities and historicizing contemporary racial relations, the report does both of these things. It locates the meaning of race in the processes through which it was constructed and distinguishes the roles of white U.S.-Americans and people of color in injustice.

The document goes on to lament that the denomination remained si-

---

40. *Facing Racism*, 9-10.

41. For example, like the EC, the PC(USA) has mandated anti-racism training for its national staff.

42. Lomax, 21.

lent about the inhumanity of slavery until 1818 and that even after that point it failed to sanction members who owned slaves.[43] Here, the report does not engage in a mere recitation of facts. Rather, it engages history as a theological act: "Remembering is a form of confession," it claims.[44] The task force insists that the church is called to recount not only the good that Presbyterians have done, but to "remember our entire history."

The report urges, "Confession is good for the soul and essential for healing and renewing our spirits."[45] Further, if to engage history is to confess, then confession necessarily calls up the question of repair. In this regard, reparations are not a mere political proposal but have deeply theological grounding rooted in biblical understanding.

In an article interpreting the work of the task force to a larger lay audience, Lomax provides a theological framework for reparations (and, in the process, raises the problem of whiteness) by deploying the story of Zacchaeus. When Zacchaeus repents, he determines to give half of his wealth to the poor and to repay anyone he has defrauded with four times what he has taken (Luke 19:8).

According to Lomax, Jesus only recognizes the authenticity of Zacchaeus's repentance by his words and behavior *together*. Only when it is clear that Zacchaeus will repay what he has stolen, and then some, does Jesus affirm Zacchaeus's salvation. Lomax speculates that it seems likely the crowd would have waited to accept the authenticity of Zacchaeus's repentance until the promised behavior was actually implemented.

Lomax's analysis becomes most poignant as he critiques white Christians' failures to follow repentant words with actions. "Is it possible," he asks, "that people of color following Jesus have watched as Zacchaeus made his descent to ground level, but are still waiting for the tangible implementation of his policy statement?"[46] Repentance can be genuine only when there is an authentic grappling with history, through which white people come to understand the harm that has been committed and from which we have benefited. Such understanding practically compels a concrete response: that of returning what has been taken.[47]

The PC(USA)'s report itself names Zacchaeus only once. But like Lo-

43. "The Report of the Task Force," 7. After this point, Native Americans drop from view in the report.

44. "The Report of the Task Force," 7

45. "The Report of the Task Force," 9.

46. Lomax, 19.

47. Lomax, 21.

max's later article, it too links Zacchaeus's restoration to fellowship with God and other humans to his act of paying reparations.

Other biblical sources provide the rationale through which the report frames its engagement with history and historical memory as confessional activity. Again and again, these sources direct those who sin and recognize their guilt to repay not only what they have taken, but several-fold beyond that (see, for example, Exod. 22:1 or Lev. 6:1-5).

It should be noted here that the Reparations Task Force does not eschew an emphasis on reconciliation. It certainly does not critique reconciliation in the terms I have in this book. But it is careful to insist that reconciliation can only be understood in the context of repentance and reparation. It states:

> Reconciliation implies repair. As followers of Jesus Christ, we, of all people, should be willing to compensate those whom we have harmed. Our verbal and written confessions, while important, are a far less than adequate means of repairing the harms done, restoring the losses, and reconciling the relationships that have been broken.[48]

Contemporary breaches in interracial relationships are located in a history of exploitation, it argues: "Breaches in human relationships cannot be repaired if there is no acknowledgement and confession of harms done and sins committed."[49] Repentance, which according to the biblical record involves word and deed, is absolutely necessary because relationships cannot be healed without material repair of the actual harms done.[50]

Here a reparations paradigm becomes most overt and complete. Racial relationships are recognized as constituted by historical and material realities. By carefully linking repair and restoration with reconciliation, the report thoroughly reconceptualizes reconciliation. The task force even points out that it is doing so when it critiques the PC(USA)'s own often-expressed hopes for overcoming division — expressions that almost always fail to give requisite attention to material realities:

> We live in hope that race and class prejudices will be overcome in our lifetimes. Yet we remain unwilling to acknowledge the sins of our fathers

---

48. "The Report of the Task Force," 10.
49. "The Report of the Task Force," 8.
50. "The Report of the Task Force," 10.

and mothers, as well as the fact that we receive residual benefits from the advantages that accrued to them because of their sins.[51]

There is an explicit connection made in this portion of the report between the material effects of our racial legacies and the profound division and brokenness that characterizes our racial relationships.

The report closes the "Reconciliation" section by chastising the church for making statements, confessions, and offering pardons for social sin without living up to them by implementing policies that could transform sinful structures. It reiterates, finally, that attempts at reconciliation are "futile" unless injustices are remembered, repaired, restored, and redressed.[52] In a formal word, then, the Task Force on Reparations admonishes the denomination and asserts a reparations paradigm for engaging relationships between Black and white Christians in the church. And, again, the denomination formally adopted this report.

The EC's process similarly reveals a theological engagement with history or historical memory that enables a shift to a reparations paradigm. In addition to affirming that historical memory is necessary for healing, Bishop Shaw also confessed that the EC had never collectively addressed slavery during the decades in which it was practiced, in order to avoid schism before the Civil War. He confessed,

> Episcopalians did not raise their voices when God would have wished them to do so. Episcopalians were owners of slaves and of the ships that brought them to this land. Episcopalians lived in the north and in the south and, as a privileged church, we today recognize that our Church benefited materially from the slave trade.[53]

In later testimony, Shaw cited some of the details of this history that have been unearthed by various dioceses. He disclosed, for example, the discovery that the oldest Episcopal church in Mississippi was built by slaves.[54]

I noted above that, in contrast to the PC(USA) report, Resolution A123 does not contain the word "reparations." In fact, when I interviewed her, Oasin specifically warned against calling the resolution a reparations document.

51. "The Report of the Task Force," 10.
52. "The Report of the Task Force," 10.
53. Shaw, 1.
54. Shaw, 3.

The reason, she said, was that doing so "misrepresents what people think they are doing."[55] She re-emphasizes that the directive is simply for studies in the complicity of the church in this history.[56]

Nonetheless, Resolution A123 and the diocesan inquiries they mandate suggest the strong possibility of an eventual adoption of reparations. Evidence of this can be seen in the testimony with which this chapter began, in which Shaw clearly sees the relationship between gathering such historical information and advocacy for reparations, and indicates the EC's belief that such knowledge will bring repentance and remedies.[57]

In addition, while no denominational decisions have been made about what to do with the gathered information, the EC's Executive Council made clear that the point of the process is for dioceses to report[58] "on how the Church can be 'the repairer of the breach' (Isaiah 58:12), both materially and relationally. . . ."[59] Such language indicates an understanding that material repair is needed and will be forthcoming in some manner as a result of an engagement with history.

Since this flurry of activity, evidence exists that at the national level these efforts have waned to a degree. Many dioceses have not yet engaged in the work required, for example. But some of them have. And while the results are mixed, there is reason to see some real transformations taking place at the local level as a result of these efforts (again, one example of which will be explored in the next chapter).

For now it is simply important to note that like the Presbyterians, the Episcopal Church recognizes engagement of history as the very activity of confession and repentance. But there are some important differences. Just as the EC has not written a longer report endorsing reparations, nowhere does it craft a general history of the evils of slavery.

But while the PC(USA) report responds positively to the question of

---

55. Oasin's clarity about the distinction between these two is not indicative of reservations she has about the issue of reparations. Rather, it is indicative of a felt need to honor each step in a longer process and not get ahead of where people are within the denomination. Personal interview, June 25, 2008.

56. Oasin.

57. Significantly, Shaw prefaces his remarks by making clear he is speaking for the whole church, not just for himself. Shaw, 3.

58. The Executive Committee meets eight or nine times in-between General Conventions to help keep the work moving forward; thanks to the Rev. Jayne Oasin for her careful explanations of the functions in this regard.

59. Resolution 2006-A123.

reparations in response to the history it presents, there is no indication of how the task force understands what reparations should be programmatic. Nor is there indication of a process by which this will be taken up further. The resolution pertaining to this issue states rather vaguely that "opportunities" should be created to "tell and hear stories remembering the past and celebrating examples of repair, restoration, reconciliation, and renewal."[60] These concepts are not concretized, nor are directions given as to when, where, and how these opportunities will take place — nor as to who is responsible to ensure that happens.

In contrast, the EC's directive is more geared toward involving the church as a whole — laity and clergy alike — in a direct engagement with its specific history, as Episcopalians at the grassroots together reconstruct their local and shared histories.

This process can be understood as having several theological dimensions. First, it generates the actual activity of confession, as people themselves are put in motion reconstructing history.

Second, it begins to create a specific venue in which discussion of concrete redress will take place, given the understanding that the authenticity of repentance can be measured only by actual material repair. And in ensuring that an infrastructure is created and an ongoing process kept in motion it embodies its theological understanding of history and reparations as a critical dimension of this work.

Despite their partiality and states of incompleteness, the theological reading of history and responses to it in both denominations' documents commend themselves to prophetic evangelicals and other mainline Protestants. This latter cohort of Christians might see in these movements a challenge to take up their own theological lenses and bring to their own respective communities/congregations a challenge to "remember [their] entire histories" — as way to put a reparations paradigm squarely into practice in regard to relations between African Americans and whites, to attend to the particular crisis of whiteness, and to contribute directly to a national conversation sorely needed about what actions we must take to repair and redress our history.

---

60. "The Report of the Task Force," 1.

The Visibility of Whiteness

At this point, it is appropriate to inquire as to the extent to which whiteness and white moral agency are acknowledged in these denominations' advocacy for reparations. For as we know from the work in the first two parts of this book, being able to specifically and unequivocally name the particular problem of whiteness is critical in our work for more adequate responses to race and for racial justice. Thus, the ways or degrees to which reparations movements are engaging and speaking to white Christians need to be considered.

On this front, there exists a significant difference between the two denominations, in large part because of the way in which they are engaging history.

Having developed a reparations paradigm, a perpetrator is clearly implied in the Presbyterian report. But, interestingly enough, the word "white" almost never appears. This absence is significant given the imperative of an honest and direct contending with the problem of whiteness in redressing harms done. But this absence does not negate the report's force. The report uses language of "offender" and "offended," and it is clear that the relationship described is that between white people and African American people. Nonetheless, a failure to use the word "white" indicates that the document does not adequately address the problem of whiteness.

Rather than using racially particular language such as "those of us who are white" or "those of us who are African American," the report uses "we" language throughout. Using such language while addressing a multiracial audience obscures who is being addressed by what issue or concept, and impedes the ability to wield particularity in the way a reparations paradigm ultimately requires.

Consider this statement, for example: "We cannot afford to live, work and worship in denial of our collective and historic sinfulness against other human beings."[61] This "we" is problematic. Not only does the part of the "we" who is African American generally not live in denial of our collective history, but in light of such history each racial group in the Presbyterian Church (U.S.A.) has a radically different relationship to the need to "confess." Who it is that really needs to confess becomes muddled. While we might know who is implied in this statement, such ambiguity allows white Christians who are addressed by this truth to distance ourselves from the statement as

---

61. "The Report of the Task Force," 10.

it slips back into a universalist ethic for talking about race (as if "we" are all equally part of the problem).

This critique is not a matter of semantics. The lack of particularity evident in the use of such "we" language and the absence of "those of us who are white" language signals that, even as the report endorses reparations, it is using a universalistic ethic where a particularist ethic is absolutely needed. We have already concluded that universalist approaches reproduce rather predictable outcomes because of the ways they flatten whiteness and misunderstand the problem of race.

The presence of a universalist ethic and reconciliation paradigm is more obvious elsewhere in the Presbyterian process. As noted above, one of the main sections of the report is inclusion of the Belhar Confession and its commendation for the church's study. In one sense, the Belhar is a strong choice for capturing white U.S. Christians' attention. By including the Belhar, the report indicts U.S. Christianity in racial injustice as seriously as the white South African Church was indicted in apartheid. This is significant since most white U.S.-American Christians can readily admit the extent to which the white South African Church was complicit in apartheid.

But in another, more substantive sense, commending the Belhar Confession for study works against making whiteness visible even as it represents a move back into a reconciliation paradigm. The sin with which the Belhar is concerned is that of making differences the basis for separation or church membership, which, like Jim and Jane Crow, was the basic logic of apartheid.

The confession's overwhelming emphasis is on interracial unity.[62] The Belhar is a reconciliation document through and through. It is also based on a universalist ethic concerned about the use of differences to divide the church.

The problem here is not the Belhar itself. Its approach may have been perfectly theologically appropriate for its time and place. But in this context the Belhar functions to wrongly describe the actual problem of race and racism as one of disunity in need of reconciliation. Despite being included as primary educational material in a pro-reparations report, nothing about it self-evidently points toward reparations.

---

62. The Belhar does embed the desire for reconciliation in the call to repair harm done: "Jesus Christ calls us to repair wrongs done to one another and to work for personal and social reconciliation and renewal." But the basic paradigm is one of reconciliation. "The Report of the Task Force," 3.

Moreover, the Belhar Confession was written by Black South African Christians — not white ones. (In this sense, it was a courageous and radical document; for Black South Africans to indict racial division was an act of subversive resistance.) This too is significant given that the Presbyterians are advocating its use in a process in which repentance and repair — which require significant work from *white* Christians — are central matters at hand. There is something discomfiting about such use that hints at the erasure of whiteness again.

At this point it is worth documenting the reason Belhar was ultimately included in the PC(USA) report. In the initial version of the report, which had been commissioned by the Advocacy Committee for Racial and Ethnic Concerns (ACREC), primarily composed of people of color, the Reparations Task Force had recommended that the church write a new confession. This confession would be included in the PC(USA)'s *Book of Confessions* and would specifically address the denomination's complicity in U.S. racial history.[63]

When the report came under consideration in 2004, the denominational Office of Assembly and Worship recommended that the PC(USA) instead simply adopt the Belhar Confession. The reason for this recommendation was to avoid the costs associated with developing a new confession.[64] From this point forward a focus on Belhar (urging that it be used for church study) — rather than on a new confession specific to U.S. racial history — became increasingly strong.

Not only does Belhar itself advocate reconciliation, further evidence of the way it diverts from a reparations paradigm emerges in descriptions of the General Assembly's discussion over whether to endorse the Belhar Confession. According to Sauceda,

> The argument made at GA was "we are at a point in time in the church where . . . our society is changing rapidly through the influx of new

63. Confessions are central in the liturgy and self-understandings of Presbyterians. The Rev. Teresa Chávez Sauceda explains that part of the Constitution of the PC(USA) is the *Book of Confessions*. It begins with the Apostles' and Nicene Creeds and includes various confessions up to 1967. The Confession of 1967 addresses the need to be agents of reconciliation and social witness amid the turmoil of the civil rights movement and the Vietnam War, but it "did not explicitly address the church's history." Teresa Chávez Sauceda, personal interview, July 28, 2008.

64. In 2004, the PC(USA) was struggling with declining membership and shrinking budgets. The message at GA was clear: "anything adopted that cost money meant something else that already had been adopted would have to be cut." Sauceda.

immigrant groups, with growing diversity of race and ethnicity in parts of the country that have never experienced it before. . . . And as we look forward to what society is going to be and ask ourselves 'are we equipped to be a church in our society and welcome everybody?' Belhar is a document that can help us do that."[65]

This argument seamlessly returns to a reconciliation paradigm. Notice here that racial separation is the problem, and inclusion and welcome are the needed remedies in an increasingly diverse world.

The original confessional posture emphasized by the report of the Reparations Task Force — which demands a look *backward* to take seriously the way the past affects our concrete material relations with one another — is completely lost in the decision to use this confession as a way to help the church move *forward* as a body that can "welcome everybody." (I want to emphasize here that Sauceda was not endorsing this view. She was simply reporting how the dialogue over whether to use Belhar had unfolded.)

If the primary concern motivating use of Belhar rather than the writing of a new confession was financial, it would be worth asking why the denomination did not then include portions of the Kairos document instead.

The Kairos document was also written in the South African context.[66] It was, however, written from a Black Power perspective and directly critiques the white South African Church's emphasis on reconciliation at the expense of Black empowerment. Kairos eloquently describes the way reconciliation used as a universal principle that can presumably be applied in any case of dissent and conflict (without distinguishing between a situation of misunderstanding and a situation of injustice) — along with pleas for peace and unity without first insisting on justice, repentance, and a radical change of social structures — becomes a principle used in a thoroughly unchristian manner.[67]

Because the basic assumption of a reconciliation paradigm universalizes the problem of racial bigotry, calls "us all" to the same kind of work, and cannot attend to the different moral cadences contained in our different

65. Sauceda.

66. With thanks to Gloria Albrecht, who raised this insight in response to an early version of this work. de Gruchy, 195-200.

67. "The Kairos Document: A Challenge to the Church" (1985). See "African Christianity: A History of the Christian Church in Africa," 10-13, http://www.bethel.edu/~letnie/AfricanChristianity/SAKairos.html.

racial identities, it becomes nearly impossible to address whiteness and white people in a forthright manner.

Thus, the fact that Belhar has become such a focal point of this work in the PC(USA) seriously undermines the strength of the reparations paradigm advocated clearly in other portions of the report of the Reparations Task Force. This disservice is especially significant because Belhar reinforces problematic understandings of racism already pervasive among white Christians that have already impeded the church's racial justice work.

The PC(USA) has not avoided work on the problem of whiteness altogether. Even *Facing Racism* states that white people created the problem of racism and that an addiction to white privilege is a far greater challenge to unity within the church than differences themselves.[68] Moreover, stronger moments of critique and awareness of the inadequacies of reconciliation continue to present themselves in denominational work on reparations, despite the questions use of Belhar raises. Consider, for example, the way ACREC describes to their fellow Presbyterians why taking Belhar seriously for study is important:

> While it is true that the Presbyterian Church (USA) has acted benevolently and graciously toward aggrieved groups of peoples within and outside of the church, and often in very practical ways, it is also true that such actions rarely served to repair and restore relationships with those groups in any meaningful way. . . . Is it possible that we have grown all too comfortable with a paternalistic way of being in relationship with aggrieved groups of people . . . ?[69]

But the picture is, at best, mixed. Moreover, while various denominational bodies are pushing awareness of white privilege, according to Sauceda, it continues to be the case that most of the energy being spent doing so has come from people of color within the denomination.[70]

Finally, on this point, ultimately even Belhar was not ratified for inclusion in the *Book of Confessions*. While the GA passed the recommendation for its inclusion in 2010, the recommendation did not receive the two-thirds

---

68. *Facing Racism*, 7.

69. Advocacy Committee for Racial and Ethnic Concerns (ACREC), "Resolution to Study the Belhar Confession for Inclusion in the Confessional Documents of the Presbyterian Church (U.S.A.)," presented to the 218th General Assembly of the Presbyterian Churches (USA), (Summer 2008): 5.

70. Sauceda.

support required by Presbyteries to pass the recommendation. Another attempt is being made at this time to try again.[71]

The point of this critique is not to discredit the reparations report. Rather, it is to suggest that even while reparations are endorsed in the report, the denomination seems to be in the midst of a conceptual transition — or in a state in which two concepts are present in a mixed and muddied manner. The PC(USA) has not moved completely from a reconciliation to a reparations paradigm, even in its reparations process. More work to overtly address whiteness specifically is thus needed to further this transition.

Moreover, given the negative views and lack of in-depth knowledge most white Christians have of the history of slavery, more work in this regard generally is needed if the church's reparations efforts are to be meaningful. On their own, white Christians will not make the leap from Belhar or words like "restore" and "repair," to robust and concrete endorsements of reparations.

Still, the work that has taken place should be seen not only as a sign of hope, but more important, as a beacon and challenge for others of us (as well those at work among Presbyterians on these matters) to continue to push in these directions: that is, toward a focus on whiteness, toward serious engagement of history, toward repentance and repair.

At this point the EC maps an interesting comparison to the PC(USA) when it comes to making "whiteness" visible. Like the PC(USA) report, with few exceptions the word "white" goes largely unused in the formal documents pertaining to reparations in the EC. Despite this omission, however, a universalistic ethic does not mitigate the EC's reparations process to the extent it does in the Presbyterian process.

For example, in Resolution A123, there is nothing vague about the use of "we." The language is specific, stating that the EC as an official body committed certain sins (at a time when Blacks were not even part of the hierarchy) and that it is the EC as a denomination that is apologizing and repenting. Shaw, for example, explains that "the Church" benefited from the slave trade.

But the visibility of whiteness in the EC process is more importantly ensured because of the way the church has insisted on engaging its specific history. This work implicitly invokes racial particularity, as this history is the same history in which race and racial differences came to be.

---

71. See http://www.pcusa.org/news/2013/4/23/belhar-confession-recommended-again-pcusas-adoptio/.

Engaging its history at the level of the dioceses implicitly invokes racial particularity, and the results will be explicit. For example, in the diocesan work being commissioned, white and Black Episcopalians are involved together in the work of historical reconstruction of their shared denominational history. Interviews I conducted with some participants in these processes made clear that working together on a shared history has made the moral differences in racial identities unavoidably clear. Meanwhile, even in local contexts in which such work might be taken up primarily by white Episcopalians (perhaps because few African American Episcopalians are present), this moral meaning of racial identity will also be able to surface because of the very nature of historical query and what it necessarily reveals. If pursued genuinely, discoveries and naming of the historical and material content of whiteness will also be unavoidable.

To the extent that this historical work continues to be engaged with a theological understanding that repentance must lead to remedies, connections will likely be drawn between the historical and material content of whiteness and the work of repair.

Attention to racial particularity was already evident in preliminary reports by some dioceses on their historical work. The Diocese of Pennsylvania, for example, specifically resolved that it will investigate, among other things, "sources of personal and family wealth from activities related to the slave trade."[72]

In its resolution to focus on education and discussions of reparations, the Diocese of Maryland includes study of white privilege as part of its educational program.[73] In its "Explanation" of the resolutions, the diocese writes, "Since emancipation, the advantage of that wealth and privilege has continued to benefit those of European descent. . . ." It goes on to recognize that people of African descent have not had access to "'white' legacies of wealth, education, good health, housing and every other aspect of life in which social and cultural institutions impact upon one's well-being. . . ."

The Diocese of New York writes of their developing understanding that "slavery is the defining experience in this country." They continue, "We are also becoming aware of the initial 'rupture' that began this country's racial

72. The Diocese of Pennsylvania, R-14-2006, "Resolution on Slavery and Racial Reconciliation in the Episcopal Diocese of Pennsylvania," 23rd Convention (November 2006). See http://www.episcopalchurch.org/social-justice_57347_ENG_HTM.htm.

73. Nancy D. Barrick and Allen F. Robinson, "A Brief History of the Maryland Reparations Task Force." See http://www.episcopalchurch.org/social-justice_57347_ENG_HTM.htm.

experience."[74] This statement could not more strongly embody a reparations paradigm. It also powerfully deploys the recognition that separation exists between us as racial beings because of the activities (slavery) in which racial differences first were given meaning.

These dioceses have moved far from a reconciliation paradigm in their increasing clarity and specificity about the nature of harms done, to whom and by whom they were done, and to whom unjust benefits have continued to accrue and on whom vestiges of slavery continue to have a negative effect. This movement represents an engaged theological posture increasingly acknowledging whiteness and bringing the problem of the moral agency of white people, past and present, into the picture in explicit ways.

Given that the EC has not yet formally endorsed reparations as a full body, nor written a formal statement on such, the EC's work on reparations might appear more modest than the PC(USA)'s. But a closer look reveals, instead, the development of a strong infrastructure, careful education processes, and practices that increasingly make racial particularity — including the problem of whiteness — unavoidably clear.

Conclusion

It cannot be overstated that both of the denominational processes are partial and incomplete. Moreover, each has encountered challenges and some indication of languishing in the past few years, subsequent to the initial activity that emerged because some committed Presbyterian and Episcopalian Christians pushed for these reparation inquiries to move forward. When I sat down with two different committees working at the diocesan level in the Episcopal Church in 2012, I heard visions that continue to be full of great hope, but also a clear indication that the processes have slowed down at the national level. (For example, while dioceses were originally to have reported back to GC in 2009, the date has continued to be pushed back and many dioceses have failed to become active in the ways mandated.)

Similarly, among Presbyterians, mandates given in the list of recommendations have been slow to come to fruition — in fact, the GA recently voted against formally including the Belhar in the *Book of Confessions*. It remains to be seen whether "repair of the breach" will actually transpire and

74. Nell Braxton Gibson, "Update on Reparations Work in the Diocese of New York." See http://www.episcopalchurch.org.

how earnestly and robustly white congregants will come along in support of these processes.

But the purpose of investigating these movements has not been to suggest they are the ideal examples to be emulated, nor to do exhaustive analysis of them (much that has gone on in these denominations has not been addressed here). I am not attempting to make a case here that we have robust evidence that Christian communities are on the cusp of a certain, more hopeful future.

But having heeded these warnings, it remains critically important that these movements be rendered visible. It is significant that reparations movements have manifested among mainline denominations at all. These are evidence of a shifting understanding of race having emerged, no doubt as a result of many hours of difficult work by those who have been committed to bringing these initiatives to the table.

Getting such initiatives to the table and securing official support in a variety of assembly-wide contexts is evidence of some kind of movement taking place. And this *is worth knowing about.* For these movements reveal to those of us stuck in the conundrums described in the first part of this book just how challenging it continues to be to secure transformation when the ways we have of thinking about, naming, and addressing "whiteness" seem to short-circuit our efforts. They also give a glimpse of concrete and *different* pathways that some have actually tried, which do hold promise for securing different approaches to our racial problem in the church.

Yet noting their weaknesses is instructive as well — reflecting on how even in reparations conversations naming "white" responsibility can be challenging, and recognizing how far our communities have to go in securing significant lay and grassroots education and buy-in (without which such movements cannot succeed).

We have no clear solution to where we find ourselves in the wake of reconciliation's failure. Even a reparations paradigm will require relentless effort, commitment, and tenacity to move us a different way down the road.

But whether they understand themselves in this way or not, these movements respond to our eleven o'clock lament! And in their responses they do not simply push for more togetherness as a solution for overcoming the "most segregated hour." They turn explicitly to causes. They assume causes require repentance. They speak biblically and theologically about repair and redress. And as a result, transformative pathways and different understandings open and come into view — which is a start.

As members of these denominations root themselves in the actual history of Blacks and whites — not only in the United States but specifically within their very own denominations — a different kind of relationship can be envisioned. This is one of the most important things that these actual efforts, unrealized as they may be, offer to the rest of us.

So who are the people who have actually been having these conversations? What have those conversations looked like? Might listening in on some of them prove inspiring and challenging as we continue to think about moving forward to a new vision of race in our faith communities and the nation more broadly?

What remains to be done is to experience a few responses to these questions. Thus, the last constructive chapter of this book invites us to hear what has transpired in one particular community as a result of their work on this painful, formative, shared history.

CHAPTER EIGHT

Becoming "Repairers of the Breach"

It was a significant moment in 2006 when the General Convention (GC) of the Episcopal Church (EC), which meets every three years, passed "Study Economic Benefits Derived from Slavery" (Resolution A123). As Katrina Browne described it in her film *Traces of the Trade: A Story from the Deep North,* African American Episcopalians had been trying for decades to get their denomination to deal with the legacy of slavery in the United States. At the 75th GC, she says, not only had folks marshaled the energy to try again. But this time the specific role, responsibility, and involvement of the denomination itself was being called to account.

Traces of the Trade contains moving and challenging testimony of these hearings as the denomination debated the resolution. Both Black and white Christians shared aloud — many urging the church to take seriously a legacy that continues to shape and form the church.

Their efforts were successful. The measure passed. And with it came a mandate that all dioceses in the EC begin to research the history of their own parish, diocese, families, and legacies. Both clergy and laity together were directed to inquire into that history as part of a journey intended to envision and establish processes for repentance and repair.

This was work the Maryland Reparations Task Force had already begun. In fact, the Diocese of Maryland had already commissioned a task force to do so, in part because the denomination had failed to pass a similar resolution at the GC in 2003 (proposed by the Diocese of California).[1]

1. See http://www.episcopalarchives.org/cgi-bin/acts/acts_resolution-complete.pl ?resolution=2003-C003.

Mary Miller remembers the audible groan that went up when a resolution in support of reparations had failed three years before the 2006 success. Those who had been laboring to take the denomination's anti-racism work to a new level were deeply disappointed. But their determination was not thwarted. As Mary puts it, "We're so used to working in the shadows in this church."[2] She and others simply went back to work.

Mary is one of a handful of white members of the historically Black parish of St. James Lafayette Square Church, the third oldest African American Episcopal parish in the nation. When Mary reported to the congregation what had happened at the GC, people were frustrated. So she asked, "Would you like to work on this so it never happens again?" The answer was a resounding yes, and thus the work began as an adult study forum at St. James. The result was a resolution to the May 2004 Maryland diocese convention that called for "diocesan conversations to take place on racism, reparations, white privilege and discrimination."[3]

The Maryland Reparations Task Force was appointed within a year and began to educate itself and organize events in the diocese. The task force's charge was to research ways "the Diocese of Maryland profited from slavery and subsequent and systemic racism and to take action found to be appropriate."[4] The task force forwarded the Maryland resolution to the GC and began networking with other diocesan-level committees to pass a denominationwide resolution at the national level in 2006.[5]

In 2012, I spent several days with former members of the Maryland Reparations Task Force. I was interested in hearing about at least three things. First, I wanted to know how they had gone about their work. This was not a group of scholars or activists necessarily (though some members of the task force are). These were Christians from a variety of walks of life, committed to their denomination and longing for a new racial conversation — one that would finally result in something different — to take hold in their church.

As I would learn, most of them did not begin the work with a clear idea about reparations. Most were converted to the importance of reparations as a result of their early efforts to educate themselves.

2. Mary Miller, interview with the author, March 1, 2013. All subsequent references to Mary and words placed in quotes are from this same interview.
3. "A Time to Love: Conversations on Reparations," produced by Phoebe McPherson (The Episcopal Diocese of Maryland, 2008).
4. "A Time to Love."
5. "Reparations Task Force of the Diocese of Maryland," summary by N. Barrick, September 17, 2008.

The second thing I wanted to know was what kind of interracial dialogues and connections had emerged as a result of their work having been focused explicitly through a reparations lens, rather than through a reconciliation one. The insights here were remarkable, even though the task force had not yet gotten clear about what kind of reparative measures it would commend before it was disbanded and reconfigured as a Truth and Reconciliation Commission (TRC) in 2008.

Third, I was interested in what Episcopalians engaged so directly at a grassroots level saw as possible or even hoped-for in terms of their diocese's and denomination's future. What do they think repair in the Diocese of Maryland should look like? What about on the national church level?

I received a variety of responses to this question. The most consistent one, however, was that their work had barely begun; engaging history deeply and truly is difficult, is slow, and involves heavy lifting.

The history and depth of complicity in slavery and its aftermath is deep in this region. Despite having been a free state during the Civil War, Maryland is a place where the living, breathing presence of centuries of racial atrocity remains very much pervasive, though rarely spoken of in mixed racial company. David Clark, a white member of the task force who is also a priest, describes Maryland as having been sympathetic to the Confederacy despite being officially "free" — as well as a place where "the Civil War isn't really over."[6]

There is much truth that has needed to be told in Maryland. And the context for telling it has not been easy. Even this many years in, the diocese is still early in the process of enacting broader, diocesan-wide education of the sort required if a case for repair is going to be made successfully.

In this chapter I present extensive transcripts from interviews with several members of this Maryland task force — women and men, African American and white American, laity and priests. My observations are augmented by insights I gained from a shorter visit and group interview with the New York Reparations Committee, another diocesan-level group.

Like the work on reparations at the national denominational level, diocesan work remains partial and ongoing. Little is certain about the future of this movement. But listening to these Christians describe what they have done and continue to do, the insights to which they have arrived, and the challenges faced as they have engaged the history and legacies of slavery was

6. David Clark, interview with the author, March 1, 2013. All subsequent references to David and words placed in quotes are from this interview.

a powerful experience. To my mind, their experience commends the reparations paradigm as a way of responding to race in the church with equal power.

The purpose of this chapter is, thus, twofold. First, it is simply to provide a further concrete example of what a reparations paradigm looks like beyond the level of theory — in an actual, live time and place, unfolding among a community of Christians longing for a racially transformed church.

When I asked Nancy Barrick, co-chair of the task force and an African American layperson, about the reparations part of the work, this longing was clear. This is about "repairing the church," she said and, among other things, "bringing the body together and giving an opportunity to know the whole story, to know the truth."[7]

From 2003 to at least 2008 and ongoing today in a slightly different form, Episcopalians in the Diocese of Maryland have actively tarried with their legacy of slavery and have done so through a paradigm explicitly considering the question of reparations. Attention deserves to be given to this group's accomplishments, as it is one of few models out there in terms of what it might look like to journey into the question of reparations in a serious way.

A second purpose of this chapter is to consider what kinds of learning have come through a multiracial justice project convened specifically through the reparations paradigm. To that end, this chapter reports extensively on the insights and disclosures these remarkable women and men were willing to share with me in response to questions I asked them about their relationships with each other, how they understand reconciliation in relation to reparations, and what they hope for in terms of concrete outcomes for this work.

The insights the task force's experience makes available are significant. It's my sense that engagement with these might further the imagination and moral vision of those of us still looking for reconciliation and seeking transformation in our own faith communities as eagerly as these faithful have sought it, but who have yet to take up quite this kind of historical journey.

"Every Parish Must, in Some Way, Participate"[8]

As already noted, the Maryland task force played a substantive role in securing passage of the denominationwide resolution (A123) re-introduced in 2006,

---

7. Nancy Barrick, interview with the author, March 1, 2013. All subsequent references to Nancy and words placed in quotes are from this same interview

8. Member of the Maryland Reparations Task Force, from "A Time to Love."

which directed each diocese to begin researching its own history. It was by no means alone in its efforts. The Diocese of Newark introduced Resolution C011, "Support Legislation for Reparations for Slavery," which also passed in 2006. And several other dioceses or members from within particular dioceses had been variously active since the 2003 failure to see A123 through the GC. Like Maryland, a handful of dioceses have also been working diligently on the issue of reparations both before and after the 2006 directive passed.

The New York Reparations Committee, for example, has produced a DVD as one outgrowth of its work: *The Diocese of New York Examines Slavery: Talking About Reparations, Repair and Reconciliation*. The film emphasizes the collective lack of awareness that exists about northern involvement in chattel slavery, and it insists that "none of us" can move forward "in strength and power" until we repair the damage that centuries of chattel slavery has wrought.[9] Under the leadership of Nell Braxton Gibson, the committee produced a study guide to accompany the DVD to educate parishes about the basic concept of reparations.

Maryland has also produced a DVD to help explain the work to its congregants. *A Time to Love* describes the significance of the national resolution this way: "so that we as the people of God can come to make a full faithful and informed accounting of the legacy we inherited and better understand how we can work both individually and collectively to repair the breach."[10] This description aptly applies to the work the Maryland task force was actively embodying even before the denomination officially embraced this call.

The same year the Maryland task force was convened (2005), it hosted a diocese-wide conversation with Dr. Raymond A. Winbush, urban studies professor at Morgan State University. Winbush is a prominent expert on reparations. His works *Should America Pay? Slavery and the Raging Debate on Reparations* and *Belinda's Petition: A Concise History of Reparations for the Transatlantic Slave Trade* are both excellent, accessible resources on the larger context for reparations. Each lays out historic and contemporary rationales for reparations, describes various efforts that have been made before on these issues (namely people of African descent have been working to secure repair since the moment slavery began), and addresses pragmatic challenges to and visions for reparations.

Twenty-seven parishes from the diocese were in attendance for the dia-

9. *The Diocese of New York Examines Slavery: Talking About Reparations, Repair and Reconciliation* (Episcopal Diocese of New York, 2008).
10. *A Time to Love.*

logue with Winbush. According to participants, he challenged them mightily to look honestly at slavery and the horrors of its aftermath in their midst. It became clear at this event, some reported, that no one even really knew how much slavery or discrimination after the abolition of slavery had impacted the diocese.[11] Generating and disseminating this knowledge became a central mission for the task force.

Two years later (2007) the task force hosted a collective viewing of *Traces of the Trade.* In *Traces of the Trade,* Katrina Browne and other members of the DeWolf family gather to trace their ancestors' participation in the slave trade — from the African continent, to Cuba, to the northern United States. The DeWolfs were the wealthiest slave trading family in the North. They were also Episcopalian.

The film indicts and challenges white U.S.-Americans, but in particular white Episcopalians and the Episcopal Church as a whole, to consider seriously not only the wealth garnered from slavery, but the long-standing impact of a failure to tell the truth about this history on white and Black communities alike.

Throughout the film, white U.S.-Americans wrestle in provocative ways with the pain of learning the vicious truth of their families' legacy, and they struggle to figure out what it means for them as "heirs of oppression" (Corlett's term) to take responsibility for it. The particular relationship of white people to white supremacy and the conundrums this relationship creates for justice-loving people who claim to value equality is faced directly and made visceral. The depth of interracial alienation that exists as a result of this history and our contemporary silences about it are laid bare; viewers of the film can actually see how deeply our racial identities are forged and constituted by these devastating legacies in which our lives continue to unfold.

The DeWolf descendants in particular are shown contending with the emotional and spiritual damage this history has done to them as white U.S.-Americans, the violence in which it implicates them still, and the way it impacts their relationship to African American communities today. Throughout the film they struggle with the question of what a material response today should look like.

It became clear in my interviews how much impact Winbush's presentation and the film had on the Maryland task force's understanding of the viable case that exists for reparations in the United States and the Episcopal Church in particular.

11. *A Time to Love.*

Not only do Winbush's work and *Traces of the Trade* expose the actual realities of slavery in ways white U.S.-Americans have rarely faced, but both make crisply clear how much these histories are with us in the present — how pervasively they press on us. Almost every interview referenced these experiences at some point, indicating how transformative they were for the task force members' own understanding of the salience and legitimacy of the question of repair and reparations.

It was also evident that this understanding has played a central role in how powerfully committed and energized the task force is in their insistence that their diocese and the denomination must deal with this history.

These experiences also brought into focus for them how urgent it is for white people, in particular, to be pressed to hear this history. After describing how difficult it can be for white people to engage, Ron Miller (co-chair of the task force, and a white, retired priest) described the importance of *Traces of the Trade* in precisely this way: "Slave bricks, slave works, all of that, and a lot of people don't want to look at that. I mean, one of the interesting things about *Traces of the Trade* is the way that the DeWolf family gradually discovered that they can look at it. . . . They weren't sure what they were into until they really, finally began to open things up . . . we all have to do that."[12] In Miller's mind white resistance to hearing the truth seems to have something to do with how overwhelming it is to recognize and admit such evil, but *Traces of the Trade* gives whites an example to emulate.

The same year the task force hosted the first viewing of *Traces of the Trade* (which they have continued to host),[13] they also submitted "a resolution putting the Diocese of Maryland on record as apologizing for its involvement and its support of the slavery of African Americans."[14] This resolution also passed, serving as a formal apology by the diocese.

As the task force members became more educated, they also began to conduct educational forums. They requested every regional bishop in the diocese to arrange local dialogues, and they showed up (without funding or a research assistant, thus as volunteers) to educate, facilitate, and otherwise support parishes in this process. Such local, grassroots effort is critical for the larger success of the diocesan process.

Says Ron,

12. Ron Miller, interview with the author, March 1, 2013. All subsequent references to Miller and words placed in quotes are from this same interview.

13. On February 28, 2013, I attended a screening of *Traces of the Trade,* sponsored by the Maryland Diocese Truth and Reconciliation Commission.

14. Ron Miller.

One of the real problems with this is to get local people to face the issue. It's one thing to bring something to convention, but if people have not wrestled with it locally, personally, it's a challenge. And so, with the help of the historiographer Kingsley Smith [diocesan historian] and Mary Klein [archivist for the diocese], data was pulled together about how old parishes are and how they might have been involved with issues of slavery. Maryland, as an old diocese, has churches that go back to something like 1685.

David Clark minced no words in describing what it was the task force wanted people to learn: "We wanted to educate them . . . [by saying to them] this [parish] was built by slaves! There were slaves on this property we are sitting on. . . . A lot of the churches [in this diocese] had that kind of beginning."

The results of these dialogues were mixed. The work was difficult. Many of the parishes with whom the task force met were overwhelmingly white. Sometimes turnout was low. "Some people showed up because of the concern with the word 'reparations,'" David explained. "[They] were going to understand what was going on so they could say, 'No we're not going to do that.'"

"Yeah," David's wife, Colleen, chimed in, "They came with their pitchforks." Nancy Barrick described the experience of facilitating this process similarly:

A number of congregations did not know that the property they were in was built by slaves. And I think many found it somewhat uncomfortable that this was so. Because, well . . . the congregations were totally white; well, the Episcopal Church is mainly white anyway, Caucasian rather. We had some good experiences . . . but lots of doubt, lots of doubt, and lots of reticence in both the white and the Black churches. Black people don't want to talk about slavery because it's painful to some, to many. And white folks don't want to talk about it because "that's over and done with." Well, both of them, both Black and white say, "It's over, why bring this up again?" And white people don't want to feel guilty because it's "Well, I didn't have anything to do with that, so why blame me?" And we tried to say, "That's not what it's all about." It's a matter of understanding what happened. Why, you can't skip over the reparations part to get to a healed body, I don't think. You have to know, like Dr. Raymond Winbush said, that "[if] someone breaks out your window, they can come to you and say, 'Oh, I'm so sorry I did that.' But somebody's got to pay for that window." And so be it.

David Clark remembers, however, that despite their reticence and having arrived "defensive," many times folks left these dialogues in a different state. He says, "And then, they left in a different mood; I mean we did a good job of educating them — at least opened their minds to other alternatives."

Nancy's husband, George, who is African American, was also on the task force. He similarly recollected positive outcomes from parish dialogues. After explaining that it's too late to re-do the past, he went on to say it's not too late to work for "changes in the next generation."

He continued:

That's a process that has to go on. It comes to each generation to become conscious of what, who they are, where they are, where they came from, and what they can project. And see it's [important] to begin the process. That's what I found great. When we, from that committee, got into discussion with a congregation that probably has [origins related to slavery], the congregation was impressed with our presentation [and then we] sat down in a circle and we talked.[15]

Nancy Barrick's description of the outcomes of these parish visits was somewhat more guarded than these two, but she describes having remained determined nonetheless. She noted in another setting, "At times our work seems futile. But I feel that this task force has a duty to be the thorn that provokes the church to action."[16] She, like most other members of the task force, also made clear that despite the challenges and alongside the determination to "be a thorn," this part of the task force's work was particularly energizing, was meaningful, and became the context out of which developed deep bonds between members of the task force itself as they did this difficult work.

The task force continued to pursue its mission during 2007 and 2008, meeting monthly for study and discussion, working with parishes, and supporting efforts made by Smith and Klein to turn the historical data collected as part of this process into the production of a book titled *Our*

15. George Barrick, interview with the author, March 1, 2013. All subsequent references to George and words placed in quotes are from this same interview.

16. *A Time to Love.*

History: Racism in the Anglican and Episcopal Church of Maryland. This book exposes the many levels in which the diocese is implicated in slavery. Besides lay leaders and clergy having themselves "owned" human beings, the work presents evidence that every Maryland church built prior to 1865 was built by enslaved persons or through direct economic dependence on such labor.

The authors note that the diocese had, with one exception, no involvement with the Underground Railroad. They describe the relationship of Episcopalians in Maryland to slavery overall as "tolerating and then accepting, depending on it and even blessing it."[17]

Breaking denial about that relationship has been the central focus of the Maryland task force. In its 2008 report to the diocese, as the task force was being reconfigured, Nancy Barrick reported on the task force's origins: "The charge was to determine 'a sense of the mind of the Diocese on the issue of restitution for slavery.' *A daunting task* [emphasis mine]."[18]

Even with the passion and commitment of members of the task force throughout its years of activity (which in many ways remain palpable though the task force is no longer commissioned in this form), such a daunting task has been slowgoing.

In 2008 the task force was disbanded, and the diocese's newly elected bishop reconfigured the vision for this work by forming in its stead a Truth and Reconciliation Commission (TRC). (More will be said about this reconfiguration below.) Some of the members of the original task force are on this commission, while others are not. At the time of my interviews, the TRC was planning a pilgrimage for All Saints' Day in the fall of 2014. This event is to commemorate 150 years since Maryland abolished slavery through the state's constitution and will involve a walk to significant sites in the diocese pertaining to its legacy of slavery. Planners intend to include a cyber-pilgrimage so that those unable to physically journey can take part as well.

This pilgrimage relates to another significant focus emphasized by the denomination as a result of the 2006 "Study Economic Benefits Derived from Slavery" resolution. Besides calling for diocesan research to report back to the denomination, the resolution also requested the presiding bishop of the church to name a Day of Repentance and hold a Service of

17. *A Time to Love.*
18. "Reparations Task Force of the Diocese of Maryland," summary by N. Barrick, September 17, 2008.

Repentance at the National Cathedral. It also requested "each diocese to hold similar services," and the TRC's pilgrimage is a response to that part of the resolution.[19]

Other dioceses have already held such services. In January 2008, a service jointly sponsored by several dioceses (New York, Long Island, New Jersey, Newark) was held in New York City. Called "Let My People Go: A Service of Liberation," it was held in conjunction with an anniversary of New York's abolition of the slave trade. According to records being kept by the Executive Council Committee on Anti-Racism of the EC, from Delaware to North Carolina, Tennessee, Virginia, and Alabama, in total about ten dioceses have either held or have planned such a service since 2006. (A similar number report having some sort of active research process underway, though this leaves dozens of dioceses as yet inactive on this issue.)[20]

The denomination held its service of repentance on October 4, 2008. However, rather than being held at the National Cathedral in Washington, D.C., as A123 had requested, it was held at St. Thomas Church in Philadelphia, the first African American Episcopal parish begun by Absalom Jones.

This choice was not without controversy. While he never could find out why the change in venue happened, Ron said he understood the logic of the choice. Namely "you can argue that if I offend you, I'm going to come to your house and apologize to you in your house." At the same time, he also understood why many people of color were disappointed. Holding the service at the National Cathedral would have been a "national statement." The apology would have had a broader impact instead of appearing to be more of a "local" affair.

Furthermore, though it is an integrated parish now, the National Cathedral is historically a "white institution." So an apology would have had a greater impact there. Again, however, Miller emphasized that he understood why St. Thomas might have made sense to some, given that it was the African American community to whom apology was being given.

Several members of the task force and many members of the diocese journeyed together to the Service of Repentance, where the presiding bishop of the denomination issued a formal apology for the church's role in slavery.

In 2009, the Rev. Canon Angela Shepherd, on staff at the Maryland

---

19. See http://www.episcopalarchives.org/cgi-bin/acts/acts_resolution-complete.pl ?resolution=2006-A123.

20. See http://www.episcopalarchives.org/cgi-bin/acts/acts_resolution-complete.pl ?resolution=2006-A123.

Diocese and co-chair of the TRC — the configuration in which this process is now taking place — reported on research to the national body gathered at the GC, thus fulfilling one dimension of the A123 directive. (Though Mary Miller notes that, at some point, the TRC is going need to sit down and write a thirty- to forty-page report to submit to the denomination.) Ultimately, however, the task force did not come to a point of commending particular reparative strategies for the diocese or the denomination before its work was brought to a formal close.

Every member of the task force implied in our discussions or stated outright that the task force's work had been reconfigured toward "reconciliation" long before it was anywhere near completion as a "reparations" project, and before they could have gotten to a point of envisioning what "repair" might actually mean. It remains to be seen as to what extent the TRC will take up the work and continue in similar directions, or engage these issues in a different manner.

But it was also clear in my interviews that the longings and commitments stirred and nurtured in the task force's relatively short tenure (just three years) generated significant loyalty among its members. As one African American member put it in 2008 (as the work was being brought to a close), "I think that this diocese, following its apology, needs to in a very intentional way determine what to do to begin the repair. It might be more than one thing, but every parish must in some way participate in the solution."[21]

Despite how unknown the future of this work is, and despite how much work remains yet undone, some things are clear to those who have actively participated: This work is urgent. This work is incomplete. This work is the responsibility of everyone.

Insights and Experiences

Some of the insights that emerged for and within the task force elucidate how a reparations paradigm enables much more adequate responses to racism than have our long-standing efforts at reconciliation. In what follows I will emphasize a few areas that speak most directly to larger questions and claims I have made in this book. Specifically, I will consider how making history central and putting reparations squarely on the table seems to have created

21. *A Time to Love.*

a forum conducive to significant and necessary transformation in white understanding, generated strong bonds among those engaged in this interracial work, and led to clarity among group members that a commitment to reparations rather than reconciliation is critical — despite the reality that a programmatic articulation of reparations ultimately remained unarticulated by the task force.

On the last issue, however, it became clear in my interviews that significant challenges remain pervasive in this work as well. Thus some of these challenges will be given attention in a final section of this chapter.

David Clark joined the Reparations Task Force because he hoped to subvert it. He admits this openly, and other members of the task force volunteered his "conversion" story as evidence of the transformative power of the process in which they participated.

When the task force was convened in 2005, David was a part-time priest in a suburban white parish. His first thought when he heard about the task force was, "Oh, this is going to be another entitlement effort." The advisory board of his church "was up in arms."[22] So he joined the committee intent on steering it in "a more conservative direction."

George Barrick described encountering David in an overcrowded room at the diocesan convention where the formation of the task force was being discussed. The room was "crowded with crazy opposition." One of the folks doing this crowding was David Clark. "David was sitting right there, and I said to him, 'Well, when I look in the mirror in the morning, I see a face . . . that has not gotten the same privileges as another one. And so if a privilege comes about, somebody paid for it, and if someone paid for it, then there is a debt. . . .'" George concluded, "The only way we were going to change this man's mind was to bring him onto the committee."

This beginning makes David Clark's transformation in the process and the way he now understands the urgency and significance of reparations work especially remarkable. David explains it this way:

> I believe that part of what happened in our committee . . . was that we finally understood there has been a great injustice that was evil and wrong done to this group of people in ways that the general public has no concept of. *Traces of the Trade* began to address it. We began to understand the need for making it right in a holy context because we acknowledged that that was really evil. And the "love each other" — that's

22. David Clark.

such an oblong blur. Define love. You know? How do you? I mean, it's just Mom and apple pie. You can't put your teeth into it, and I think where the reparations committee got traction was in beginning to deal with the reality of the need for some reparation of that evil.

Taking history seriously got David's attention.

Colleen Clark, who is also white, had different motivations for joining the task force. She hails from a family that held sugar plantations and enslaved men and women in Haiti, from which her ancestors had to flee after a slave insurrection. When they arrived in South Carolina they returned to their enslavement practices.

Thus, Colleen described the work of the task force in very personal terms. She recognized even as a young person the immorality of her family's treatment of an African American maid. She explained, "I saw the home that the maid lived in, which wasn't a home at all; it was a shack. I just, I had . . . I was overwhelmed with it. . . . I thought, 'I can't deal with this.' . . . So I wanted to get involved for that reason, maybe for that reason alone."[23]

It was evident that the way the task force framed its work created a forum in which whites could *and had* to name and respond to their own relationships to white supremacy. The significance of this cannot be overstated.

This significance has nothing to do with a misguided concern about attending to white people's needs or hurt when the harm to people of African descent should be the focus. On the contrary, it has everything to do with that harm — to the extent we are speaking of framing racial justice that enables, generates, and even demands outlets for the silence, denial, repression, and deformation that has long constituted white U.S.-American identity and culture and that impedes work on repentance and repair.

In the New York committee's production, African American psychologist Joy DeGruy Leary poses these questions in regard to our unnamed histories of slavery: "How has this affected Europeans? What must it do to your humanity to have to bear it, to have to hide such ugliness? To keep such an awful secret and to try to control for it everywhere?"

Colleen Clark was speaking about precisely this when she described repeated, unwelcome discoveries in her life of how distorted white culture is — how distorted within her own family. In another account she described being with an aunt and uncle from deeper south.

---

23. Colleen Clark, interview with the author, March 1, 2013. All subsequent references to Colleen and words placed in quotes are from this same interview.

They were so good to us kids and, you know, I just I loved them dearly. But I remember we went to church. . . . We're supposed to be thinking wonderful thoughts, okay? And this car passed my uncle and it was driven by a Black man, and if you could've heard the tirade that came from [my uncle's] mouth. . . . I just sat back there. . . . "This isn't the uncle I know. What . . . whoa . . . what is going on?" I had never heard that kind of hate. . . . You think this person's this wonderful, loving person, and then you see this evil side of them, or this side that's . . . it's like, "Oh my god."

She continued, clearly in pain, "It's thinking one thing and finding out something terribly different that's really evil in your mind." This is an account of white woundedness and deformation.

DeGruy Leary continues by saying that if some people of European descent finally get to a point where the cost and tensions become so great they start to say, "I'm getting ready to tell this ugly secret," then a shift and opportunity is finally created for people of African descent and the entire nation to finally mend and heal.[24] In DeGruy Leary's analysis this can happen — and only happen — when we engage history honestly.

Thus, in contrast to the inability of a reconciliation paradigm to bring whiteness into view, a reparations paradigm does so unequivocally and centrally. The possibilities this opens are visible in the different, but equally important, kinds of transformation such emphasis on whiteness enabled for David and Colleen Clark: for David a radically different view of the legitimacy of reparations work; for Colleen an immediate recognition that here was a forum in which to respond to what she already knew to be malformed in her own white experience.

This assessment — concluding that reparations enable a critical dimension for white transformation that may be relatively new in anti-racist work in the church — came up in my conversation with Ron Miller as well.

Having served the church for decades (usually within African American parishes) and married to Mary, who has been an anti-racist activist in the church for just as long, Ron remembers well the many but always short-lived attempts at racial transformation the church has tried over the decades. Honing in instead, however, on what our white ancestors have done, he said, might move whites to the point where we recognize that actually healing this history is going to happen only when we see and repay the debt that began there and continues to accumulate.

24. *The Diocese of New York Examines Slavery.*

Ron said, "I've been ordained since 1964, and every decade there's been work on racism and it never goes anywhere. They do it for a while [then] they say, 'Okay, well that's done for now.' And then they come back five years later and say, 'Oh . . . relations between races are not good; we need to do something about that.' And they do it for a while but it never really moves on, and I think part of the clue for moving it on is, in fact, to take the step to open conversation and *then to discuss the questions of reparations* [emphasis mine]."

When I asked Ron why he thinks reparations might be the key to moving on, he responded,

> Well, I think . . . that's the skeleton in the closet. I mean, they, white people are afraid of what it's going to cost them. And they'll go through the motions and think they'll be changed, but until we have really looked at what it's cost people of color and let *them* talk to *us* about it. . . . I mean, that's the issue really is to hear folks.

In short, transformation will come when white people hear well enough that we actually *get it* and realize that moving to anywhere new will require letting it cost us something.

On this front Mary Miller seems somewhat hopeful as well. She's been through at least four rounds on various race relations committees, but this time around, she said, is different because the framing of this work actually requires dealing seriously with white privilege. "[This reparations discussion] is grabbing a hold, I think, because we white folks are seeing ourselves in a different place than we've ever been before. Before the reparations piece it's just been [about] 'getting along' and catching up with the obvious lacks in our judicial and social systems. And there's still some of that, but that's a piece of where reparations comes in, of course."

Reparations work in Maryland has inarguably engendered a different kind of conversation, one we have not typically had in church contexts even when we have talked endlessly about race. If the experience of this small group of passionate advocates is any indication, the way reparations enables a different self-understanding and mode of response for white folks in regard to our relationships to whiteness has real conversion power. It remains to be seen whether it has staying power.

That a forum established through an emphasis on history as the starting point for understanding race (rather than on valuing difference and inclusion) has enabled a different contending with whiteness to transpire is particularly stunning when we consider the terrain on which a discussion of reparations necessarily takes place — terrain that is much more difficult and demanding of whites than is the terrain on which reconciliation places us.

Given the violence and blood-soaked ground on which we stand and necessarily acknowledge when we take up history, reparations has us look squarely in the face at the evil and inhumanity packed into whiteness in the United States.

It seems reasonable to expect that such work might generate more division than would the work of reconciliation. But while it is certainly the case that this diocese has a long way to go before a majority embraces the notion of reparations (and thus no strong causal conclusions should be made here), it was notable to me how cohesive and committed to each other this group of individuals seemed to be.

I shared this observation during the interviews. Noting that task force members seemed to be a tightly knit group, I asked how they would explain why an ostensibly more difficult and painful conversation might generate greater connection rather than greater division and mistrust. How is it that so much talking about — tarrying with — such devastating histories led to such deep regard for one another? How could it be that an issue as divisive as reparations seemed to have yielded robust interracial relationships?

A portion of David Clark's response to these questions emerged in the quote shared above, in which he almost disparages the idea of interracial dialogue convened under the province of "love" or "reconciliation" as an "oblong blur" that does not deal with the actual evil in our midst. In fact, David said, "The 'let's love each other' message denies the reality of the evil that has been done and continues to be done as a result of slavery."

Colleen Clark insisted that reparations work is precisely the kind of work required to generate such connections. "That's how you heal," she said, "by talking about it. . . . It's the same thing as when my first husband died. I didn't heal by not talking about all of that. I had to talk about it and talk about it and talk about it . . . over and over. It's grief work. It's the same thing with the reparations. You don't heal and you don't get beyond without talking about it."

The kind of talking being implied here has a particular cadence and purpose, given the terrain on which these conversations took place. Denial, it would seem, makes genuine connection more difficult and actual division thus more likely.

And given the significant unawareness or ignorance of racial history among whites, denial (whether active or passive) is a normative state in white culture. Thus, any work on race that hopes to be effective must directly confront and shake up denial's ability to continue to exist. It would seem that framing our interracial work through a reckoning with history and reparations accomplishes this. Whiteness is given no cover and denial is impossible when careful historical work on slavery and its legacies becomes the shared interracial project.

George and Nancy Barrick described having become deep and fast friends with David and Colleen Clark during their time on the task force. Recalling George and David's first encounter, that is somewhat surprising. It also merits some commentary given my insistence in chapter 2 that interracial dialogue — which depends on or requires people sharing their stories — is something of which we should be wary, an expectation that places an undue burden on people of color.

It is clear that much storytelling went on among this group. Nancy described sitting down with people to eat together and the need for everyone to get out of their comfort zone "to know who we are as human beings and that each of us has God in us. I have God in me as you do in you. And how he expresses himself through us is different. I can't do what you do, and you probably can't do what I do, and maybe there are some things we can do together. But we need to understand that. And communication is the name of the game."

Ron Miller said that part of the work on either side is to "let me tell you my story and [for you to] identify with it." George said that the discussions on reparations generated "an opportunity to have a different perspective because of our different conditions. And I think that's the thing: that all of us need to see each other."

Other interviewees described their engagement in similarly community-oriented, humanizing terms. These kinds of references sound strikingly similar to those we might expect to hear in reconciliation discussions, given the assumptions of reconciliation that getting to know and coming to embrace one another across our differences is the work.

Yet I remain convinced that the kind of storytelling described here yielded something different precisely because it was not engaged through a reconciliation paradigm.

In hearing their longer accounts reflecting on white conversion, the rupturing of veils of denial and silence, and how they moved to a place of passionate commitment, it seems clear that storytelling proved authentic and efficacious. I am inclined to argue that this could be the case only because whiteness and unjust white benefits were, necessarily, given no cover by anyone in the group — and could not be because of the nature of the project. This is quite different from engaging in abstract dialogue about how we are all "human underneath our differences," because the dialogue was riveted on a truthful telling of a shared and difficult history and its impact in the present.

The raw and painful revelations that emerged in the task force's story-telling were intrinsic to the ethos that resulted among these Christians. I do not believe this could have been achieved with the goal of storytelling so that Nancy and George's "differences" from David and Colleen's "differences" could be better understood and embraced.

Furthermore, the task force avoided the risk of making Nancy and George's differences as African Americans the object of inquiry for David and Colleen — a dynamic that already frames our work in relation to differences, which is then compounded by the conundrums of white racial identity.

Instead, David and Colleen's own relationship *to their own history* was one shared focus. And the distress the terrain of that history placed them in meant they could not, ultimately, separate that history and their relationship to it from the impact it has had on Nancy and George's stories (who have themselves had very different racial and class experiences despite both being Black). This also meant the four understood they were shaped by and nurtured in a context in which a norm had already been established that assumed, as heirs of oppression (all four) Nancy and George had a right to expect something from David and Colleen.

Such framing means the storytelling and dialogue of which I was so critical when taking place through a reconciliation paradigm has a radically different resonance in a reparations paradigm. This is not to say that simply convening under the umbrella of reparations will mitigate any and all challenging interracial dynamics. Those can transpire in any context in which whites are engaged with people of color.

But in contrast to the many environments of which I have been part, in which interracial dialogue is the convening focus and leads, too often, to a saccharine environment that precludes actual relationships, it was clear that the reparations focus of this work significantly mitigated the extent to which dialogue could privilege a white perspective. No doubt this raw environment played a primary role as members of the group came to regard each other so deeply.

At the diocesan-level something similar, though less pronounced, may be emerging — if slowly. Each member reiterated that there is a long journey to go before he or she would describe the outcome of this work as certain, let alone realized. But each also indicated that the kinds of conversations generated by this movement were new within the diocese.

Ron Miller cautiously assessed evidence that the task force had changed some white Christians' minds on things. He said, "It's still an open question [the question of where white folks in the diocese are as a result of this work]. But . . . I think they're probably a little more open. I mean, I would say, I don't think the barriers are getting higher and sharper." Mary Miller said that there has "been a shift in terms of the ease of talking in public" (in terms of interracial talking).

One significant event may provide evidence that the barriers are not only not getting "higher and sharper," but may even be coming down slightly. Mary, Ron, and David Clark each separately indicated that the election of the first African American diocesen bishop, Bishop Eugene Sutton, in 2008 was partially an outgrowth of the task force's work.

They did not claim credit for this election, so to speak. Nor did they claim that white Christians have somehow all come to a clear anti-racist awakening. Rather, their assessment pertained to a shifting climate and improved awareness developing among whites as a result of the dialogues on diocesan history.

Mary Miller was particularly careful to emphasize that in this, as with all anti-racist progress made in the diocese, it was the work and advocacy among African Americans that was central. (She also noted that talking reparations demands also "remembering the good stuff." In this case she was referring to the faithful witness of three African American parishes, in each of which Thurgood Marshall's family had been part.)

But given the racial demographics of the Episcopal Church and how heavily whites outnumber Blacks in the diocese, Bishop Sutton's election would not been successful without substantive white support. Again, none of the interviewees made a direct, causal connection between their work and this election, but they each, independently, raised Sutton's election as a notable "first" that may have been supported by their diocese-wide work.

A final significant insight here pertains to the attempts of the task force to actually arrive at a shared understanding of what "reparations" is or could ultimately mean. And this insight spills over into some of the most challenging dimensions of this work, as well as into a critique of reconciliation that every member of the task force, much to my surprise, made clearly.

Given how fraught the very word "reparations" can be, a significant part of the actual work of this task force — both among themselves and as they worked with parishes — was to come to a shared understanding of reparations. When I asked what they envisioned or hoped for in terms of future diocesan or denominational reparative responses, each interviewee had some difficultly answering.

Two things were interesting about this. First, it became clear that working through diverse views and reactions to the word "reparations" had itself been a meaningful and important part of their process. Strikingly similar descriptions came up in my conversation with the New York Reparations Committee in response to this same question.

The New York committee, borrowing from work done in the UCC, defines "reparations" in the facilitator's guide they produced to accompany their DVD:

> Reparations is the process to remember, repair, restore, reconcile and make amends for wrongs that can never be singularly reducible to monetary terms. The process of reparations is "an historical reckoning involving acknowledgment that an offense against humanity was committed and that the victims have not received justice."[25]

The New York committee explained that nearly their first full year of work together was taken up just in hashing out their various assumptions about what reparations might mean. But despite how time consuming this dialogue was, *this was work they deemed as having been well worth their time.*

Something akin to the way dialogue about a shared history facilitated authentic interracial relationships in Maryland happened in New York precisely through the committee's difficult, loaded, contentious conversations about how to think about reparations in the first place. The clarifying honesty of engaging "reparations" and the terrain on which it set them led to greater cohesiveness as a group than they might have developed had "repair" not been the critical framework through which they engaged in dialogue.

Second, what also became clear is that there remains among both groups diverse ideas about the notion of reparations themselves, and a lack of clarity about any concrete proposals. Ironically, reparations themselves may be the most incomplete portion of the work.

---

25. Quoted in the facilitator's guide, *The Diocese of New York Examines Slavery: Talking About Reparations, Repair and Reconciliation*, 2008; original author Bernice Power Jackson, *Reparations: A Process for Repairing the Breach: A Study and Discussion Guide for Local Congregations, Associations and Conferences.*

Mary Miller in Baltimore and the Rev. Dr. Mary Foulke, a white member of the Reparations Committee in New York, each describe their view that one way the church should think about repair and "what is due" is to think in terms of resources and support for Black congregations.

According to Mary Foulke, many African American Episcopal churches "are languishing" because of a lack of resources, support, and attention from the denomination. In areas where there is no wealth, these churches are simply closing. "I would like to think about what it would mean to look at reparations in relation to that," she said.[26]

Mary Miller echoed this perspective when she described the process of coming to a shared vision of reparations at St. James, as at first folks responded to the word "reparations" in a variety of ways, "from soup to nuts." Once they moved past any suspicion that repair meant an individual payment to someone, even those most averse to talking about "dollars" were willing to say reparations must mean resources being used for the good and benefit of all.

Thus, to the extent the good and benefit of all has not been the case relative to race in the EC, repair must be the response. "We finally zeroed in on our definition, which simply said 'repairing what's broken,'" Mary said, and St. James has continued to use that definition for themselves. "It's an Episcopal church so it has troubles in the parish. . . . [We go] looking for what's broken and what we might be able to do to help fix it. Repair it. And that's where things have continued to be."

David Clark seemed clear, at first, that in the course of the task force's discussion "reparations" did not primarily mean a financial response:

> King Cotton was a lot of money, and Black people made cotton king. And there's no way you could ever repay that financially, so then we got into, "Okay, we're not talking about money reparations — we're not going to give everyone $40 and a mule." They were promised that, they should've had it, they didn't get it, but we can't as a government or a church, especially with the financials, give everybody a paycheck. We have to do something different. And so one of the issues that we got to was, "Well, what can you do different that would make it right?" And as I recall we talked about some education resources, some schools, some special accommodations.

26. Conversation with the author, Spring 2013.

But David's memory of the discussions was rather vague. He did speak with more nuance later, suggesting that as reparations were not being conceived as payments to individuals, then concrete, resource-intensive forms of repair could be conceptualized: "It doesn't matter what you give; it's not going to be enough. So it's better to give of your time, of your effort, and also to help and to give money within the social context — I guess money in the sense of buildings and stuff like that. But building things and providing opportunities [as opposed to individual payments] . . . because it goes much further."

Early in our interview Nancy Barrick explained that whites have had "ladders" to get where they are, while Black folks have had to "crawl." When I asked her later what kind of ladder she thought might be needed to repair and redress this history, her first response was that different communities would need to identify specific needs in their own contexts: "First of all each community needs to find out about themselves, learn about themselves, and then they can decide what it is that they can do within their own community that will . . . foster a good relationship or repair any damages."

Her response was consistent with the clarity among this group that reckoning with actual realities of our history is a first and central step that is not to be short-circuited. Indeed, it was at this point that Nancy made her first reference to the fact that the task force had only begun to get far enough into the work to think about "ladders" when it was reconfigured, against the desires of the members, into a TRC.

A diversity of perspectives on what reparations might actually be in the future remained throughout the task force's work. Indeed, an open-ended and unarticulated notion of such responses continues to be present in Maryland, as well as in the larger denomination's formal statement of supporting reparations.

But despite this part of the work being the most incomplete dimension of the project, every task force member was as clear and direct as David Clark about one understanding of reparations. Repentance and reparation must come before reconciliation, they each insisted. If they do not, reconciliation is simply not meaningful activity.

This sentiment was echoed by the New York committee as well, even as it too remains as unfinished and various in its notions of reparations as does Maryland. Said Mary Foulke directly in response to my question to that group about what reparations might mean, whatever they end up looking like in form "we must have reparations before we can be reconciled."

Challenges and Limitations

The matter of the unfinished character, myriad diversity, and incompleteness of the work as it pertains to concrete reparations proposals brings into view real challenges that do exist in a reparations paradigm. It also speaks to some of the ways the pervasive presence of reconciliation paradigms continues to impede the advent of something racially new taking root in the church.

Given that the convening concept is reparations, it is striking, perhaps even ironic, that both Maryland and New York were unable by this point to cohesively envision possible reparations proposals. In a conversation I had with Raymond Winbush while in Baltimore, Winbush described having been asked by a group of Quakers with whom he had been in dialogue what they could do as a form of reparations. He had no problem making a concrete suggestion right away: "Put ten African American young people through college," he told them (my paraphrase). "That would be a form of reparations."[27]

None of the reparations work I have encountered in the Episcopal Church even begins to approach such concrete and specific forms of repair. Yet given the arguments of this book, such specificity ultimately will be essential to keep reparations work from falling prey to the same muddled and vague set of outcomes to which much of our anti-racism and reconciliation work has.

There are a number of reasons getting to specificity will prove challenging. The very nature of denominationwide resolutions (true for most Protestant denominations) works against the success of such specificity because of how denominations tend to be structured. On the one hand, it can be important for denominations to pass resolutions from the top down. Doing so puts the significance of such resolutions on the map and happens because of the committed work of advocates who insist their denominations respond to their concerns. There is value in such resolutions.

On the other hand, a top-down process also means resolutions get passed in regard to which many members of a given denomination may not even be particularly aware, let alone feel a real investment. Yet we know that for buy-in to be cultivated in regard to something as difficult as reparations, folks not only have to engage it, but they are likely going to have to engage it for a substantive period of time. This is precisely why the grassroots work being done in Maryland has been so critical (and so energizing). For a national resolution to become alive and meaningful, it must take fire with passion and conviction on the local level.

27. Conversation with the author, March 1, 2013.

At that same point, however, another structural challenge to reparations work enters. Those working at the grassroots level often do so in unfunded or underfunded capacities. As volunteers they simply do not have the infrastructure or resources — which could only come from the "top" — to make and implement decisions about reparations themselves. In this way it makes perfect sense that the Maryland task force's most effective and compelling work was that of educating parishes — other clergy and other laity.

That kind of work lends itself well to being done and responded to at the grassroots level. But the next step, commending reparations themselves — any commendation of which would be resource and infrastructure intensive — is an innately different kind of task, with very different kinds of challenges. This challenge then, I suspect, is going to be continually encountered in reparations work. It will require creativity and commitment to move through such difficulties, see reparative projects implemented, and otherwise ensure that this work does not end by merely engaging history over and over without ever actually responding to and redressing it.

However, another critical issue emerged in Maryland that tempers the comments I just made. Quite simply, despite the challenges that are innate to this work (those just described), it is far too early in any of these movements to simply conclude that the difficulty of coming to a concrete proposal about reparations means that such specificity will never come.

In any difficult venture, we only ever know what kind of work might actually be possible or result if and after we first take the steps needed prior to even begin being able to envision, let alone implement, the next steps. Remember David Clark's story. From a hypothetical vantage point looking at "what might be feasible down the road," who would imagine he would have come to a place of assessing reparations as meaningful and urgent work for white Episcopalians? His arrival only emerged because he took prior steps out of which something new became possible.

In a similar way, it became overwhelmingly clear to me that something powerful, organic, and transformative was indeed happening in the active years of the Reparations Task Force in Maryland. Much more important, the participants themselves were clear about this as well. The fact that this group did not or had not yet gotten to the point of commending a specific reparations program should not be seen as evidence they could not have eventually done so. They were still in the process of actually taking prior steps necessary to the emergence of any meaningful specificity.

In many ways this explains why the reparative possibilities they did talk about remained so vague. Notably, none of them implied they had come anywhere close to nearing the end of the new, exciting, difficult journey on which they had embarked. Quite the contrary, each repeatedly described the work as having barely begun and as ongoing, since they themselves had much more to learn and understand before arriving at the point where meaningful recommendations could be made.

And this possibility, that the work was still in its infancy and thus unfairly "judged" in terms of what it did not specifically recommend, leads to a brief discussion of one of the most serious challenges in reparations work: namely the constant pressure and presence of reconciliation paradigms in our churches.

Bishop Sutton disbanded the task force after being elected in 2008 and — to a person — every task force member, including those who have chosen to continue serving in the newly configured TRC (most have not), spoke of this with great lament. Mary Miller, who is part of the TRC, described it as "a sadness." The bishop, she said, "put the reparations and the anti-racism work on the shelf for two-and-a-half years. And the reparations folks particularly felt the traction was lost."

Ron Miller explained that part of the reason the work was halted was because Bishop Sutton had a vision acquired from Desmond Tutu and the TRC process in South Africa. (Note that this resonates deeply with the turn in the Presbyterian process, which also quickly moved to the South African context and lost energy shortly thereafter.) Ron lamented thus, "We had an ongoing, working task force . . . and were really ready to move parishes along when the bishop was elected and consecrated. He thanked us for all we had done and closed it down."

This loss of direction and energy was palpable not only in regard to the actual cessation of the task force for two years, but also in regard to the reconciliation framework under which the journey was being reinitiated. I was unaware of any of this backstory, or how and why the task force was now a TRC, before speaking to these members of the task force. Thus, the interviewees' critiques of reconciliation were not prompted by the arguments I have made in this book.

But consistently in the interviews it was precisely when I asked about the relationship of reconciliation and reparations that this account of their work having been "shut down" emerged, along with the sense of loss and bitterness many of them continue to bear about this and the new configuration of the process.

George Barrick explained with the gleam of conviction in his eyes that "during the reparations [meetings], it was energy. [Even] the word 'Jim Crow' was energized. I'd like to know where the energy is [now]. If we could just bring that in and convert it to reconciliation."

Steve Swift, a white member of the TRC, was not part of the original task force and had little knowledge of it. Thus it is particularly interesting how much his observation resonates with what George perceived: "I think [the TRC is] struggling to find out what to do. I mean, the pilgrimage is what's carrying them right now. But what will be involved later, I don't know. I don't know that the commission knows. The bishop has asked us, asked the commission, to leave reparations alone for a while. I don't know the rationale for that . . . but [the TRC is] clear that their focus is not to be that."

Other members of the task force, as well as the Rev. Canon Angela Shepherd, who put me in contact with folks for interviews, described Nancy Barrick as one of the most important movers and shakers in the reparations processes. When I asked Nancy about reparations relative to reconciliation, she described the emergence of the TRC and said, "I'll be honest, it doesn't move me." When I asked her why, she responded, "It just doesn't move me. I don't think they're . . . They're not pushing. They're just . . . I don't know what they're doing . . . and I'm on it [the TRC]."

George Barrick augmented Nancy's response: "I won't say 'mis-,' but I think there's a 'dis-interpretation' of what the [reparations] committee was . . . because of a lack of awareness of what was being accomplished." Both George and Nancy expressed their suspicion that the work was halted because a lot of people are still so wary of the word "reparations." But in the transition to the TRC, Nancy said, the "focus" of this work became utterly different in ways that simply do not generate the kind of authentic truth telling, passion. and commitment that was present in initial group.

The task force members' sense of loss also came out more specifically in regard to the actual assumptions contained within reconciliation. Each indicted reconciliation as contributing to the "fuzziness" of the TRC's focus today. David Clark's words, quoted above, re-enter here: too much "Mom and apple pie" and not enough attention to actual "evil."

Ron Miller cautioned me when I asked him about reconciliation work in the diocese — perhaps interpreting me as advocating the notion of reconciliation — by saying, "One caution, some people are rejecting the use of the word "reconciliation," since we were never reconciled. . . . Racial 'conciliation,' or race relations is a more accurate description of what we're dealing with. . . . We have never been 'one,' and reconciliation assumes that we're restoring something."

Colleen Clark simply said that were the commission actually working on something concrete with a specific outcome in mind, she would be happy and eager to become involved again. But her sense (with which David Clark agreed) was that the TRC was not going to be interested in the concrete.

Given that I did not interview anyone on the TRC (aside from Steve Swift, Nancy Barrick, and Mary Miller, who have agreed to serve on the new committee), I want to be cautious about insinuating more than can be known about what the TRC might be up to or how those who have convened it envision this work. Frankly, I did not explore that.

Moreover, I saw evidence of the possibility that a different notion of reconciliation may be at work in Maryland than that which I have critiqued so heavily in this book. Shepherd, who co-chairs the TRC, said that from her perspective "the window for reparations has passed," something she sees as a "tragedy." But she went on to be clear that in her understanding reconciliation means "becoming reconciled to the history." This understanding of reconciliation has a different cadence than that which I have identified as typically informing Protestant reconciliation talk. It is definitely not reparations talk, but it also is not a framing of the problem over the flat terrain of difference and inclusion.

In fact, Shepherd, who is African American, also told me that she is deeply critical of "cultural competency" training to the extent it does not or cannot get into the history that we have to face.

In addition, in her capacity as co-chair, she has also been working to raise awareness and engagement of white privilege throughout the diocese, and she deeply values the historical work the Reparations Task Force has done. She continues to screen *Traces of the Trade* at the diocesan level — not your typical reconciliation resource. In short, it may be that the "reconciliation" taken up in the TRC work ends up informed by the reparations work that preceded it, despite Shepherd's clarity that the reparations window itself has closed.

A final area of challenge in the whole of this process remains the least surprising. As much as reparations can enable significant white transformation, such transformation requires white people to actually engage. And it is clear and unfortunate, but predictable, that the biggest impediment to reparations work (as well as the reason the work requires so much heavy lifting) is simply because of white resistance. In fact, on the weekend I arrived Shepherd, who has an expertise in working on white privilege with white folks, had just canceled a workshop on white privilege because of a lack of participants.

Mary Miller, who has such a long and broad view of race work within the Episcopal Church, expressed a deep sense of what remains true about white engagement and how much remains to be done to push, cajole, convince, and otherwise fire-up white Christians on reparations work — or virtually any other racial justice work within the diocese. What was true fifty years ago remains true today, she said: "The most active people in the work itself, on the diocesan level, are African Americans. . . . Whenever I stop and think about it, the only faces I see are young African Americans."

Conclusion

Could prophetic evangelicals in intentional communities engage in historical work as deep as the work described herein? If they did so, would similar pathways open to the kinds of transformations that reparations work — with all its partialness and incompleteness — began to open in Maryland? Could Christians in any number of contexts within mainline Protestantism decide to push and advocate for a new framing of their work, pursued through a reparations paradigm? If they began to study, research, explore, and lay bare the histories and legacies in which the lives and work of all our communities in this nation unfold, what would happen? What might *become* if the many Christians longing so deeply for racial transformation in the church reframed their thinking and emulated the journey taken by these folks in Maryland (and pockets of others in New York, North Carolina, Delaware, and elsewhere)? Does having become convinced that the only way to break through the seemingly endless cycles of work on race that have so rarely led us somewhere new mean it is time to try something radically different?

Might Stephen Rose's description of what the Black Manifesto made possible in 1969 still echo in our spirits as prophetically speaking of something that is today still possible: ". . . the demand is just; the time is right; and a proper response by the white churches would be the painful prelude to something like an appropriate commencement of something new in America"?[28]

Short of sheer unwillingness by whites to imagine the viability of a serious conversation and engagement of the sort undertaken by the Maryland task force on these matters, I find no reason whatsoever to conclude that it could not be thus.

Reparations work offers no easy or quick response to the crisis of white supremacy, racial alienation, and racial injustice in our faith communities,

---

28. Stephen C. Rose, "The Manifesto and Renewal," *Christianity and Crisis* 29 (May 26, 1969): 142.

nor in our nation as a whole. Like other responses, it too contains significant and daunting challenges. There are no obvious or complete models out there yet for how to do it and see it all the way through.

Yet the testimony and witness of what this small but courageous group of men and women began — and the ways this beginning in a very short period of time radically reconfigured their senses of self, their notions of what might be possible, and their clarity about the truth telling to which Christians are called — has gripped me. I believe it should grip other justice-seeking Christians as well.

In different geographical contexts and in different community configurations, what it might look like to take up the question of reparations for slavery will no doubt be different. A reparative conversation in Iowa, given the history of this state, would generate very different trajectories of complicity and legacy than has a conversation about the history of Maryland.

Whether a group of Christians living in an intentional community think about research into and responses to their own histories relative to where they come from or to the place they dwell together now; whether a given body is reporting back to a denomination or merely seeking to network with and encourage or challenge other similarly minded prophetic Christians; there are numerous forms in which serious engagement of reparations for slavery might manifest.

But these questions and historical truths — along with our massive denial and silence about them in white contexts — surround us all in this nation at every turn, regardless of geographical context. Thus, engaging in reparations work is something that we all can do. I would take it a step further and insist, in fact, that the ways in which we are surrounded means that reparations work — specifically reparations for slavery and repair of the gaping wound that remains present among and between white and Black Christians — is work to which we have a biblical obligation.

Finally, I would say with profound conviction and without equivocation that *that* work — that new (and yet old) and differently framed (though long-framed this way by African Americans) work — in our Christian communities might have the power to transform the church.

Such transformation might move from denominations to parishes to intentional Christian communities in ways we could never — if we tried to do so from our current vantage point without having first walked boldly into the work itself — begin to imagine. And so, simply put, it is time to take those first steps.

Conclusion

A reparations paradigm does not offer a full blueprint or a set of step-by-step instructions to be followed to help our faith communities, civic communities, and nation as a whole transform and become the kind of world we who long for justice want them to be.

Even if we are fully persuaded that taking up — or, better put, joining in — work advocating reparations for slavery or bringing a reparations paradigm to other racial justice work would enable more adequate engagement, there is no easy route from here to there.

Nonetheless, a reparations paradigm does make some things very clear. It insists we look carefully at where we are now, in this historical moment, and at the ways the legacies we inherit continue to shape and inform our relationships across lines of racial difference and to strengthen unjust contemporary social structures that subjugate some while benefiting others. It insists that before we begin to easily, or even cautiously, speak of being reconciled, some things are required first.

Those of us whose identities have been forged and continue to be shaped by white supremacy in this nation, and who have inherited the heavy weight of ancestral complicity in its legacies, need to repent. We need to apologize and take responsibility. And repentance and apology, if the model of Zacchaeus holds anything for us, need to be made meaningful with concrete actions and programs for repair.

We must become "repairers of the breach" who figure out how to begin paying back, several-fold when possible, what has been taken. We must do

251

so even while cognizant that the atrocities that constitute our racial history can never be fully repaired.

The denominational work explored in this book is still very much in process in terms of what reparations for the sins of racism may eventually yield. Indeed, it is too soon to know whether and to what extent reparations will actually result and, more important, whether white Christians who are part of these communities will become convinced of the necessity and legitimacy of reparations for racial justice, let alone authentic reconciliation.

What is clear, however, is that a significant shift in understanding racism and the requisite activities to pursue racial justice is critical. The basic premise and logic of reconciliation — even while it holds before us a theological vision worth affirming — simply cannot accomplish the work that white Christians need to be about alongside their African American, Latino/a, Native American, Asian, and Asian American brothers and sisters.

The urgency of these matters makes it worth deep and sustained effort to imagine the possibility that something new is required of us.

What might we see if we try to envision a future that not only includes reparations for slavery, but a reparations paradigm successfully deployed and sustained over time by white Christians in many areas of racial justice work — by prophetic evangelicals, mainline Protestants, Roman Catholics, and a faithful cloud of others? What would it look like if we fully traded our inclinations toward charity for justice and hospitality for mutual regard and moral due — reconstituting and reforming the very basis of our interracial relationships in ways that lead to both individual and structural change?

What if we try to envision a future in which an authentic process of repentance has taken place — one going beyond formal apologies from church leaders and successfully bringing along a majority of laypeople — and in which concrete forms of repair have been realized?

Imagining all of this, what would then happen if we tried again the exercises described at the beginning of chapter 2? Would the responses of white people participating in a process of naming unique and positive characteristics of their racial identity be different? Might it be safe to hypothesize that white Christians who have been active, authentic participants in the work shaped by a reparations paradigm would, at least, not be so baffled by the questions?

Having engaged and acknowledged the historical realities and the material contexts in which our white racialization takes place, having taken the risk of confessing and working directly against the legacies of our racial histories as they live on in the present, might white Christians actually even be able to point to unique and positive choices we have made and are continuing to make collectively about who we want to be as racial beings?

We are a long way from even having taken some of the earliest steps into this journey. But despite how far away we are from this vision — and even while there is much that needs to shift in the understanding of white Christians who still long for racial reconciliation — there are murmurings and stirrings afoot among mainline Protestants and prophetic evangelicals that suggest an embrace of a reparations paradigm is not unthinkable.

Indeed, it is my fervent hope that some of us who have been working on these issues for a long time and who know well precisely the places at which our work gets "stuck" — who feel the frustrations that so much effort and passion has secured so little substantive and sustained transformation — will recognize in these pages Spirit-filled options worthy of being pursued, new directions worthy of being considered.

The irony of such a radical possibility is this: if we risk actually letting go of a reconciliation paradigm and in its stead embrace fully a reparations paradigm (with all of the uncertainty and work that doing so will require), perhaps then the long, slow journey into racial reconciliation might more truly be able to begin.

Index